£3.25

D1492424

THE VIOLENT EFFIGY

THE VIOLENT EFFIGY
a study of Dickens' imagination

John Carey

Faber and Faber 3 *Queen Square London*

First published in 1973
by Faber and Faber Limited
3 Queen Square London WC1
Printed in Great Britain by
Western Printing Services Ltd, Bristol
All rights reserved

ISBN 0 571 10239 5

© 1973, John Carey

CONTENTS

Dickens is infinitely greater than his critics. The point needs stressing because critics can, with unusual ease, appear intelligent at his expense. Shortcomings, ultimately irrelevant, in his own intelligence account for this, plus the presence of worthless elements in even his best novels. What makes him unique is the power of his imagination and, in Kafka's phrase, its 'great, careless prodigality' – careless, because extending itself typically into odd angles and side-alleys of his subject. To take a single example, when Mrs. Jarley's caravan rolls into town one sultry afternoon, Dickens' narration passes swiftly over houses, inns and bystanders and lights on some insects: 'the flies, drunk with moist sugar in the grocer's shop, forgot their wings and briskness, and baked to death in dusty corners of the window.' Festive and forlorn in rapid succession, they are very Dickensian flies, and it took Dickens to notice them at all.

The second fact to bear in mind is that Dickens is essentially a comic writer. The urge to conceal this, noticeable in some recent studies, can probably be traced to a suspicion that comedy, compared to tragedy, is light. Comedy is felt to be artificial and escapist; tragedy, toughly real. The opposite view seems more accurate. Tragedy is tender to man's dignity and self-importance, and preserves the illusion that he is a noble creature. Comedy uncovers the absurd truth, which is why people are so afraid of being laughed at in real life. As we shall see, once Dickens starts laughing nothing is safe, from Christianity to dead babies. His instinctive response to tragic pretensions may be gauged from an early letter, in which he announces that he has just moved into a hotel room previously occupied by the celebrated actor Charles Kean:

I am sitting at this instant in his wery chair!!! I was bursting into the water-closet this morning, when a man's voice (of tragic quality) cried out – 'There is somebody here.' It was his. I shall reserve this for his Biographer.

Humankind's attempts to surround its puny concerns with gravity and decorum seemed to Dickens hilarious. Contemplating them he was overcome, he confessed, by that 'perverse and unaccountable feeling which causes a heart-broken man at a dear friend's funeral to see something irresistibly comical in a red-nosed or one-eyed undertaker'. Institutions and organizations and the structure of government upon which civilized society depends provoked him to scornful merriment. Yet the effect of his mirth is curiously not sardonic. His investigation of fools and hypocrites radiates enjoyment. His comic figures claim our affection. The laughter, though devastating, revels in what it exposes. It is this crucial aspect of his genius that is omitted by moralistic critics who see in Quilp only 'a study in sadistic malice' (the phrase is from Dr. and Mrs. Leavis' *Dickens the Novelist*), or in the portrayal of Fagin only 'horror at the corruption of innocence'.

Dickens' inability to take institutions seriously is one reason for believing that we shall miss his real greatness if we persist in regarding him primarily as a critic of society. There are other reasons, too. As has often been remarked, he warmly favoured the hanging of disaffected natives in Jamaica and the blowing of mutinous sepoys from the mouths of cannon. In America he regretted the 'melancholy absurdity' of giving blacks the vote, and objected besides that 'exhalations not the most agreeable arise from a number of coloured people got together.' These traces of prejudice, though venial when placed in their historical perspective, are not encouraging if one wishes to recommend Dickens for his enlightened social views. A more serious drawback, in this respect, is his inconsistency. He reflects the popular mind in that he is able to espouse diametrically opposed opinions with almost equal vehemence. He urges compassion for the occupants of prison cells, yet feels outraged when convicts are given better accommodation than impoverished working men. In the *History of England* he wrote for his children he includes a lecture on the wickedness of warfare which, he insists, can never be 'otherwise than horrible'. But when he recounts the havoc King Richard wrought among the Saracens 'with twenty English pounds of English steel', or celebrates the exploits of 'bold Admiral Blake' who 'brought the King of Portugal to his senses', it appears that the horrible side of war has somehow slipped out of sight. 'He was very much a man of one idea,' affirmed his friend John Forster, 'each having its turn of absolute predominance.' Almost any aberration, indeed, from drunkenness to wife-beating can be found eliciting at various times both Dickens' mournfulness and his amused toleration. It is noticeable, too, that though he customarily laments the inadequacy of the successive systems of Poor Relief, he congratulates those who would never deign to accept it. In *Our Mutual Friend* persons seeking public charity are likened to 'vermin', while old Betty Higden, fleeing it, remains a 'decent person'. By encouraging this distinction Dickens could hardly ease the lot of the destitute, yet consideration for the destitute was commonly his cry. It seems clear that in reality he believed in 'independent self-reliance' just as firmly as Lord Decimus Tite Barnacle, yet Lord Decimus is ridiculed for adhering to that belief in *Little Dorrit*. It has caused some surprise, too, considering the picture of industrialism presented in *Hard Times*, that Dickens should have paid tribute at a public banquet the year before the novel appeared to:

the great compact phalanx of the people, by whose industry, perseverance, and intelligence, and their result in money-wealth such places as Birmingham, and many others like it, have arisen.

These inconsistencies, and they are widespread, would be damaging if Dickens were prized as a social theorist. But they are symptomatic of a flexibility which, if he is regarded as an imaginative writer, becomes vital. It is this that impels him to see his dominant objects and landscapes – his locks and cages and crumbling mansions, his effigies and corpses and amputated limbs – in sharply contrasting lights. Precisely relevant here is Keats' argument about the poetic character: that it is essentially amoral and unprincipled: 'It has as much delight in conceiving an Iago as an Imogen.' Dickens, though more apologetically, recognized in himself the same bond between imagination and inconsistency: 'the wayward and unsettled feeling which is part (I suppose) of the tenure on which one holds an imaginative life'.

Regarding Dickens as an imaginative writer does not entail marking down his work as a sort of fanciful vacation from 'real' experience. That might, admittedly, be the case if we were to accept the pronouncements about literature and reality offered in Mr. Robert Garis' influential study *The Dickens Theatre*. Mr. Garis regrets, in the first place, Dickens' tendency to 'show off his style'. It strikes him as an offence against '*good taste* and *good manners*',

and would not be acceptable, he intimates, in the pieces of prose
composition submitted by his own students. But his more substan-
tial reason for deciding that Dickens is not a 'serious' writer like
George Eliot is that we are not allowed to see the 'inner life' of his
characters. We are not invited to analyse their motives or attend
upon their cogitations. This disqualifies Dickens as a serious writer,
Mr. Garis explains, for 'we expect serious drama and serious
literature in general to enact an approach towards human beings
which accords with the way we approach the people we know in real
life, when we are taking them seriously.'

That Mr. Garis has a very cramped idea of literature will be
apparent, yet something like it hovers behind many of the complaints
about Dickens' 'unreality'. The power of imaginative literature to
refashion the seen world, to fracture and recast the reader's circum-
scribed notions about what constitutes the 'real', seems to have no
place in Mr. Garis' calculations. The reader, he supposes, will be
secure in the conviction that he has exhausted the available ways of
'taking people seriously' before he starts his book, and he will expect
the author not to venture outside these. Literature, on this reckoning,
will restrict itself to imitating those views of other people's affairs,
satisfying both to our curiosity and to our self-esteem, which
acquaintances occasionally favour us with in moments of confidence.

Yet Mr. Garis, in denying Dickens' novels the status of serious
literature, probably does them less of a disservice than the critics
who labour to unearth their 'meanings', as if great works of art were
to be cherished, in the last resort, for whatever moral droppings can
be coaxed from them. The fruits of this approach often provide the
strongest argument for its discontinuance. Mr. A. E. Dyson, for
instance, proposes as the kernel of *David Copperfield* the information
that 'the best marriages are between two deep yet not passionately
tormented friends of opposite sexes.' The objection to this is not so
much its banality as that it belongs to a species of discourse and a
mode of thought quite distinct from that in which Dickens' powers
operate upon us. In consequence it is ludicrously unlike the gains
which are actually to be reaped from entering the imaginative world
of *David Copperfield*.

The main subject of the following chapters, then, will not be
Dickens' morals, social criticism or alleged inferiority to George
Eliot, but the workings of his imagination.

DICKENS AND VIOLENCE

In Dickens' travel book *Pictures from Italy* he describes how on February 21, 1845, he, 31 guides, 6 saddled ponies and a handful of tourists made an ascent of Mount Vesuvius. The local people warned him it was the wrong time of year, especially for a night ascent. Snow and ice lay thick on the summit. Characteristically he ignored the advice of these 'croakers', as he called them. His wife and another lady and gentleman had to be carried in litters. Dickens went on foot. As the party approached the top, blundering in the darkness over the broken ground, half suffocated with sulphurous fumes, Dickens' description of the sheets of fire, and the red-hot stones and cinders flying into the air 'like feathers', becomes more and more excited. 'There is something', he relates, 'in the fire and the roar, that generates an irresistible desire to get nearer to it.' Not that this desire was felt by the others. While Dickens, a guide and one other crawled to the edge of the crater, the rest of the party cowered below in the hot ashes yelling to them of the danger. 'What with their noise,' writes Dickens,

and what with the trembling of the thin crust of ground, that seems about to open underneath our feet and plunge us in the burning gulf below (which is the real danger, if there be any); and what with the flashing of the fire in our faces, and the shower of red hot ashes that is raining down, and the choking smoke and sulphur; we may well feel giddy and irrational, like drunken men. But we contrive to climb up to the brim, and look down, for a moment, into the Hell of boiling fire below. Then, we all three come rolling down; blackened and singed, and scorched, and hot, and giddy: and each with his dress alight in half-a-dozen places.

On the way down one of the tourists falls – 'skimming over the white ice, like a cannon-ball' – and almost at the same moment two of the guides come rolling past. Dickens is offended, unreasonably enough, by the cries of dismay the other guides send up. Luckily all three casualties are eventually recovered, none of them badly injured.

The anecdote is typical of Dickens. Typical of his disregard for other people – his 'hard and aggressive' nature, 'impetuous' and 'overbearing', in Forster's words; typical of his enormous and unquenchable desire for activity, for something which would use up his dynamic energies; and typical of his fascination with fire as a beautiful and terrible destroyer, a visible expression of pure violence. In Rome on Easter Sunday he watches St. Peter's stuck all over with fireworks, and records his sense of exultation at seeing great, red fires suddenly burst out from every part of the building, so that the black groundwork of the dome 'seemed to grow transparent as an eggshell'. Railway trains and steamboats excite him as moving fires. In his American travel book he describes the engine which takes them across the country as a thirsty monster, a dragon, yelling and panting along its rails, scattering a shower of sparks in all directions. Crossing the Atlantic on board the *Britannia* in 1840 he was impressed at night by the way light gleamed out from every chink and aperture about the decks 'as though the ship were filled with fire in hiding, ready to burst through any outlet, wild with its resistless power of death and ruin'.

In *Dombey and Son* the railway train becomes a fiery animal with 'red eyes, bleared and dim in the daylight', which smashes Carker when he unwisely steps on its track. It 'struck him limb from limb, and licked his stream of life up with its fiery heat, and cast his mutilated fragments in the air'. But fire had been used to express violence in the novels before this. In *Oliver Twist*, in the scene where Nancy suddenly braves Fagin and Sikes, the signs of human passion – Nancy stamping her foot and going white with rage – are reinforced when she seizes Fagin's club and flings it into the fire, 'with a force', Dickens notes, 'that brought some of the glowing coals whirling out into the room'. It's as if the human actors are inadequate to embody the violence of Dickens' idea, and he has to bring in fire to express it. This scene is recalled when Sikes murders Nancy. Afterwards he lights a fire and thrusts his club into it. Dickens vivifies the moment with an incandescent detail: 'There was hair upon the end, which blazed and shrunk into a light cinder, and, caught by the air, whirled up the chimney.' Running away from his murder, Sikes suddenly comes upon a conflagration:

The broad sky seemed on fire. Rising into the air with showers of sparks, and rolling one above the other, were sheets of flame, lighting the atmosphere for miles around, and driving clouds of smoke in the direction where he stood.

It is, in fact, a house on fire, and Dickens fills in the circumstances with his usual enthusiasm for such subjects – the 'molten lead and iron' pouring white-hot onto the ground, and so on. The episode seems an arbitrary intrusion, quite redundant so far as the plot is concerned, unless one sees it as a projection of the violence and torment within Sikes. Similarly in Peggotty's abode, when David Copperfield comes upon the lustful Steerforth snarling about 'this Devil's bark of a boat', the malcontent seizes a piece of wood from the fire and strikes out of it 'a train of red-hot sparks that went careering up the little chimney, and roaring out into the air' – just to impress upon the reader the dangerous state he's in. Fire spells peril as well as passion. In *Bleak House*, Esther first comes upon Ada and Richard 'standing near a great, loud-roaring fire' with a screen 'interposed between them and it'. Our sense of destruction reaching towards youth and beauty becomes definite when this fire is given 'red eyes' like a 'Chancery lion'.

The violence of a mob, which always intensely excites Dickens, is repeatedly conveyed through its fiery antics. In *Barnaby Rudge* the molten lead on Bill Sikes' house recurs in the magnificent scene where the rioters burn down Mr. Haredale's mansion:

There were men who cast their lighted torches in the air, and suffered them to fall upon their heads and faces, blistering their skin with deep unseemly burns. There were men who rushed up to the fire, and paddled in it with their hands as if in water; and others who were restrained by force from plunging in, to gratify their deadly longing. On the skull of one drunken lad – not twenty, by his looks – who lay upon the ground with a bottle to his mouth, the lead from the roof came streaming down in a shower of liquid fire, white-hot; melting his head like wax.

Later in the novel, when Newgate prison is stormed, the mob build a fire against the main gate, and men can be seen in the middle of the flames trying to prise down the red-hot metal with crowbars. The same mob howls and exults as Lord Mansfield's Law library, with its priceless collection of manuscripts, goes up in flames. Seeing the violence directed against a prison and the law should remind us how much Dickens, the Dickens who was to write *Little Dorrit* and *Bleak House*, is imaginatively on the side of the rioters and wreckers, despite the dutiful expressions of dismay with which he surrounds the scene. 'I have let all the prisoners out of Newgate, burnt down Lord Mansfield's, and played the very devil,' he wrote exultingly to Forster, 'I feel quite smoky.' Similarly in *A Tale of Two Cities* the chateau, symbol of aristocratic oppression, is fired in a scene reminiscent of the St. Peter's firework display. At first the chateau begins 'to make itself strangely visible, by some light of its own, as though it were growing luminous'. Soon flames burst out of the windows, rents and splits branch out in the solid walls 'like crystallization', and lead and iron boil in the marble basin of the fountain. The 'illuminated village' rings its bells for joy.

Even when a mob can't actually burn things, Dickens gives it bits of fire to signify its rage and frenzy. The mob which hunts down Sikes is 'a struggling current of angry faces, with here and there a glaring torch to light them up'. Similarly, if a character can't be supplied with a blazing house to symbolize his violence, the fire can be conveyed in the imagery. When, in *Little Dorrit*, Mrs. Clennam is eventually goaded beyond endurance by Rigaud, she defies him, Dickens says, 'with the set expression of her face all torn away by the explosion of her passion, and with a bursting from every rent feature of the smouldering fire so long pent up'. Mrs. Clennam, like the steamship *Britannia*, shows fire at every porthole. Introducing Krook, the villainous rag and bottle dealer in *Bleak House*, Dickens draws attention to 'the breath issuing in visible smoke from his mouth, as if he were on fire within'. Unlike Mrs. Clennam and the *Britannia*, Krook does, of course, literally explode later in the novel, leaving nothing but oily soot on the walls of his room. Dickens regularly spoke of his own industry and his need for strenuous exercise in the same fiery terms. 'I blaze away, wrathful and red-hot,' he reported, at work on *The Chimes*. 'If I couldn't walk fast and far I should just explode.'

Great Expectations is another novel which plays with fire. The blacksmith's furnace, with its red-hot sparks and murky shadows, and its two giants, Joe and Orlick, one good, one bad, is an imaginative touchstone in the book. Walking home at night Pip notices the furnace 'flinging a path of fire across the road'. Out on the marshes the torches of the search party are intensely seen. 'The torches we carried, dropped great blotches of fire upon the track, and I could see those, too, lying smoking and flaring . . . Our lights warmed the air about us with their pitchy blaze.' Pip's sister is murderously struck down by a blow on the head at a moment when, Dickens notes, 'her face was turned towards the fire.' Pip sees the face of Estella's mother 'as if it were all disturbed by fiery air', like a face passing behind 'a bowl of flaming spirits in a darkened room'. Dickens intends this as an index, of course, of the criminal passions that lurk within. Miss Havisham goes up in flames, 'shrieking, with a whirl of fire blazing all about her, and soaring at least as many feet above her head as she was high'. She had, of course, tempted providence by becoming so fond of Joe's blacksmith song about fire 'soaring higher', which Pip taught her. The image of her rouged corpse with fire bursting from its head had so strong an appeal, it seems, that Dickens attached it, rather gratuitously, to Magwitch as well. The disguise Magwitch contrives for leaving London includes a 'touch of powder', which suggests to Pip:

the probable effect of rouge upon the dead; so awful was the manner in which everything in him, that it was most desirable to repress, started through the thin layer of pretence, and seemed to come blazing out at the crown of his head.

Miss Havisham on fire, and the fire of Joe's smithy, fuse in Pip's mind. Delirious, after his own narrow escape from being burned in Orlick's lime-kiln, he dreams of an iron furnace in a corner of his room, and a voice calling that Miss Havisham is burning within. Pip's sick fancy recalls Esther Summerson's dream, striking in one so uninflammable, that she is a bead on a 'flaming necklace' in 'black space', praying to be released from 'the dreadful thing'.

Joe is a good character, of course: the repository of those natural, human affections that Dickens dwells upon with such patronizing approval. His association with fire warns us that in Dickens' imaginative landscape fire is not simply the sign of violence and destruction. It is a leading characteristic of Dickens' mind that he is able to see almost everything from two opposed points of view. In his thinking about society this often makes him look confused and hypocritical, as we have noted. Even a major Dickensian property like the prison is viewed at different times as a hideous deprivation of freedom and as a snug retreat from the world. Some of the prisoners released from Newgate by the mob, creep back and 'lounge about the old place'. For them it's home. So, too, with fire. A violent, though enthralling destroyer on the one hand, it also becomes, in the innumerable cosy Dickensian inn parlours with their blazing logs, a natural accompaniment to comfort and security. The fire of Joe Gargery's forge represents the safety of the childhood home. It flings a path of fire across Pip's road as a friendly, domestic warning to turn him aside from his ruinous ambitions. With something of the same purpose, no doubt, it tries to cremate Miss Havisham, who has done her best to make Pip rebel against the values of home and fireside.

The episode in *The Old Curiosity Shop* where Nell and her grandfather make a brief excursion into the industrial midlands neatly illustrates Dickens' two ways of looking at fire. A lurid glare in the sky hangs over the neighbourhood, and the wanderers meet a factory worker, imagined by Dickens as a sort of smoky goblin, who lets them spend a comfortable night in the ashes beside his furnace. This touching scene is strangely out of key with the way the factory is described. It is said to be full of the 'deafening' noise of hammers. Men move 'like demons' among the flame and smoke, 'tormented by the burning fires', and drag from the white-hot furnace doors sheets of clashing steel, 'emitting an insupportable heat, and a dull deep light like that which reddens in the eyes of savage beasts'. The factory worker proves communicative about his own particular fire. It has been alive, he says, as long as he has. He crawled among its ashes as a baby. It's his 'book' and his 'memory': he sees faces and scenes among its red-hot coals. In Dickens' terms this marks him as a good character. Only virtuous people in the novels practise this species of fire watching. We recall Lizzie Hexam in *Our Mutual Friend* who develops her imagination by looking at red-hot embers, in strong contrast to her selfish brother Charlie who wants to better himself by reading books. The fire in this episode, then, is both nurse and destroyer; the fire of home and the fire of Hell.

Dickens, who saw himself as the great prophet of cosy, domestic virtue, purveyor of improving literature to the middle classes, never seems to have quite reconciled himself to the fact that violence and destruction were the most powerful stimulants to his imagination. To the end of his career he continues to insert the sickly scenes of family fun, and seriously asks us to accept them as the positives in his fiction. The savages and the cynics, the Quilps and the Scrooges, who have all the vitality, are, in the end, tritely punished or improbably converted. His public championship of domestic bliss became so natural to him that he persisted in it even when his own actions wildly belied it. Starting a new magazine in 1859, he seriously proposed to call it *Household Harmony*, despite the fact that he had recently separated from his wife, had personally announced in the newspapers that she was an unsatisfactory mother disliked by all her children, and was himself having an affair with the actress Ellen Ternan. When Forster pointed out that the proposed title would be met with derision, Dickens was surprised and irritated.

With so much of his imaginative self invested in his violent and vicious characters, and so much of the self he approved of vowed to the service of home and family life, Dickens has a particular weakness for villains whose express intention it is to smash up happy homes. Silas Wegg in *Our Mutual Friend* walks to the Boffin house each evening in order to gloat over it like an evil genius, exulting in his power 'to strip the roof off the inhabiting family like the roof of a house of cards'. It was, says Dickens, 'a treat which had a charm for Silas Wegg'. For Dickens too, to judge from the vigour of the image. Steerforth, in *David Copperfield*, smashes the pure Peggotty home by seducing Little Em'ly. The old converted boat in which the Peggottys pursue their blameless existence is blown down on the night of the storm which drowns Steerforth. David finds him next morning, lying appropriately 'among the ruins of the home he had wronged'. Even Gabriel Varden in *Barnaby Rudge* indulges in some miniature home-smashing. Mrs. Varden has been in the habit of putting her voluntary contributions to the Protestant cause in a collecting box shaped like a little red-brick dwelling house with a yellow roof. When the riots show how mistaken her allegiance has been, Gabriel throws the little house on the floor and crushes it with his heel. So much for little houses, militant Protestants and meddling females. Apart from the home, the main haunt of Dickensian snugness is the inn. Of the Maypole Inn in *Barnaby Rudge* he writes: 'All bars are snug places, but the Maypole's was the very snuggest, cosiest and completest bar, that ever the wit of man devised.' A rhapsodic description of its neat rows of bottles in oaken pigeon-holes, and its snowy loaves of sugar follows. It's appropriate that this veritable temple of snugness and security should be selected by Dickens for one of his wildest home-wrecking scenes. When the mob arrive at the Maypole, equipped with their usual flaring torches, they smash the glass, turn all the liquor taps on, hack the cheeses to bits, break open the drawers, saw down the inn sign and are divided in opinion whether to hang the landlord or burn him alive. Dickens' tone is predominantly comic, and there is no mistaking the pleasure with which he elaborates the details of pillage and destruction.

Early in his career Dickens began to produce narratives in which the figures who are regarded with the most intense fellow feeling are the murderers. He habitually speaks about murderers' mental habits with extraordinary self-confidence, as if he were one himself. The consequences of murder, he asserts in *Bleak House*, are always hidden from the murderer behind a 'gigantic dilation' of his victim, and rush upon him only when the blow is struck. This 'always happens when a murder is done'. Similarly he is adamant that murderers like Sikes, who do not give 'the faintest indication of a better nature', really do exist. 'That the fact is so, I am sure.' From where, we wonder, could he get such certainty? The conformist part of him repudiated his murderers with horror. But the artist delved with fascination into their responses, and particularly into how they feel when hunted down or at bay. In *Master Humphrey's Clock*, for instance, we find a first-person narrative in which Dickens casts himself in the role of a child slayer, telling what it was like to murder his brother's son. He stabs him in a garden, and as he does so he is struck not only by the look in his victim's eyes, but also by the eyes which seem to watch him, even in the drops of water on the leaves. 'There were eyes in everything.' He buries the child in a piece of ground which is to be newly turfed, but when the lawn has been completed over the grave he is haunted by visions of the child's hand or his foot or his head sticking up through the grass. He sits and watches the secret grave all day. 'When a servant walked across it, I felt as if he must sink in; when he had passed, I looked to see that his feet had not worn the edges.' Eventually he has a table set out on the lawn, and puts his chair directly over the grave, so that no one can disturb it. When he is entertaining some friends at this table, though, two great bloodhounds come bounding into the garden and circle about it excitedly, ending up snuffing at the earth directly under his chair. As his friends dragged him away, he says, 'I saw the angry dogs tearing at the earth and throwing it up into the air like water.' Bill Sikes, like this murderer, is haunted by eyes after his slaying of Nancy, and it is his dog's eyes gleaming from behind the chimney pot that send him plunging to his death. ' "The eyes again!" he cried in an unearthly screech.' Similarly the elder Mr. Rudge, who has little to occupy himself with in the novel besides galloping furiously through the night, is brought to life for a moment when Dickens shows him remembering the circumstances of the murder he committed. He recalls how his victim's face went stiff, 'and so fell idly down with upturned eyes, like the dead stags' he had often peeped at when a little child: shrinking and shuddering . . . and clinging to an apron as he looked.' The flash of childhood recollection at the moment of murder is instantly convincing: the one convincing sentence about Mr. Rudge in the entire book. Again, Jonas Chuzzlewit isn't generally a figure we feel Dickens has managed to get inside. He is viewed from above as a vile, cringing specimen with whom we can all feel virtuously disgusted. But in the few pages where he commits murder he suddenly becomes the recipient of Dickens' imaginative sympathy. The details of the blotched, stained, mouldering room with its gurgling water-pipes in which Jonas locks himself are intently conveyed. When he unlocks the long-unused door in order to slink off and murder Montague Tigg, Dickens makes the reader attend to his tiniest movements:

He put the key into the lock, and turned it. The door resisted for a while, but soon came stiffly open; mingling with the sense of fever in his mouth, a taste of rust, and dust, and earth, and rotting wood.

We know even what the murderer's mouth tastes like. After the murder, Jonas keeps fancying himself creeping back through the undergrowth to peer at the corpse, 'startling the very flies that were thickly sprinkled all over it, like heaps of dried currants'. The simile – added in the manuscript – shows Dickens' imagination entrapped by the scene, like Jonas'. But Jonas has to commit murder to get promoted from the status of a routine Dickensian villain and earn himself a page or two of great literature. No other human experience – least of all the positive human experiences, like being in love – will arouse Dickens to such intense imaginative sympathy as the experience of being a murderer. One of his most vivid studies in this mode is Fagin on trial for his life – a very different matter from Fagin in the death cell a few pages later, where he is transformed into a gibbering wretch for the unctuous Oliver to pity. Fagin's sensations in the courtroom are recorded as scrupulously as Jonas Chuzzlewit's:

He looked up into the gallery again. Some of the people were eating, and some fanning themselves with handkerchiefs; for the crowded place was very hot. There was one young man sketching his face in a little notebook. He wondered whether it was like, and looked on when the artist broke his pencil point, and made another with his knife, as any idle spectator might have done . . . There was an old fat gentleman on the bench, too, who had gone out, some half an hour before, and now come back. He wondered within himself whether this man had been to get his

dinner, what he had had, and where he had had it . . . He fell to counting
the iron spikes before him, and wondering how the head of one had been
broken off, and whether they would mend it or leave it as it was.

Here the hypersensitivity, combined with a strange feeling of
detachment, common to people who find themselves at the centre of
an accident, are conveyed by Dickens with absolute seriousness of
intent and perfect artistic honesty. The temptation to use Fagin as
the occasion for lofty moralizing is withstood, though Dickens
succumbs to it soon afterwards. Oliver's reactions after the trial are,
by contrast, wholly preposterous: ' "Oh! God forgive this wretched
man!" cried the boy with a burst of tears. . . . Oliver nearly swooned
after this frightful scene, and was so weak that for an hour or more,
he had not the strength to walk.' Dickens could furnish this type of
saintly confection in unlimited quantities, but the triumphs of his
art stick out of it like islands, and there is no difficulty about distinguishing them.

Before Oliver's visit Fagin's mind is seized with the details of
how murderers are disposed of: 'With what a rattling noise the drop
went down; and how suddenly they changed, from strong and
vigorous men to dangling heaps of clothes.' A keen interest in the
different methods of executing men, and the precise manner of each,
was another aspect of Dickens' preoccupation with violence. The
guillotine stands in the foreground of *A Tale of Two Cities*. Charles
Darnay, in the condemned cell, realizes he has never seen it, and
questions about it keep thrusting themselves into his mind: 'How
high it was from the ground, how many steps it had, where he would
be stood . . . which way his face would be turned.' Dickens could
have enlightened him. When in Rome he went to see a man guillo-
tined, and has left a minute account of the whole affair, from the
behaviour of the various members of the crowd to the appearance of
the scaffold: 'An untidy, unpainted, uncouth, crazy-looking thing . . .
some seven feet high, perhaps: with a tall, gallows-shaped frame
rising above it, in which was the knife, charged with a ponderous
mass of iron.' The prisoner appears on the platform, barefoot, hands
bound, the collar and neck of his shirt cut away. A young, pale man,
with a small dark moustache, and dark brown hair.

He immediately kneeled down, below the knife. His neck fitting into a
hole, made for the purpose, in a cross plank, was shut down, by another
plank above; exactly like the pillory. Immediately below him was a
leathern bag. And into it his head rolled instantly.

The executioner was holding it by the hair, and walking with it round the scaffold, showing it to the people, before one quite knew that the knife had fallen heavily, and with a rattling sound.

The head is set up on a pole – 'a little patch of black and white' for 'the flies to settle on'. The eyes, Dickens notices, are turned up, 'as if he had avoided the sight of the leathern bag'. He stays on to see the scaffold washed down, observing 'There was a great deal of blood,' and to get a closer look at the body.

A strange appearance was the apparent annihilation of the neck. The head was taken off so close, that it seemed as if the knife had narrowly escaped crushing the jaw, or shaving off the ear; and the body looked as if there were nothing left above the shoulder.

The eager, graphic brilliance of the writing throughout hardly prepares one for the moral stance Dickens hastily adopts at the end, complaining that the crowd were callous, and that several attempts were made to pick his pocket during the spectacle.

In July 1840 Dickens was one of the 40,000 people who witnessed the hanging of the murderer Courvoisier. Writing of it later he is again hot against the pickpockets, and stigmatizes the disgraceful behaviour of the crowd, whose motives for being there, he leaves us in no doubt, are altogether more reprehensible than his own. Opposed in principle to capital punishment, he plainly cannot admit to himself that he watches it out of curiosity, like everyone else. When Mr. and Mrs. George Manning were hanged together in 1849 on top of the Horsemonger Lane Gaol, Dickens was in attendance again to see them 'turned quivering into the air'. He recalls the curious difference in appearance between the two dangling bodies: 'the man's, a limp, loose suit of clothes as if the man had gone out of them; the woman's, a fine shape, so elaborately corseted and artfully dressed, that it was quite unchanged in its trim appearance as it slowly swung from side to side'. In Switzerland he went to see a man beheaded, and writes an account later in *Household Words*. The victim sits tied to a chair on a scaffold, and the executioner uses a huge sword loaded with quicksilver in the thick part of the blade.

It's plain that Dickens derives a considerable thrill, too, from visiting localities where executions and murders have occurred. The only thing that redeemed the city of Norwich, in his eyes, was its place of execution, 'fit for a gigantic scoundrel's exit'. After a tour of the prison at Venice he writes, 'I had my foot upon the spot, where . . . the shriven prisoner was strangled.' In the Tombs Prison in

New York he has himself conducted to the yard where prisoners are hanged: 'The wretched creature stands beneath the gibbet on the ground; the rope about his neck; and when the sign is given, a weight at its other end comes running down, and swings him up into the air – a corpse.' Dickens preferred this method to the English – 'far less degrading and indecent'. By the time he visited America again, a former acquaintance of his had been able to assess its advantages. This was Professor Webster of Harvard, hanged for murdering a colleague, portions of whose body he had concealed about his lecture room. Dickens eagerly inspected the scene of the crime, sniffed the unpleasant odours of the furnace – 'some anatomical broth in it I suppose' – and peered at the 'pieces of sour mortality' standing around in jars. In *Sketches by Boz* he relates how he often wanders into Newgate Prison 'to catch a glimpse of the whipping place, and that dark building on one side of the yard, in which is kept the gibbet with all its dreadful apparatus'. Dennis the hangman in *Barnaby Rudge* provides Dickens with ample opportunity for anecdotes about the dreadful apparatus and its operation. The first feature of Dennis to which Dickens draws attention is his neck, with its great veins 'swollen and starting'. A neck for stretching, as Dennis himself would say, and at the end of the novel it is stretched – unlike that of the real-life Dennis, who was reprieved. Several aspects of the execution scene show that Dickens' imaginative powers have been aroused: Dennis between two officers, unable to walk for terror, his legs trailing on the ground; the room into which the prisoners are taken to have their irons struck off, so close to the gallows that they can plainly hear people in the crowd outside complaining of the crush; and the gallows itself, its black paint blistering in the sun, and 'its nooses dangling . . . like loathsome garlands'.

A form of violence more exotic and, to Dickens' way of thinking, more amusing than capital punishment was cannibalism, and we can see his thoughts straying towards it on several occasions. He was introduced to the subject by his nurse, Mary Weller, who used to take a fiendish delight in terrifying him with the story of a certain Captain Murderer whose practice it was to get his tender young brides to make a piecrust into which he would then chop them up, adding pepper and salt. The resultant pie he would eat, with his teeth filed sharp by the blacksmith for the occasion. He was finally thwarted by a bride who took deadly poison just before he killed her, so that after his meal he began to swell and turn blue, and went on swelling until he blew up with a loud explosion – an early version of Krook in *Bleak House*. The Fat Boy in *Pickwick Papers* has similar tendencies. He is about to consume a meat pie when he notices Mary, the pretty housemaid, sitting opposite. He leans forward, knife and fork in hand, and slowly enunciates: 'I say! How nice you look.' 'There was enough of the cannibal in the young gentleman's eyes', Dickens remarks, 'to render the compliment a double one.' When Hugh in *Barnaby Rudge* has the delicious Dolly Varden and haughty Emma Haredale at his mercy, imprisoned in a closed carriage, he insists on speaking of them as delicate, tender birds, and stares into the carriage, we are told, 'like an ogre into his larder'. Furthermore Dickens is just as excited as Hugh and his confederates at the sight of tempting, helpless femininity, and hardly conceals the fact. 'Poor Dolly! Do what she would, she only looked the better for it, and tempted them the more. When her eyes flashed angrily, and her ripe lips slightly parted, to give her rapid breathing vent, who could resist it?' Not Dickens, we gather, who is evidently salivating freely. It is by far his sexiest scene, which makes the cannibalistic hint more worth noting. Even Pecksniff, in *Martin Chuzzlewit*, has a cannibalistic impulse when forcing his attentions on the maidenly Mary Grant, having first got her alone in a wood, as Hugh does with Dolly Varden. Mary struggles but, Dickens comments, 'she might as well have tried to free herself from the embrace of an affectionate boa-constrictor.' Pecksniff clutches one of her hands, despite her attempts to pull it free, and gazes at it speculatively, 'tracing the course of one delicate blue vein with his fat thumb'. Eventually he holds up her little finger and asks, 'in playful accents', 'Shall I bite it?' But the tearful, trembling Mary doesn't get nibbled after all: Pecksniff kisses the finger and lets her have it back. In both these scenes the flutterings of female distress and the humbling of female pride are evidently so appetizing to Dickens that it is really hypocritical of him to pretend that the two men concerned are thorough rogues with whom he has no sympathy. But as usual he can preserve his moral composure only by foisting his violent imaginings onto another character, whom he then condemns for imagining them. A further edible heroine is Estella – or so it seems to Miss Havisham, who eyes the girl 'with a ravenous intensity', 'as though she were devouring the beautiful creature.' In *Bleak House* the cannibal is the dyspeptic Vholes. Given to regarding Richard 'as if he were making a lingering meal of him', he finally quits the novel with a gasp, suggesting that he has 'swallowed the last morsel of his client'. Opponents of legal reform defend Vholes' livelihood as though he and his relations were 'minor cannibal chiefs' threatened by the abolition of cannibalism. 'Make man-eating unlawful, and you starve the Vholeses!' Pip in *Great Expectations* is likewise an edible hero. Magwitch, on the marsh, is immediately tempted by his plumpness: ' "You young dog," said the man, licking his lips, "what fat cheeks you ha' got . . . Darn Me if I couldn't eat 'em".' He refrains, however, and instead tells Pip about the young man whom he is with difficulty holding back from tearing out Pip's heart and liver and eating them, roasted. Uncle Pumblechook's mouth seems to water too, at the sight of the succulent boy, and he takes pleasure in informing Pip that if he had been born a pig Dunstable the butcher would have come along and seized him under his arm and taken out his penknife from his waistcoat pocket and killed him for pork. 'He would have shed your blood and had your life.' 'I'm a going to have your life!' declares Orlick, later in the novel, when he has Pip all ready trussed up in the sluice-house on the marsh: 'He leaned forward staring at me, slowly unclenched his hand and drew it across his mouth as if his mouth watered for me.' It's unusual to find a hero who has such difficulty keeping himself out of the stomachs of the other characters.

Dickens' need to express his violent and murderous instincts through his fiction can be seen, of course, as early as *Pickwick Papers*. But there the tales of savagery and slaughter are kept apart from the main narrative and are quite untouched by the humour which pervades it. In the tale called *A Madman's Manuscript*, for example, Dickens tries to imagine himself into a demented wife-slayer: 'Oh! the pleasure of stropping the razor day after day, feeling the sharp edge, and thinking of the gash one stroke of its thin bright edge would make!' Another of the inset tales concerns a man who murderously avenges himself for the imprisonment of himself and his family in the Marshalsea. This, it has been conjectured, may mean that Dickens' resentment against society over his father's imprisonment is one of the roots of his violence. But the *Pickwick* tales, particularly *A Madman's Manuscript*, are forced and melodramatic, because Dickens' sense of humour, his greatest gift as a novelist, simply switches off when he starts to tell them. Not until the writing of *The Old Curiosity Shop* in 1840 did he create an embodiment of his violence who could also express his black and anarchic laughter. This embodiment was Daniel Quilp, a magnificent invention who is able to embrace all the variations of violence Dickens can desire.

Quilp is both dwarf and giant – a dwarf in body, with a giant's head. For teeth he has a few discoloured fangs, and he is so filthy that when he rubs his hands together the dirt drops off in pellets. Much of his time is spent in driving to ludicrous excess the components of Dickensian cheeriness. Conviviality trails a hair-raising image of itself around with it. Food consumption, for instance, is an indispensable accompaniment of Dickensian bliss. Quilp approaches meals with horrible ferocity. He eats hard-boiled eggs shell and all. He devours 'gigantic prawns with the heads and tails on'. He chews tobacco and watercress at the same time, and bites his fork and spoon until they bend. He smokes pipes of hideous strength, and forces his guests to do the same, warning them that otherwise he will put the sealing-waxed end in the fire and rub it red-hot on their tongues. He drinks boiling spirit, bubbling and hissing fiercely, straight from the saucepan. He pinches his wife black and blue, bites her, and keeps her in constant terror of the ingenious punishments he devises. For all this she is utterly infatuated, and tells her lady friends that they would all marry Quilp tomorrow if they had a chance. What's more, Dickens implies that she is right. His corrected proofs show that Quilp was originally meant to have a child by Sally Brass – an earnest of his exceptional virility. When amused, Quilp screams and rolls on the floor. He delights in tormenting animals as well as people. Finding a dog chained up he taunts it with hideous faces, and dances round it snapping his fingers, driving it wild with rage. He keeps a huge wooden figurehead of an admiral, sawn off at the waist, in his room, and diverts himself by driving red-hot pokers through it. He is, in short, a masterpiece of creative energy in comparison with whom Little Nell and her grandfather and all their part of the novel are so much waste paper.

Dickens was never able to create a second Quilp, but bits of him turn up in the other novels. His treatment of his wife is reflected in Flintwinch in *Little Dorrit*, who shakes Mrs. Flintwinch by the throat till she's black in the face, and twists her nose between his thumb and finger with all the 'screw-power of his person'. Cruncher in *A Tale of Two Cities*, who flings boots at his wife because she insists on saying her prayers, has Quilpish quality too. Quilp's taste for boiling spirit is something he shares with the maddened rioters in *Barnaby Rudge*. When a vintner's house catches light they lap up the scorching liquor which flows along the gutters, dropping dead by the dozen, rolling and hissing in a lake of flame, and splashing up liquid fire. Already in *Pickwick Papers*, in the story of the goblins and the sexton, the goblin king had drunk blazing liquor, his cheeks and throat growing transparent as he swallowed it. And the thrill of blistering beverages survives in *Our Mutual Friend*. Jenny Wren, saddled with a sottish parent, invents a short way with drunkards:

When he was asleep, I'd make a spoon red-hot, and I'd have some boiling liquor bubbling in a saucepan, and I'd take it out hissing, and I'd open his mouth with the other hand – or perhaps he'd sleep with his mouth ready open – and I'd pour it down his throat, and blister it and choke him.

Quilp piercing the admiral with a red-hot poker is recalled in David Copperfield's vindictive fantasies relative to Uriah Heep. When Heep is audacious enough to fall in love with Agnes, David is tempted to seize the red-hot poker from the fire and run him through the body with it. That night he dreams so vividly that he's actually done this that he has to creep into Heep's bedroom to make sure he's still alive. Pip in *Great Expectations* recalls how Orlick drew a red-hot bar from the furnace and 'made at me with it as if he were going to run it through my body'. According to Dickens, one of his nurse's ghoulish tales featured a lady who slew her husband with a heated poker, so his interest in this topic began early.

Quilp is Dickens' way of avenging himself upon the sentimental set-up of *The Old Curiosity Shop*, upon all that part of his nature that revelled in angelic, plaster heroines, the deaths of little children, and touching animals. To aid her in her assault on the readers' hearts, for example, Nell has a little bird in a cage. Quilp threatens to wring its neck. He is salaciously inclined towards Little Nell herself, gloats over her blue veins and transparent skin, and invites her to become the second Mrs. Quilp. Nell trembles violently, much to Quilp's amusement. When he takes over Nell's grandfather's house, he chooses her own little bed to sleep in. Dickens offers violence to his own sexless heroine in these passages, and with aggressive enjoyment. Quilp's reduction of his wife to a mass of bruises gives an outlet to Dickens' punitive feelings towards women, which he felt the need to repress when speaking about them in his own person. In *Martin Chuzzlewit*, reporting that Jonas actually struck his wife,

Dickens soars into virtuous indignation and the second person singular – always a bad sign with him: 'Oh woman, God beloved in old Jerusalem! The best among us need deal lightly with thy faults.' After the strain of such noble attitudes Quilp would clearly be a relief.

Both before and after 1840 Dickens attempted to create violent villains, but none ever rivals Quilp, because their violence seems stuck on, not essential to their natures, as Quilp's is. Monks, for instance, in *Oliver Twist*, has fits, writhes on the ground, foams at the mouth, bites his hands and covers them with wounds, and entertains the Bumbles to the accompaniment of thunder and lightning. But he lacks Quilp's humour and energy. On the one occasion he tries to hit Oliver, he falls over. Uriah Heep has an isolated moment of violent power. This is in the scene with David where he tells him he has Agnes' father, Mr. Wickfield, under his thumb:

'Un – der – his thumb,' said Uriah, very slowly, as he stretched out his cruel-looking hand above my table, and pressed his own thumb down upon it, until it shook, and shook the room.

Heep is a boy of 15, and nothing in his cringing gait or starved appearance suggests a figure who could shake a whole room merely by pressing the table with his thumb. In this instant he is about to turn into an altogether different and more violent creation, but Dickens doesn't forget himself again.

Thomas Wright notes that Quilp's mother-in-law Mrs. Jiniwin was modelled on Dickens' mother-in-law Mrs. Hogarth. Quilp was, in a sense, Dickens himself, as seen through his mother-in-law's disapproving eyes. In his last completed novel Dickens drew another violent villain, also to some degree a self-portrait – Bradley Headstone. Headstone's jealous love for Lizzie Hexam is usually taken to reflect Dickens' feelings for his young mistress Ellen Ternan, and the location of Headstone's school, Edgar Johnson has noticed, parallels that of the house, Windsor Lodge, which Dickens had rented for Ellen. Comparing Headstone with Quilp's fine demonic rapture allows us to see how much has been lost over the years. Headstone is presented as a man of terrible passions which lurk beneath a respectable exterior. When moved, his lips quiver uncontrollably, blood gushes from his nose, his face turns 'from burning red to white, and from white back to burning red', and he punches a stone wall until his knuckles are raw and bleeding. When he hears of Lizzie's marriage he throws a fit, and bites and lashes about. As he sleeps, red and blue lightning and palpitating white fire flicker about his bed. On one of his particularly bad nights Dickens shows him sitting in front of the fire, 'the dark lines deepening in his face . . . and the very texture and colour of his hair degenerating'. Despite all these alarming physical symptoms, though, Headstone is utterly helpless and ineffective. He has no weapons against Eugene Wrayburn's cool irony, which goads him almost to madness. There is no glimmer of humour about him or his presentation. Compared to Quilp, he is a lamb for the slaughter. He is sexually null too. His desire for Lizzie is a dry, theoretic passion. There is nothing to show he even notices her body, as Quilp does Nell's.

The trouble is that Headstone is only partly a vehicle for Dickens' love for Ellen. He also has to serve as a diagram for certain social developments that Dickens deplores. From humble origins he has raised himself by hard work and is now a schoolmaster. Dickens, formerly a hearty advocate of universal education, now sees it as the breeder of pedantry and social pretensions. Once educated, the lower classes get above themselves. In his decent black coat and waistcoat Headstone looks, Dickens says, like a workman in his holiday clothes. He might have made a good sailor if, when a pauper child, he had taken to the sea instead of to learning. As it is, his learning is merely mechanically acquired. Needless to say, Dickens doesn't explain what the alternative ways of acquiring learning might be. When Headstone has committed, or thinks he has committed, murder, he is made into a model to illustrate another of Dickens' pet social theories: that the murderer is never sorry for his crime. All Headstone can think about is how he might have got rid of Wrayburn more efficiently. Dickens is no longer an opponent of capital punishment. Headstone proves a failure because he is fabricated out of his author's social prejudices, instead of being impelled, as Quilp is, by his author's savage humour, self-criticism and emancipation from the cant and sentimentality that were always threatening to kill Dickens' art.

It would be wrong to conclude that because Headstone is a violent character, and is disapproved of by Dickens, Dickens has grown disillusioned with violence. On the contrary, he retains to the end his perfectly simple faith in a strong right arm. Nicholas Nickleby is the first of the heroes to exercise his virtuous muscles on evil-doers. Though slight in appearance – John Browdie refers to him as a whipper-snapper – he makes an impressive showing when struck across the face by Squeers: 'Nicholas sprang upon him, wrested the weapon from his hand, and pinning him by the throat, beat the ruffian till he roared for mercy.' Mr. Lenville is the next victim: 'Nicholas ... suffered him to approach to within the requisite distance, and then, without the smallest discomposure, knocked him down.' To complete the act Nicholas picks up Mr. Lenville's ash stick, breaks it in half, tosses him the pieces, and makes his exit. There follows a fine dramatic encounter between Nicholas and the dastardly Sir Mulberry Hawk: 'Stand out of the way, dog,' blusters Sir Mulberry. Nicholas shouts that he is the son of a country gentleman, and lays Sir Mulberry's face open from eye to lip. Finally Nicholas confronts the arch villain, Uncle Ralph. ' "One word!" cried Ralph, foaming at the mouth.' But Nicholas, distrustful of words, knocks down Ralph's elderly fellow-conspirator Arthur Gride instead, picks up Madeline Bray, and rushes out with, as Dickens puts it, 'his beautiful burden in his arms'. Granted this is a very early novel, but the victory of righteousness is no less physical, and no less theatrical, at the end of *Martin Chuzzlewit*. Old Martin rises against Pecksniff and strikes him to the ground, 'with such a well-directed nervous blow, that down he went, as heavily and true as if the charge of a Life-Guardsman had tumbled him out of the saddle'. The soldierly simile here is, of course, meant to give the violence an especially decent flavour. A similar motive prompts Dickens to remind us, at the end of *Our Mutual Friend*, that John Harmon's 'seafaring hold was like that of a vice', and that he takes a 'sailor-like turn' on Silas Wegg's cravat, preparatory to knocking Silas' head against the wall. There is something healthy and patriotic about a sailor, which makes it all right to assault a cripple. Eventually Wegg and his wooden leg are carried downstairs and thrown into a muck cart. By such summary means is evil expelled from a Dickens novel.

We notice, in these examples, how the writing deteriorates once the violence becomes virtuous. The military images are shoddy subterfuge. Hopelessly dignified, the good characters brandish their sticks or fists, and the villains tumble. Dickens beams complacently. It is a dutiful, perfunctory business. Riot, murder, savagery have to be there before Dickens' imagination is gripped.

2

DICKENS AND ORDER

In one of his papers in *The Uncommercial Traveller* Dickens recalls a visit he paid to a Welsh clergyman who had been responsible for collecting and burying the corpses of the passengers and crew of the Australian trading ship, the *Royal Charter*, which went down off the Welsh coast in October 1859. Dickens was always intrigued by corpses, but the paper contains a surprising amount of ghoulish curiosity even for him. He eagerly examines the stains on the church floor which mark where the bodies were laid out. He is interested to learn that the laundry marks on the clothes of the female corpses often showed that they were wearing garments which were the property of other passengers, indicating that they must have dressed in great haste and agitation. But what chiefly appeals to Dickens throughout is the orderliness and efficiency with which the clergyman has managed to sort out the corpses, document them, accommodate among his 'neatly arranged papers' the numerous letters from their bereaved relatives, bury them and, if necessary, dig them up again. 'He had', Dickens explains, 'numbered each body in a register describing it, and had placed a corresponding number on each coffin, and over each grave.' Exhumed corpses qualified for a second burial service before they were reburied. Dickens inspects two coffins which happen to be awaiting occupants, and is pleased to report that they are 'neatly formed'. The exhumed travellers, he records with satisfaction, did not smell, or, as he puts it, there was 'no offence in the poor ashes when they were brought again to the light of day'.

Neatness, orderliness and personal cleanliness, even among corpses, were passionate concerns of Dickens. We recall how in *Bleak House* Jo the crossing sweeper is taken off for a bath and arrayed in clean linen to get him ready for the touching death scene which Dickens has in store. Indeed any child from a poor background in a Dickens novel who finds itself suddenly washed and laundered has good reason to suspect that its days are numbered. But Dickens' worship of order and cleanliness has a much more profound effect on the novels than these details suggest. In his family life his concern with neatness was obsessive. Each morning he went upstairs to inspect the drawers in his daughters' bedroom, and left notes reprimanding any untidiness. If, when he was in the garden, the wind ruffled his hair, he would rush indoors to brush it. At Gadshill the villagers found themselves running footraces and playing cricket under Dickens' meticulous supervision. 'Method in everything' was his watchword. He valued absolute punctuality, and demanded it from his children and servants. In Italy he was greatly irritated by the dirt and slackness of the foreigners, but was glad to see that the railway was gradually introducing punctuality and order even there. England seemed 'wonderfully neat' on his return. When he decided to sample the 'innocent vivacity' of the Carnival at Rome he was pleased to find that the streets were vigilantly patrolled by dragoons, and that any carriage that got out of line was quickly escorted back to its place by a mounted trooper.

Untidy streets disgusted him. In *Our Mutual Friend* he inserts a paragraph complaining about the waste paper which blows about the streets of London. In Paris, where the cost of living is high, he explains, the inhabitants have 'sharp stomachs', so nothing is wasted. 'Human ants creep out of holes and pick up every scrap.' The implication is that a little starvation wonderfully improves a city's appearance.

Well-ordered public institutions were another of his specialities. He visited them untiringly. His American journal is full of sentences like 'There is a good stone prison here,' 'There is a bomb-proof fort here,' 'In the suburbs there is a spacious cemetery: unfinished yet, but every day improving.' He is enchanted to find how well run the South Boston lunatic asylum is: 'Every patient in this asylum sits down to dinner every day with a knife and fork.' On the other hand in the prison at New York he notices that one of the prisoners has left his clothes scattered about the floor of his cell, and asks the gaoler, 'Don't you oblige the prisoners to be orderly?' Inspecting the factory girls at Lowell he is relieved to find that their virtues include cleanliness. 'The rooms in which they worked', he adds, 'were as well ordered as themselves.' It is always a pleasure to Dickens to 'see the humbler classes of society careful of their dress

and appearance', as he puts it. Indeed, that is one of his standard
tests for distinguishing between the deserving and undeserving poor.
We need to remember this side of Dickens which yearns to see people
regimented, uniform in their behaviour, obeying rules. Opposed to it
always is the violent and anarchic side of him. The strength of each
side is determined by the strength of its opponent. When we hear
Dickens fulminating against statisticians and political economists,
against the wickedness of reducing human beings to ratios and
percentages, we should remind ourselves that it is a tendency in
himself that has aroused his anger. This helps to explain the intensity of that anger, and the exaggeration and misrepresentation which
mar his onslaughts on the percentage experts.

When Dickens visits establishments which cater for the cultural
or bodily welfare of the English lower classes the result is displeasing
not only because the tone reeks of condescension but also because
the concern with hygiene and orderliness eclipses everything else.
The Britannia Theatre at Hoxton, which put on pantomimes and
melodramas for working-class audiences, earned Dickens' commen-
dation because, thanks to the modern ventilation system, the
working classes like the Welsh clergyman's corpses, did not smell
when they were gathered together there, as they often did in the
commoner places of public resort. The remarkable achievement of
depriving the lower orders of their unwholesome odour Dickens
ascribes to the fact that the builders of the theatre have, as he puts it,
ingeniously combined 'the experience of hospitals and railway
stations'. The facetious tone he puts on to describe the plays he
sees there makes it plain that he regards them as absolute trash; but
he does not count this against the Britannia Theatre in the least. On
the contrary, the implication is that they are excellently adapted to
the occasion, and that for an audience of this class it would be
pretentious to produce anything else. A similar blend of hygienic
concern and jovial patronage distinguishes Dickens' account of his
visit to the Self-Supporting Cooking Depot for the Working Classes
in Commercial Street, Whitechapel. He chuckles at his own condescension in eating a fourpenny-halfpenny meal side by side with
the lower orders, and is loud in his applause of the 'neat and brisk
young woman' who takes the money, the 'neat smartness' with
which the waitresses dress and do their hair, and the 'pleasant and
pure' appearance of the cutlery. 'I dined at my club in Pall-Mall', he
adds, 'a few days afterwards, for exactly twelve times the money, and

not half as well.' From this we are meant to conclude, of course, that the working classes should be grateful for their neat cooking depot, rather than that they should wonder why they are twelve times poorer than Dickens.

In the novels neatness is frequently a sign of virtue. When Nicholas Nickleby is employed by the Cheeryble brothers he proves his worth by entering items in a ledger. Tim Linkinwater the clerk watches with great anxiety and then triumphantly announces that Nicholas has demonstrated his worthiness. 'He dots all his small i's and crosses every t as he writes it.' There are the feats that single out the Dickensian hero. In *Our Mutual Friend* John Harmon, disguised as John Rokesmith, exhibits his heroic qualities in the scene where he reduces Mr. Boffin's chaotic correspondence to order:

Relinquishing his hat and gloves, Mr. Rokesmith sat down quietly at the table, arranged the open papers into an orderly heap, cast his eyes over each in succession, folded it, docketed it on the outside, laid it in a second heap, and, when that second heap was complete and the first gone, took from his pocket a piece of string and tied it together with a remarkably dexterous hand . . . All compact and methodical.

'Apple-pie order!' applauds Mr. Boffin, and congratulates the hero on keeping his hands clean of ink. A comparable ordeal awaits the virtuous Tom Pinch in *Martin Chuzzlewit*. Mr. Fips takes him to a room containing 'boxes, hampers and all sorts of lumber' and several thousand books 'scattered singly or in heaps'. Pinch spends a few chapters setting things to rights, and then Dickens shows us the proud result:

He had got the books into perfect order now, and had mended the torn leaves, and pasted up the broken backs, and substituted neat labels for the worn out letterings. It looked a different place, it was so orderly and neat.

So, too, Arthur Clennam, the hero of *Little Dorrit*, proves his mettle by sitting in Daniel Doyce's counting-house and 'getting the array of business documents into perfect order'. The vagueness in all these episodes is remarkable. The reader gains no inkling of how the accounts of a firm are actually kept, or of what the merits of different accounting methods might be. Nor does he acquire any confidence in Dickens' understanding of these matters. The neatness is self-justifying, unrelated to any real occurrences in the world of finance, and does not extend beyond elementary gestures like dotting i's and typing papers in a bundle. It is what one would expect in a novel written for a child.

Neatness in household affairs is obligatory for Dickens' heroines, and seems chiefly to consist in keeping jams and pickles on their appropriate shelves and carrying around a little bunch of keys. Taking over at Bleak House, Esther Summerson reports:

> Every part of the house was in such order, and every one was so attentive to me, that I had no trouble with my two bunches of keys: though what with trying to remember the contents of each little store room drawer and cupboard; and what with making notes on a slate about jams, and pickles, and preserves, and bottles, and glass, and china, and a great many other things: and what with being generally a methodical, old-maidish sort of foolish little person; I was so busy that I could not believe it was breakfast time when I heard the bell ring.

The tidiness of the virtuous Esther is contrasted with Mrs. Jellyby's sluttish ways, and with the 'shabby luxury' amidst which the irresponsible Skimpole lives. Esther notices at once that Mr. Skimpole's hair is 'carelessly disposed' and his neckerchief loose, after which it is only to be expected that he will turn out thoroughly bad and betray Jo the crossing sweeper. Bella Wilfer in *Our Mutual Friend* tells her parents delightedly that she and her husband live in 'the charmingest of dolls' houses' and 'are economical and orderly, and do everything by clockwork'. And though she protests to her husband that she wants to be something much worthier than a doll in a doll's house, it's plain that Dickens finds her most delicious simply as that. He is enchanted by her neat little ways about the house, much as one might be about the antics of some small animal or particularly ingenious clockwork toy. She puts on 'trim little wrappers and aprons', and when she has written a letter she folds it and seals it and directs it and wipes her pen and wipes her middle finger – almost human, in fact. Another occupant of Dickens' dolls' house is Ruth Pinch in *Martin Chuzzlewit*, remarkable as much for her scrupulous neatness as for the modest palpitations her heart undergoes whenever John Westlock approaches. 'Pleasant little Ruth!' ogles Dickens, 'Cheerful, tidy, bustling, quiet little Ruth! No doll's house ever yielded greater delight to its young mistress, than little Ruth derived from her glorious dominion over the triangular parlour and the two small bedrooms.'

The violent, anarchic side of Dickens, however, despised neatness. He associated it with mean spirit, lack of ambition, contented lower-middle-class respectability. In this mood we can find him sneering at the very characteristics he esteems elsewhere. Tim Linkinwater in *Nicholas Nickleby* is presented as a model of clerkly virtue because he is methodical, punctual and utterly satisfied with his lot. In 44 years he has never slept out of the office once; he has opened the safe every morning at 9, and made his final rounds at half past 10 every night, 'except on Foreign Post nights, and then twenty minutes before twelve'. There is little doubt that Linkinwater is one of the elect. But in a paper called 'Thoughts about People' in *Sketches by Boz* Dickens introduces another neat, methodical clerk called Mr. Smith who, like Linkinwater, is punctual in his habits and varies his routine only on Foreign Post nights. But this clerk, because Dickens' mood has changed, is assessed quite differently. 'Poor, harmless creatures such men are,' Dickens writes, 'contented but not happy; broken spirited and humbled, they may feel no pain, but they never know pleasure.' Likewise, the methodical habits which were apparently so admirable in Esther Summerson are suddenly seen from a different angle when they appear in someone like Miss Tox in *Dombey and Son* or Miss Peecher the schoolmistress, Bradley Headstone's admirer in *Our Mutual Friend*:

Small, shining, neat, methodical, and buxom was Miss Peecher . . . A little pincushion, a little housewife, a little book, a little workbox, a little set of tables and weights and measures, and a little woman, all in one. She could write a little essay on any subject, exactly a slate long, beginning at the left-hand top of one side and ending at the right-hand bottom of the other, and the essay should be strictly according to rule. If Mr. Bradley Headstone had addressed a written proposal of marriage to her, she would probably have replied in a complete little essay on the theme exactly a slate long.

The only differences between Miss Peecher and Esther Summerson are that Miss Peecher is lower class and better educated, yet the features which are used to recommend Esther, make Miss Peecher paltry, arid and ridiculous. The Gradgrind children in *Hard Times* are similarly neat and educated: 'They had a little conchological cabinet, and a little metallurgical cabinet; and a little mineralogical cabinet; and the specimens were all arranged and labelled.' Exactly as Tom Pinch would have arranged and labelled them, we feel sure, if he had had the ordering of it. And Gradgrind's house has modern ventilation and is fireproof from top to bottom just like the Britannia Theatre which so captured Dickens' enthusiasm. But in *Hard Times* neatness and hygiene have mysteriously become disreputable because the novel is written by the side of Dickens which favours dirt, imagination and circus performers.

Again, the facility for arranging papers neatly which constituted a large part of the sterling qualities of John Harmon and Arthur Clennam, tells heavily against Carker, the villain of *Dombey and Son*. In Carker neatness is supposed to be obscene. He has 'long nails, nicely pared and sharpened'. 'A natural antipathy to any speck of dirt' makes him watch motes of dust as they fall, and 'rub them off his smooth white hand or glossy linen'. His house is said to be 'beautifully arranged and tastefully kept', with 'well ordered offices'. However Dickens hints that there is a lurking sensuality beneath all this clean living which makes the neatness a kind of self-indulgence. The pictures in Carker's house, we are told, 'do not commemorate great deeds, or render nature in the poetry of landscape, hall or hut', but are 'of one voluptuous cast – mere shows of form and colour'. This curious phrase is presumably meant to set our minds running on galleries of erotica, but Dickens is so mealy-mouthed about it, and so preposterous in his account of what works of art might properly depict, that it would be a very willing reader who felt any antipathy towards Carker on this score. Hardly more successful in alienating the reader's affections is the idea that Carker resembles a cat. Cat images are dropped on him heavily and repeatedly from the time of his first appearance, and there is an obvious effort to supply him with a symbolic bird in the shape of Edith Dombey. During their stormy interview, we learn, 'she plucked the feathers from a pinion of some rare and beautiful bird, which hung from her wrist by a golden thread, to serve her as a fan, and rained them on the ground'. As Carker becomes more threatening, 'He saw the soft down tremble once again, and he saw her lay the plumage of the beautiful bird against her bosom.' But Edith, with her haughty nostrils and operatic poses – not to mention the pistol tucked in her bodice – is anything but birdlike, and would look almost as out of place in an aviary as she would among real human beings. So the attempt to discredit Carker by making him out to be a savage feline succeeds no better than the attempt to discredit him because of his dirty pictures.

Other figures, besides Carker, show Dickens' awareness that excessive cleanliness can be a symptom of sexual or moral inadequacy. The lawyer Jaggers in *Great Expectations* washes his hands in scented soap after interviewing every client. After a particularly shady case he washes his face and gargles and scrapes his nails clean as well. At dinner he deals out clean plates, knives and forks for every course, and drops the ones his guests have just used into two baskets on the ground. Mrs. Gargery, in the same novel, unhappily married to the spineless blacksmith, deliberately makes the house uninhabitable when she feels particularly strongly that her husband's return for her services is inadequate. Her method is to 'put on her coarse apron', take bucket and pail and set about cleaning her home so ferociously that her husband is driven into the back yard where he stands shivering till she has finished. Both Jaggers and Mrs. Gargery are employing soap and water in a very oblique way. Jaggers tries to clean his mind with it. Mrs. Gargery punishes her husband with it for failing in his marital duties, and at the same time exorcises her own cravings. The widowed Mrs. MacStinger in *Dombey and Son*, another frustrated lady, uses it to revenge herself on her lodger Captain Cuttle for his refusal to become her second husband. When Florence visits him, she finds it is one of 'Mrs. MacStinger's great cleaning days'. The Captain is miserably marooned on a chair with his legs drawn up in a room where everything else is sodden with soap and water. Once we recognize that in Dickens excessive cleanliness can be a character's way of trying to expunge guilt and ungratified sexual desires, it might well render us suspicious of David Copperfield's aunt Betsey Trotwood. David watches her 'put on a coarse apron' like Mrs. Gargery, and wash up the tea things:

She next swept up the crumbs with a little broom (putting on a pair of gloves first), until there did not appear to be one microscopic speck left on the carpet; next dusted and arranged the room, which was dusted and arranged to a hair's-breadth already.

This should be enough to make us uneasy, even without Aunt Betsey's constant attempts to drive the virile donkeys and their male guardian off her little patch of front lawn. Sure enough, we discover before very long that Aunt Betsey is indeed unhappily married. Her husband mysteriously wanders the countryside, turning up occasionally to get money from her on the little patch of lawn in the moonlight. He has the good grace to die of his excesses shortly before the end of the novel.

Dickens' regard for public order prompted utterances strikingly at odds with the cheery, charitable views that can be found in the novels. He deplored the English nation's 'morbid sympathy for criminals'. He favoured flogging for bigamists and for offenders who molested ladies coming out of chapel. After siding for a time with devotees of abolition, he championed capital punishment. When Thomas Smethurst, the surgeon, was convicted of murder in 1859, Dickens declared 'I would hang any Home Secretary, Whig, Tory, Radical, or otherwise, who should step in between so black a scoundrel and the gallows.' He encouraged the belief that criminals constitute a separate species, fit only for extermination. Students of the criminal intellect, he explained in *Edwin Drood*, perpetually misread it 'because they persist in trying to reconcile it with the average intellect of average men, instead of identifying it as a horrible wonder apart'. *Hunted Down* alerts its readers to the great error of supposing that murderers have consciences, or are at all put out by their dastardly destruction of honest citizens. The French landlady in *Little Dorrit* remarks, with Blandois in mind:

That there are people whom it is necessary to detest without compromise. That there are people who must be dealt with as enemies of the human race. That there are people who have no human heart, and who must be crushed like savage beasts and cleared out of the way.

Dickens applauds the speech, throwing in a taunt at the 'amiable whitewashers' of criminals in England. Blandois is duly 'crushed' by a falling house at the book's end. Remarkably, this follows closely upon a sermon about Christian forgiveness by Little Dorrit. The tender sentiments in the novels seldom bear comparison with Dickens' practice. *David Copperfield* pathetically presents its little hero as he traipses the Dover Road, 'against whom house-doors were locked and house-dogs barked'. Dickens, residing on the Dover Road, kept large dogs chained each side of his entrance gate to discourage such vagrants. In this sense Harold Skimpole who, though he turns Jo out of doors, weeps over the song about a boy 'Thrown on the wide world, doom'd to wander and roam', is practically a self-portait. For 'the ruffian class' Dickens recommended perpetual imprisonment. The term, as he uses it in *The Uncommercial Traveller*, appears to cover habitual thieves, street-corner loiterers, and persons who throw stones at railway carriages – 'an act of wanton wickedness with the very Arch-Fiend's hand in it'. On one occasion he had a girl taken into custody for using bad language in the street, and made it clear – to the embarrassment of police and magistrate – that he wanted her sent to prison. In Paris he handed a drunken coachman over to the authorities, and was surprised to find the man turning up at his lodgings a considerable time later, to get a police-certificate signed confirming that he had returned the one-and-a-half-francs fare to Dickens. 'He had been in prison ever since!' Dickens wrote to Forster, 'Isn't this admirable?' It would be foolish, of course, to sneer at Dickens' rigour. The courage and public spirit he displayed in these incidents were better suited to ridding the streets of violence and obscenity than either tolerance or reluctant quietism. But it should be remarked that his passion for law-enforcement waned once the law struck at his own interests. The contract he entered into, early on, with the publisher, Richard Bentley, seemed increasingly unrewarding to him as his own market-value went up. In this situation the anarchic part of his nature quickly asserted itself. 'This net that has been wound about me so chafes me, so exasperates and irritates my mind,' he wrote, 'that to break it at whatever cost . . . is my constant impulse.' Very much what the ruffian class might feel. Though Bentley yielded, the law was entirely on his side.

That portion of Dickens' character which enjoyed seeing people ordered and regimented made him a particularly ardent admirer of the Metropolitan Police force. Founded by Peel in 1829 it was part of a movement of reform which, during Dickens' lifetime, completely remodelled the English police system, bringing to it a new efficiency and a new measure of public respect. G. A. Sala, Dickens' colleague, recalls that he had 'a curious and almost morbid partiality for communing with and entertaining police officers. . . . He seemed always at ease with these personages, and never tired of questioning them.' In Inspector Bucket, in *Bleak House*, Dickens created the first police detective in English fiction, partly basing him on Inspector Charles Frederick Field, a personal acquaintance, who was probably the most celebrated detective of his time. Dickens was partial to nights out with the police. Under the protection of several officers he would visit slums or thieves' dens or houses of ill repute, regularly entranced by the firm, knowing air with which his uniformed escort handled the various shifty or impertinent characters they came across. One of these occasions, written up in *The Uncommercial Traveller*, took him to Liverpool's dockland, 'a labyrinth of dismal courts and blind alleys', as he puts it, 'kept in wonderful order by the police'. Dickens, a police superintendent and three

officers, break in on several householders in the hope of finding
evidence of prostitution or theft. Even when they draw a blank, as
they usually do, it's clear that Dickens considers that the householders, all of whom he describes in facetious and disparaging terms,
are lucky to have got away with it this time, rather than that they
have any cause for complaint. If they live in dismal courts and alleys,
the implication is, then they must expect the police and attendant
journalists to come tramping through their house whenever the
fancy takes them. As Philip Collins has noted, the imperturbability
of the British policeman soon became a legend with the middle
class: a favourite topic in *Punch*, for example. Dickens is entranced
by it. In *Our Mutual Friend* we find the Police Station, with its
bright light, and inside:

> the Night-Inspector, with pen and ink, and ruler, posting up his books in a
> whitewashed office, as studiously as if he were in a monastery on the top of
> a mountain, and no howling fury of a drunken woman were banging her-
> self against a cell-door in the backyard at his elbow.

We notice that it is a mark of virtue in the police officer that he
doesn't go and see if anything can be done for the drunken woman.
It shows his dependability, and his refusal to have the wool pulled
over his eyes by the lower classes. When Wrayburn and Lightwood
come into the station and want to see the body in the mortuary, the
Night-Inspector takes a lamp and conducts them: ' "Now, gentlemen," ' he says, 'showing not the slightest consciousness of the
woman, who was banging herself with increased violence'. Esther
Summerson, in *Bleak House*, visits a similar police station:

> Mr. Bucket took me in and sat me in an arm-chair, by a bright fire. It was
> now past one, as I saw by the clock against the wall. Two police officers,
> looking in their perfectly neat uniform not at all like people who were up
> all night, were quietly writing at a desk; and the place seemed very quiet
> altogether, except for some beating and calling out at distant doors under-
> ground, to which nobody paid any attention.

And quite right too, we deduce. The same splendid inhumanity,
the triumph of discipline and uniform which enabled one human
being simply to ignore the misery of another, greatly attracted
Dickens in soldiers, as well as police officers, as we can see from the
account of Barnaby's capture in *Barnaby Rudge*. Barnaby sees a
body of men approaching, and realizes from their 'orderly and
regular mode of advancing' that they are soldiers. 'They advanced

steadily; neither quickening their pace as they came nearer, nor raising any cry, nor showing the least emotion or anxiety'. They overpower Barnaby in a rapid 'business-like way', and set off again with him in their midst:

Tramp, tramp. Tramp, tramp. Heads erect, shoulders square, every man stepping in exact time – all so orderly and regular – nobody looking at him – nobody seeming conscious of his presence.

Dickens plainly wants us to feel that it's a grand thing that men can be converted into automatons so effectively. In this respect he contrasts markedly with Tolstoy, who describes a somewhat similar scene in *War and Peace*. Pierre is captured by the French in Moscow, and kept for several weeks in a shed with other prisoners. During the imprisonment discipline relaxes; the guards chat with their captives and the French corporal in charge keeps trying to share his pipe with Pierre. But on the morning of the French evacuation everything is suddenly brisk again. The French soldiers have their helmet chinstraps fastened, which alters their familiar faces. The corporal won't listen, when Pierre tries to ask him about a sick prisoner, and the man's face is so different from before that Pierre wonders whether it really is the corporal he knew, or some stranger.

In the changed face of the corporal, in the sound of his voice, in the agitating, deafening din of the drums, Pierre recognized that mysterious callous force which drove men against their will to murder their kind . . . To be afraid or to try to escape that force, to address entreaties or exhortations to those who were serving as its tools, was useless.

After this it is hard not to conclude that Dickens' excitement over the orderly 'tramp, tramp' of the soldiers' feet is childish and a little disgusting. Nevertheless, it is a commonly felt excitement, cognate with the impulse that draws crowds to tattoos and colour-troopings. If it lessens Dickens as a human being, it greatly strengthens him as a novelist that he can appeal to those deep and never-quite-extinguished responses which make liberal intellectuals feel queasy. Throughout his life he remained a connoisseur of efficient militarism, quick to applaud its manifestations, from the neat gaiters adopted by some Zouave troops he came across in France, to the three regulation cheers bellowed by the crew of the Prince Consort's yacht when the French emperor went aboard at Boulogne. He remarked upon 'the prodigious volume of them, and the precision, and the circumstance that no man was left straggling on his own account either before or afterwards'. Almost as good as gunfire.

Characters not actually in the police force or the army who yet enforce law and order in their particular spheres are also likely to receive large quantities of Dickens' approbation. Miss Abbey Potterson, the landlady of the Six Jolly Fellowship Porters in *Our Mutual Friend*, is a case in point. Her public house is presented as a little haven of civilization beleaguered by waste and darkness. From the outside it looks like a 'lopsided wooden jumble' by the river side, practically afloat at high water, and hemmed in by a 'wilderness' of narrow courts and alleys. But the diminutive bar inside, 'not much larger than a hackney coach', is a sort of beacon of snugness (characteristically, Dickens once considered opening a novel in the lantern of a lighthouse). Snugness positively 'gushed forth', writes Dickens, through the glass partition which divided it from the 'rough world'. Miss Potterson's rule in this cosy corner is arbitrary and fierce. '*I* am the law here, my man,' she tells recalcitrant customers. Dickens is warmly attracted by her authoritarian manner. It is backed up, he says, by 'the possibility of physical force' in the shape of a muscular pot-boy, who stands ready at closing time as the customers file out 'in the best order; Miss Abbey standing at the half-door of the bar, to hold a ceremony of review and dismissal'. Miss Potterson's idyllic little police state is also a symbol of security, a miniature fortress. When Lizzie Hexam leaves it after a visit, she finds herself in 'the river-side wilderness' immediately, and hears behind her 'the rattling of the iron-links, and the grating of the bolts and staples under Miss Abbey's hand'.

We notice that the compactness and security of the Fellowship Porters are emphasized by two comparisons. It's so small and self-contained that it might easily go off on wheels: it is 'not much larger than a hackney coach'. And it's such a bright little box of snugness amidst its wild surroundings that it's rather like a boat – practically afloat at high water. Mrs. Jarley's neat home in *The Old Curiosity Shop* does literally go off on wheels – it's a caravan. 'A smart little house upon wheels, with white dimity curtains festooning the windows,' and gleaming paint and a bright brass knocker. Nervous Nell and her grandfather find safety there (in the later *Doctor Marigold* the fugitive girl preserved in a caravan acquires extra pathos from being deaf and dumb). At night the steps leading up to Mrs. Jarley's front door are taken away, once the occupants are inside, to cut the van off from the rest of the world. Nell, lying in bed, hears the driver, George, rustling his straw underneath the floor, where he sleeps, and this gives her 'an additional feeling of security'. Guard-dog George is Mrs. Jarley's version of the Potterson pot-boy. As well as being on wheels the Jarley home, like the Fellowship Porters, has affinities with a boat.

One half of it – that moiety in which the comfortable proprietress was then seated – was carpeted, and so partitioned off at the further end as to accommodate a sleeping place, constructed after the fashion of a berth on board ship.

Boat and caravan repeatedly converge in Dickens' mind. In America, for instance, steaming down the Ohio on board the *Messenger*, he reported to Forster on the accommodation – 'just as clean and just as large as that caravan you and I were in at Greenwich Fair last past'. *Going Into Society* starts among the marsh-lands and market-gardens around Deptford, with Mr. Magsman's wooden house on wheels laid up for the winter near the mouth of a muddy creek, its funnel smoking cosily. Only temporarily out of the water, we are made to feel.

Nell's romance of security – living in a boat, which is also on land, which is also cut off from the ground at night like a nest – is carried further in *Dombey and Son*. Florence Dombey, fleeing from her father's home after he has hit her, runs through the London streets, says Dickens, 'like the sole survivor on a lonely shore from the wreck of a great vessel'. Florence, like Nell, finds her land-boat, this time Solomon Gills' ship's instrument shop, with its effigy of a wooden midshipman standing at the door (the effigy really *did* stand outside a shop in Leadenhall Street), and friendly Captain Cuttle inside, complete with hook hand and marine terminology to give the whole enterprise a nautical flavour. The Captain soon has a room at the top of the house prepared for her. 'It was very clean already; and the Captain being an orderly man, and accustomed to make things ship-shape,' says Dickens, makes a bed on the couch, and converts the dressing table into 'a species of altar', with his two silver teaspoons, his telescope and a number of other curiosities laid out on top of it. This altar to domestic snugness can also be matched in *The Old Curiosity Shop*, incidentally, where the brown-faced, sunburnt redeemer-figure who later turns out to be Nell's great-uncle, arrives at his lodgings with a temple made of polished silver in a trunk, and exhibits it to the fascinated Dick Swiveller.

Into one little chamber of this temple he dropped an egg, into another some coffee, into a third a compact piece of raw steak from a neat tin case, into a fourth he poured some water. Then, with the aid of a phosphorus box and some matches, he procured a light and applied it to a spirit-lamp which had a place of its own below the temple; then he shut down the lids of all the little chambers; then he opened them; and then, by some wonderful and unseen agency, the steak was done, the egg was boiled, the coffee was accurately prepared, and his breakfast was ready.

We may be excused for thinking that the altar of snugness and the temple of breakfast are more genuine components of Dickens' religion than the biblical passages with which he garnishes death beds. At all events Captain Cuttle does his best to turn Florence's lodgings into a land-ship for her. He talks to her as if they were afloat together. ' "The whole row o' dead lights is up, for'ard, lady lass," observed the Captain, encouragingly, "and everythink is made snug." ' After Walter's return he gets another room ready for her which he transforms, says Dickens, 'into a species of land cabin', adorned with a model of a Tartar frigate which is hung up over the chimney-piece. There Florence lives, 'like a quiet bird in a cage, at the top of the old Instrument-maker's house.' Again, in *Bleak House*, when Esther is in Deal with her maid Charley, she remarks: 'Our little room was like a ship's cabin, and that delighted Charley very much.' The land-ship doesn't invariably shelter a girl. The maudlin hero of *The Poor Relation's Story* fancies himself in an idyllic counting-house fronting the Thames, its windows 'shaped like the stern windows of a ship', seemingly about to slip out on the tide like Miss Potterson's bar. The signalman's cabin at *Mugby Junction*, aglow with friendliness and the smell of oil, recalls 'a cabin in a Whaler'.

But the last of Dickens' land-ships, with a girl-bird safe inside, occurs in *Edwin Drood*. Rosa Bud, pursued by the hypocritical, opium-smoking John Jasper, flees to her lawyer Mr. Grewgious at the Inns of Court, and is soon snugly housed at the top of Furnival's Inn, while Mr. Grewgious patrols the iron railings outside, 'occasionally looking in between the bars', we are told, 'as if he had laid a dove in a high roost in a cage of lions, and had it on his mind that she might tumble out'. Her other protector is the sunburnt, blue-eyed Mr. Tartar, ex-First Lieutenant in the Royal Navy, who lives at the top of Staple Inn, having chosen his room because he often knocks his head against the ceiling and it reminds him of being on board ship. He grows scarlet runners on lines and stays rigged out of his

window, walks along the gutters and goes below through the window
as if it were a companionway. His chambers are 'the neatest, the
cleanest, and the best-ordered chambers ever seen under the sun'.
They are meticulously scrubbed – every inch of brasswork polished
and burnished till it shines like a mirror; his sitting room is 'like an
admiral's cabin'; his bedroom fitted all over with lockers and drawers,
'like a seedsman's shop', where everything has its place – shelf,
bracket, hook and drawer each providing 'snug inches of stowage'.
He keeps paint and varnish ready to obliterate stray fingermarks.
'No man-of-war was ever kept more spick and span.' 'The whole
concern,' Dickens concludes, 'had a sea-going air . . . so delightfully
complete' that it 'might have bowled away gallantly with all on
board, if Mr. Tartar had only clapped his lips to the speaking-
trumpet that was slung in a corner.' Rosa, evidently falling in love
with Mr. Tartar, tells her friend Helena:

'It is like the inside of the most exquisite ship that ever sailed. It is like –
it is like –'
'Like a dream?' suggested Helena.
Rosa answered with a little nod.

It is in fact the completion of a dream that began with Mrs. Jarley's
caravan.

A ship on land, or strictly a ship up in the air, is the most powerful
image of neatness and security, then, that Tartar's tidiness suggests
to Dickens, and it is an image that throws back tendrils to Miss
Potterson's bar, and Nell in the caravan and Florence Dombey
aboard Captain Cuttle's craft. But apart from being like something
on a ship, Tartar's bedroom with its lockers and drawers is said to be
'like a seedsman's shop', and this image of innumerable cosy compartments, a multiple snuggery, every wall crammed with security,
relates to an earlier novel also. In *Great Expectations* little Pip, much
in need of security, finds himself envying Uncle Pumblechook, who
is a corn-chandler and seedsman by trade.

It appeared to me that he must be a very happy man indeed, to have so
many little drawers in his shop; and I wondered when I peeped into one
or two on the lower tiers, and saw the tied-up brown paper packets inside,
whether the flower seeds and bulbs ever wanted of a fine day to break out
of those jails and bloom.

It is a beautiful moment not only intrinsically but also because it so
finely mirrors the boy's dilemma, wanting the safety of home, but

wanting adventure. This makes him realize that the little drawers,
which are such deliciously snug homes for the seeds that he envies
Uncle Pumblechook their possession, are also prisons. It comes at
the exact point in the novel when Pip, his curiosity aroused, is going
to play at Miss Havisham's for the first time, and has accordingly, for
the first time in his life, just said good-bye to Joe, his father figure: 'I
had never parted from him before.' Drawers, cupboards, warm
nooks, have imaginative attraction for any homesick child, but it
takes an adolescent to recognize their limiting side as well. And the
drawers of a seedsman's shop in particular, convey this cramping
power, since they can crush within their tiny confines a garden, or a
forest. We should remember in this context that Florence Dombey,
snug within Captain Cuttle's land-ship, was also compared to a
bird in a cage – Dickens' commonest image for imprisonment. And
Mr. Grewgious, too, in *Edwin Drood*, looked in through the bars of
Furnival's Inn to see Rosa cosily caged behind them. Once we come
to recognize this sinister doubleness or reversibility which lurks
within even Dickens' snuggest images of order and security, we shall
find it easier to understand how the writer who craves for a bird
bride in a ship-shape home, is also the writer who needs to celebrate
destruction and anarchy. Likewise it is possible to see how Dickens
could be drawn both to a murderer, and to a policeman who sits
impassively listening to the yells and banging of his victims.

Besides being a land-ship and a seedsman's shop, Tartar's neat
little hide-out is in the Inns of Court, and this third feature also
relates it to one of Dickens' imaginative obsessions. From the start
the Inns of Court fascinated him. A conglomeration of tiny chambers,
all ingeniously interlocking, each self-contained, they were like a
seedsman's shop with human beings for seeds. But this meant that
they were like a prison as well, and throughout his career we find
Dickens vacillating between these two aspects of the Inns. The paper
called 'Chambers' in *The Uncommercial Traveller* paints the black
side. The Inns, says Dickens, Gray's Inn, Lincoln's Inn, Barnard's
Inn, Staple Inn and the rest, are a 'shabby crew', a 'dust-heap'.
The rooms are like tombs, like cells; the staircases rotten and falling
into dust; grimy windows full of To Let notices; doorposts 'inscribed like gravestones'; 'scowling, iron-barred, prison-like' passages; rusty padlocks; squalid little areas outside inhabited by rank
grass, cats, rats, flies and soot. The tenants are a prey to solitude and
suicide, and it is often months before anyone breaks in and finds

their corpses. These are the Inns of Court we find in *Pickwick* too. Sergeant Snubbin's chambers are heaped with papers, 'without any attempt at order or arrangement'; the furniture is rickety; doors rot on their hinges; dust flies from the carpet in clouds at every step. Jack Bamber, who is said to have gone 'half crazy' with loneliness in the Inns, tells Pickwick about the tenant who had a stroke and wasn't found for 18 months, 'a very dusty skeleton in a blue coat', and about the man in Clifford's Inn who smashed the lock off a closet and found the last tenant standing bolt upright in a corner with an empty arsenic bottle in his hand. In *Martin Chuzzlewit*, though, the Inns are transformed. 'There are snug chambers in those Inns,' observes Dickens, and in John Westlock's snug chambers in Furnivall's Inn he locates the idyllic little supper party where John entertains Tom and Ruth Pinch and finally loses his heart to Ruth. Likewise David Copperfield finds that Traddles has set up house in his chambers at 2, Holborn Court, Gray's Inn, with his 'bright-looking bride' Sophy and her five sisters from Devonshire. They all live, neat and snug, in three rooms at the top of a 'crazy old staircase'. David finds it 'pleasantly fanciful', and so plainly does Dickens, to think of six pretty girls living 'in that grim atmosphere of pounce and parchment, red-tape, dusty wafers, ink-jars, brief and draft paper'; and Traddles uses the nautical image to sum it up that we should expect from a forerunner of Mr. Tartar. 'We have put to sea in a cock-boat, but we are quite prepared to rough it.' In *Bleak House* Dickens switches back to the deathly aspect of the Inns. Mr. Vholes is to be found, along with a good deal of dry-rot and dirt, behind a black door in Symond's Inn – a 'woe-begone inn, like a large dust-bin of two compartments and a sifter'. Richard lives next-door, surrounded by 'dusty bundles of papers', with his name 'in great white letters on a hearse-like panel'. Neatness breaks in even here, however. The lovely Ada, like Sophy Traddles, sets up house in Richard's chambers. When we next see them Richard is about to die in Ada's arms, and though, unlike Jo the crossing sweeper, he doesn't need a bath, his room has been tidied up to give a proper dignity to the event. 'The room was made as airy as possible', Esther notices, 'and was darkened, and was very orderly and quiet.' Barnard's Inn, where Herbert Pocket has chambers in *Great Expectations*, displays what are by now Dickens' standard symptoms of dirt and decay in the Inns: dismal trees, dismal sparrows, dismal cats, cracked glass, To Let notices, soot, dry-rot, and a staircase 'slowly collapsing into sawdust'. But Herbert has a waiter bring up dinner, and the introduction of domestic items – plates and dishes – into Herbert's musty apartment gives the meal, Pip finds, 'a certain gipsy character' which makes it 'delightful'. Traddles used the same image 'a capital little gipsy sort of place' to describe what the neat, domestic Sophy had made of his crazy little garret, and it helps us to see how Dickens could have the same snug feeling about setting up house in an Inn of Court and setting up house in Mrs. Jarley's caravan.

Tartar's neat rooms in *Edwin Drood*, then, because they are a ship on land, and a seedsman's shop, and a set of chambers in an Inn of Court, unite three of Dickens' most powerful images of security and order. Moreover when we trace these images back through Dickens' writing we find that each of them is two-edged, able to signify imprisonment as well as security. As if he were unwilling to relinquish either side of the imaginative potential of the Inns of Court even in *Edwin Drood*, Dickens places in the chambers which adjoin Mr. Tartar's dream-ship at Staple Inn the solitary Neville Landless. When Canon Crisparkle visits Landless, the underside of the dream-ship is abruptly revealed:

An air of retreat and solitude hung about the rooms and about their inhabitant. He was much worn, and so were they. Their sloping ceilings, cumbrous rusty locks and grates, and heavy wooden bins and beams, slowly mouldering withal, had a prisonous look, and he had the haggard face of a prisoner . . . On the cracked and smoke-blackened parapet beyond, some of the deluded sparrows of the place rheumatically hopped, like little feathered cripples who had left their crutches in their nests.

We have been in these rooms before. They were the setting for Jack Bamber's stories as long ago as *Pickwick*. And here they are still, with only a wall between them and the dream-ship which, if Dickens had lived to finish *Edwin Drood*, they too might have become. Already, when the novel prematurely ends, Tartar is offering to rig lines and stays for scarlet runners from Neville's window and to push some boxes of mignonette and wallflower along to his parapet with a boathook.

The most shipshape, literally, of Dickens' land-ships is Peggotty's house in *David Copperfield* (containing the Biblical Ham: a Noah's Ark was among little Dickens' favourite toys). The 'wonderful charm' of the boat-house for him, David says, is precisely that it 'had never been intended to be lived in, on dry land'. It has the enchantment of improvisation, caught even in the little looking-glass in David's room 'framed with oyster-shells'. The enchantment, too, of neatness. 'It was beautifully clean inside,' David remembers, 'and as tidy as possible. . . . The walls were whitewashed as white as milk, and the patchwork counterpane made my eyes quite ache with brightness.' Yet it is really just an old black boat with 'an iron funnel sticking out of it for a chimney' and a wooden outhouse for pots and kettles, situated on a piece of waste land, a 'desolate flat', in the vicinity of gas-works, ship-breakers' yards, 'and a great litter of such places', as David puts it. It has, in other words, in addition to its other enchantments, the enchantment of junk.

In this it has affinities with Staggs' Gardens, where Polly Toodle the wet-nurse lives in *Dombey and Son*, the novel which immediately preceded *Copperfield*:

Staggs's Gardens was a little row of houses, with little squalid patches of ground before them, fenced off with old doors, barrel staves, scraps of tarpaulin, and dead bushes; with bottomless tin kettles and exhausted iron fenders thrust into the gaps. Here, the Staggs's Gardeners trained scarlet beans, kept fowls and rabbits, erected rotten summer houses (one was an old boat), dried clothes and smoked pipes.

The old boat made into a summer house clinches the resemblance to Peggotty's domain, just as the scarlet runners recall Tartar. It is the rich humanity of improvised junk that Dickens is drawing on. The Toodles, like the Peggottys, reaffirm the natural human affections in the face of Dombey on the one hand and Murdstone on the other. When Dickens later tries to celebrate the replacement of Staggs' Gardens by 'healthy public walks' and other 'wholesome conveniences', the writing goes flat at once.

Another of these junk-littered Dickensian wastelands is encountered by Nell and her grandfather on their way out of London in *The Old Curiosity Shop*. They pass through:

brick-fields, skirting gardens paled with staves of old casks . . . mounds of dockweed, nettles, coarse grass and oyster shells . . . small garden patches bordering the road, with many a summer house innocent of paint and built of old timber or some fragments of a boat, green as the tough cabbage stalks that grew about it, and grottoed at the seams with toadstools and tight-sticking snails.

Here we have the same components, the summer-house made out of an old boat, the fences made of barrel staves, even the oyster

shells which framed David Copperfield's looking-glass. But typically
Dickens has turned his junk over, and is showing us the dark side of
his image. This landscape is alien and comfortless, and as if to drive
the point home Quilp, the nominal villain of the novel, owns a
dilapidated summer-house. It stands on a piece of blighted waste
ground which he calls The Wilderness, 'a rugged wooden box,
rotten and bare to see, which', Dickens writes, 'overhung the river's
mud, and threatened to slide down into it'. Reverting, in other words,
to a boat; and Quilp's trade – ship-breaker – recalls the ship-
breakers' yards beside which Peggotty's houseboat stands. Another
sinister summer-house figures in *The Black Veil* when the surgeon,
on his way to the hanged man, passes through a waste land of
stunted trees and stagnant water, with here and there 'a miserable
patch of garden-ground with a few old boards knocked together for a
summerhouse, and old palings imperfectly mended with stakes
pilfered from the neighbouring hedges'. Dilapidated wooden houses,
'like horrible old packing cases', which seem to have 'got aground' on
the river's mud, occur too in an account Dickens sent to Miss Coutts
in 1853 of a pestilential slum he had visited called Hickman's Folly –
it adjoined *Oliver Twist*'s Jacob's island. The Hickman's Folly
public house was called 'The Ship Aground' – 'wonderfully appropriate', thought Dickens. Wonderfully suggestive, too – though some
ten years elapsed before it materialized – of Miss Potterson's mud-
environed pub 'all but afloat at high water', and the fascinating
muddle of 'vessels that seemed to have got ashore, and houses that
seemed to have got afloat' over which it presides.

We can, then, put the ramshackle wooden house beside the land-
ship and the seedsman's shop and the Inns of Court. Like them it
powerfully attracted Dickens' imagination. Like them it is double
edged. It can represent squalor. Or it can represent improvisation:
the amiable human impulse to fabricate comfort and order out of
junk.

When in *Barnaby Rudge* Gashford conducts Hugh and Dennis to
the rebel hide-out, they pass through a suitably villainous looking
neighbourhood called Green Lanes, to the west of Tottenham Court
Road, which has several of the features familiar to us by now as
components of the Dickensian waste land. Stagnant pools, coarse
grass, the upright posts of palings and ramshackle wooden huts. But
it has one or two arresting aspects as well. 'Poverty', Dickens writes,
'has its whims and shows of taste, as wealth has. Some of these cabins

were turreted, some had false windows painted on their rotten walls; one had a mimic clock, upon a crazy tower of four feet high, which screened the chimney; each in its little patch of ground had a rude seat or arbour.' Gashford and the others approach the house they are making for 'by means of a tottering plank which crossed the ditch in front'. Twenty years were to pass before Dickens wrote *Great Expectations*, but these details clearly add up to an early version of Wemmick's house at Walworth. Approached by way of a collection of black lanes and ditches, Wemmick's house is 'a little wooden cottage' with the top 'cut out and painted like a battery mounted with guns'. 'I think it was the smallest house I ever saw,' comments Pip, 'with the queerest gothic windows (by far the greater part of them sham).' It is entered by way of a plank across a ditch, which Wemmick refers to as a drawbridge. Like the Green Lanes huts, it has a bower with seats in its patch of gardens, and a miniscule pond and fountain.

As Tartar's rooms at Staple Inn are the culmination of the landship in Dickens' writing, so Wemmick's makeshift castle is the full and final flowering of all Dickensian ramshackle summer-houses – the last word in improvisation. Despite the dry-rot, which makes food eaten in it taste like a bad nut, it is the scene for an elaborate show of order, neatness and punctuality. Every night at 9 o'clock Wemmick fires a miniature cannon. Every morning he crosses the drawbridge at 'half-past eight precisely'. There is 'a neat little girl in attendance', and the first thing Pip hears in the morning is Wemmick cleaning his boots. While it thus rivals the Peggotty home in cleanliness, the wooden castle is also supposed to be a haven of human feeling like Staggs' Gardens where Polly Toodle the wet-nurse lives. Wemmick keeps his aged parent in the castle and treats him with exemplary kindness and consideration. During working hours at Mr. Jaggers, on the other hand, he prides himself on being ruthless. As they walk to the office together Pip sees Wemmick getting harder and dryer and tighter in the mouth the further they leave the castle behind. It is this aspect of Wemmick that reveals the castle's seamier side, for Wemmick's whole livelihood depends on a denial of sympathy with his fellow men, a denial represented by his hauling up the drawbridge each time he goes in. 'After I have crossed this bridge, I hoist it up – so – and cut off the communication.' Once in the castle Pip says that he feels 'as snugly cut off from the rest of Walworth as if the moat were thirty feet wide by as many deep'.

The castle with its battlements and its gun and its military routine is snug from one point of view, but from another it is a pathetic device for negating the ties that bind mankind together. The novel tells how Pip eventually finds that he is not snugly cut off, even from the convict Magwitch, who so disgusts him. On the contrary, he owes Magwitch everything. The gun which Wemmick fires each evening from his fortress across the waste ground plainly recalls the warning gun which Pip heard across the marshes at the start of the novel, and which was fired from the prison ships when a convict escaped. Pip tells us that Wemmick's gun 'went off with a bang that shook the crazy little box of a cottage as if it must fall to pieces', and this threatening image prefigures the return of the convict into Pip's life, which will teach him that snugly isolated castles are a ramshackle pretence.

Perhaps, though, we are being too hopeful, or too allegoric, in suggesting such a salutary 'meaning' for Wemmick's castle. There's no hint of adverse criticism from Dickens. On the contrary, he seems to want us to feel that Wemmick's plan for restricting his human sympathies is innocent and diverting. Wemmick is treated throughout with the patronizing affection which Dickens reserves for good lower-class characters, and is married off to Miss Skiffins at the end as a reward. It's open to us to see his castle with its flag and gun as harmless playthings – like Uncle Toby's fort or Hawser Trunnion's garrison in the books Dickens loved as a child: imitations of the world's order and rigour, rendered innocuous by a soft heart.

In Boulogne Dickens stayed two summers on the estate of a genial Bonapartist called M. Beaucourt, which presents some Wemmick-like features. M. Beaucourt's map showed the property as 'about twice the size of Ireland', and Dickens walked three miles in search of 'the bridge of Austerlitz', before discovering it immediately outside the window. 'The Château of the Old Guard', apparently 'about two leagues' from the house, was likewise run to earth within yards of the front door, 'upside down and greenly rotten', with a guardsman in painted effigy flat on his face beside it. Dickens was immensely tickled by all this, and also went into raptures over his landlord's neatness and improvisation – his 'genius for making tasteful little bedrooms in angles of his roofs', and endowing every nook with pegs and cupboards. If Wemmick's castle has vestiges of Beaucourt's, it's the likelier that Dickens meant it to be all harmless fun.

But we should not be surprised by now to see this doubt arising

over how to take Wemmick's castle. We have seen that it is Dickens'
gift to react to things in contradictory ways, and to observe the
menacing shadows which are cast even by neatness, order and
security.

3

DICKENS' HUMOUR

In one of his *Uncommercial Traveller* papers Dickens recalls the Theatre Royal at Chatham to which he used to be taken as a child:

Richard the Third, in a very uncomfortable cloak, had first appeared to me there, and had made my heart leap with terror by backing up against the stage-box in which I was posted, while struggling for life against the virtuous Richmond. It was within those walls that I had learned as from a page of English history, how that wicked king slept in war time on a sofa much too short for him, and how fearfully his conscience troubled his boots ... Many wondrous secrets of Nature had I come to the knowledge of in that sanctuary: of which not the least terrific were, that the witches in Macbeth bore an awful resemblance to the Thanes and other proper inhabitants of Scotland; and that the good King Duncan couldn't rest in his grave, but was constantly coming out of it and calling himself somebody else.

The passage takes us straight to a crucial aspect of Dickens' humour, which is his ability to see through pretence. Faced with theatrical conventions which are usually accepted without question – the idea of one actor playing several minor roles, for instance – he insists on taking a crushingly literal look at them. He suddenly refuses to co-operate in the normal, everyday conspiracy by which, for the sake of art or good manners, we all agree to put on an act, to accept the fake as real. The child in the passage has not been educated to accept falsehood, and is utterly literal. He merely observes what the adult eye would gloss over, and the result is funny. Of course the child is being laughed at to some extent too. Dickens is encouraging us to smirk at his innocence. But because we smirk we find the child endearing, whereas the actors, once revealed to us through the child's literal eyes, appear mere buffoons. The double effect of smirking at the viewer and despising the viewed is highly characteristic of Dickens' humour and recurs endlessly in the tales concerning innocent children, like *Oliver Twist*, *David Copperfield* and *Great*

Expectations. Pip, for example, goes to Mr. Wopsle's great aunt's school, and attends the quarterly recitations given by Mr. Wopsle.

What he did on those occasions was to turn up his cuffs, stick up his hair, and give us . . . Collins' Ode on the Passions, wherein I particularly venerated Mr. Wopsle as Revenge, throwing his bloodstained sword in thunder down, and taking the War-denouncing trumpet with a withering look. It was not with me then, as it was in later life, when I fell into the society of the Passions, and compared them with Collins and Wopsle, rather to the disadvantage of both gentlemen.

The same factors operate here as in the first example. The absurd disparity between the feeble Wopsle and the attitudes he strikes is quite hidden from the child, who finds the performance impressive. At the same time his innocent eye observes Wopsle closely, so that the reader is given information enough to feel superior both to Wopsle and to the child. Dickens' sardonic comment about Collins at the end brings into the open his criticism of us for being taken in by the posturings of art instead of sharing his own realistic vision. The self-important way in which, in this last sentence, Pip gives us to understand that he has seen life and knows a thing or two about passion now is evidently not intended to be funny by Dickens. Dickens could smile at himself as a lad, but found it more difficult to smile at himself as a man.

The deflatingly literal treatment of dramatic art is carried on extensively in *Nicholas Nickleby*, of course, in the episodes with Mr. Vincent Crummles and his travelling players. Here the innocent child viewer has been removed, and it is Dickens as narrator who takes a literal look at the play:

There was a gorgeous banquet, ready spread for the third act, consisting of two pasteboard vases, one plate of biscuits, a black bottle, and a vinegar cruet; and, in short, everything was on a scale of the utmost splendour and preparation.

Nearly all the humour of the Crummles episode, like this sample, consists of seeing what is actually there instead of what convention has agreed to pretend is there. We feel superior to the stage banquet, because we know it isn't a real banquet, though equally we should feel superior to it if it was, because then we'd know it was out of place on a stage. Crummles tells Nicholas about the actor they once had in their company who, when he played Othello, instead of blacking only his face and neck, as was usual, insisted on blacking himself all over. The banquet is absurd because it complies with the usual dramatic conventions, and the actor is absurd because he doesn't. However the same literal viewpoint produces the Othello joke, since it is literalism which inquires why, if Othello was all black, the actor portraying him shouldn't be.

Literalism also allows Dickens to see through ceremony and regalia. In an *Uncommercial Traveller* paper he wonders how we can consider ourselves more cultivated than savage tribes when we tolerate the absurd rituals of our parliamentary procedure. No medicine man could produce anything so 'supremely ludicrous' as 'two Masters in Chancery holding up their black petticoats and butting their ridiculous wigs at Mr. Speaker'. He refers with relish to a tribe who, it was reported, 'never could see the Missionaries dispose of their legs in the attitude of kneeling, or hear them begin a hymn in chorus, without bursting into roars of irrepressible laughter'. In this mood, too, he causes Volumnia Dedlock in *Bleak House* to remark that she is sure Mr. Tulkinghorn is a Freemason, 'and wears short aprons, and is made a perfect Idol of, with candlesticks and trowels'.

But it is not only the ceremonies of religion – the missionaries kneeling – that Dickens' blunt commonsense finds ludicrous. He can't really take the doctrines of Christianity either. In *Pickwick*, Weller senior complains of the 'Methodistical' teaching with which Stiggins has been filling his wife's head.

She's got hold o' some inwention for grown-up people being born again, Sammy; the new birth, I thinks they calls it. I should wery much like to see that system in haction, Sammy. I should wery much like to see your mother-in-law born again.

But it was Christ, not Stiggins, who said 'Except a man be born again, he cannot see the kingdom of God.' Dickens is at liberty to think it ridiculous; but he is not at liberty to think it ridiculous and consider himself a Christian. He used to become quite savage, however, when people suggested he wasn't. That the ceremonies of Christianity had a vital spiritual meaning, he did not seriously accept. In *Sketches by Boz* we find him sneering at a curate who 'got out of bed at half past twelve o'clock one winter's night, to half-baptise a washerwoman's child in a slop-basin'. On the other hand he feels qualified to indulge in a little preaching at the baptism of Paul in *Dombey and Son*:

It might have been well for Mr. Dombey, if he had thought of his own dignity a little less; and had thought of the great origin and purpose of the ceremony in which he took so formal and so stiff a part a little more. His arrogance contrasted strangely with its history.

Dickens' arrogance over the washerwoman and the slop-basin does not show up too well either, we may think. Besides, the 'great purpose' of baptism, for him, was merely social. When he wrote to Landor asking him to be his second son's godfather, he remarked that, even if the 'realities had gone out of the ceremony', it was still a way of bringing old friends together. Elliotson, the other selected godparent, thanked Dickens for absolving him from the 'religious duties', since he would not have been prepared to instruct the child that 'the maker of the Universe once came down and got a little jewess in the family way.' Attending a nonconformist meeting Dickens was outraged to find the speaker recommending that a pauper should say to a gentleman: 'I am the son of a Prince! *My* father is the King of Kings. *My* father is the Lord of Lords.' These perfectly orthodox claims seemed to him subsersive of proper class-relations. He liked his religion vague and dignified, and complained of the 'disgusting and impious familiarity' with which more enthusiastic worshippers addressed their Redeemer. From the spiritual fervour inherent in Christianity, he recoiled. Those who tried to force the Scriptures into everyday life appeared canting humbugs, and blasphemous to boot. They go to make up his troupe of comic nonconformists: Stiggins, Melchisedech Howler and the rest. On the other hand, those who shut themselves away to cultivate the life of the spirit, he considered supersititious wastrels. On his American trip he came upon the communal grave of some Trappist monks who had founded a convent in a desolate spot, and had all fallen victims to the climate: 'in which lamentable fatality', he comments, 'few rational people will suppose, perhaps, that society experienced any very severe deprivation'.

The hearty literalism with which Dickens, when in gamesome mood, approached the theatre and religion can be found too in his jokes about pictures and statues. The inn sign of the Magpie and Stump in *Pickwick* depicts, says Dickens, 'the half-obliterated semblance of a magpie intently eyeing a crooked streak of brown paint, which the neighbours had been taught from infancy to consider as the "stump".' The painting appears ridiculous not only because, seen literally, it is like any painting, only streaks of paint;

but also because the magpie's pose, 'intently eyeing' the stump, is reasonless. The unnatural poses in which artists arranged their sitters, and the odd paraphernalia they surrounded them with, comprised another aspect of painting which Dickens took a cool, literal look at. In *Our Mutual Friend* Mr. Twemlow's rooms contain a portrait of his noble relative, Lord Snigsworth:

a full-length engraving of the sublime Snigsworth over the chimney-piece, snorting at a Corinthian column, with an enormous roll of paper at his feet, and a heavy curtain going to tumble down on his head.

Like the child at the theatre, Dickens here refuses to translate the conventions of the medium into the significances they are intended to carry. So, too, with the representation of perspective, where the artist paints something shorter than it really is to indicate that it is receding from the eye. While ridiculing Miss La Creevy's paintings in *Nicholas Nickleby*, Dickens includes 'a charming whole-length of a large-headed little boy, sitting on a stool with his legs foreshortened to the size of salt-spoons'. Another absurdity of painted figures, literally considered, is that they retain their attitudes or expressions indefinitely. A portrait's smile can be nothing but a fixed smile. In *Sketches by Boz* Dickens describes a painted vase which shows 'a party of boors carousing: each boor with one leg painfully elevated in the air, by way of expressing his perfect freedom and gaiety'.

Dickens was, indeed, deeply suspicious of painting and statuary. In Italy he felt that the raptures fellow tourists went into over figures like Bernini's 'breezy maniacs' merely showed they had been taken in by the guide-books. In Bernini's figures, he complained, the 'smallest vein, or artery, is as big as an ordinary forefinger.' His own admiration was reserved, he said, for what was 'natural and true'. It seems astonishing when we consider the magnificent distortions of the figures Dickens himself creates in prose, that he should have wanted to restrict pictorial art to the lifelike. Moreover, he strongly objected to the lifelike when a painter supplied it. Millais' painting of Christ in the carpenter's shop provoked him to furious sarcasm because instead of 'etherealising' and 'ennobling' its subject as Art ought, it dared to portray a lower-class family as a lower-class family: 'such men as the carpenters might be undressed in any hospital where dirty drunkards, in a high state of varicose veins, are received.' So much for the natural and true. Again, had Dickens considered his own art and related it to painting, he could hardly have maintained his objections to the ugly and the distorted. But theoretical thinking was not much in his line. Once he started imagining, on the other hand, he became instantly acute. In *Hard Times* a 'government officer', intended by Dickens as a representative of the newly formed Department of Practical Art, and presented as a monster of pedantry, asks a class of schoolchildren whether they would paper a room with representations of horses.

After a pause, one half of the children cried in chorus, 'Yes, sir!' Upon which the other half, seeing in the gentleman's face that Yes was wrong, cried out in chorus, 'No, sir!'

Even the children who have given the right answer can't explain why it's right:

'I'll explain to you, then', said the gentleman, after another and a dismal pause, 'why you wouldn't paper a room with representations of horses. Do you ever see horses walking up and down the sides of rooms in reality – in fact? Do you?'

'Yes, sir!' from one half. 'No, sir!' from the other.

'Of course no,' said the gentleman, with an indignant look at the wrong half.

Dickens evidently doesn't realize that his government officer's standards for judging art are much the same as his own. It isn't 'natural and true' for horses to walk up walls. Nor for camels to kneel on tables, for that matter, but in *Our Mutual Friend* Dickens extracts a lot of humour from the silver camels which adorn the Veneerings' dining table. 'A caravan of camels take charge of the fruits and flowers and candles, and kneel down to be loaded with the salt.' The government officer would have found this comic, too; and the comedy depends on mistaking an artifact for what it represents.

The literalism which sees silver camels as real camels also allows Dickens to extract comedy from idioms and titles by taking them at face value. The idiom which refers to persons of celebrity as 'lions', for example, is taken literally during Mrs. Leo Hunter's party in *Pickwick*. The puny journalist Pott is referred to as 'the slumbering lion of the Eatanswill Gazette', and Mrs. Hunter is said to have provided refreshments for 'only the very particular lions', and left the smaller animals to take care of themselves. Dickens had already worn this joke rather thin in a paper called 'Some Particulars Concerning a Lion' in *Sketches by Boz*. The same logic lies behind the scene in *Oliver Twist* where Bumble presents Oliver to the Board in charge of the workhouse:

Eight or ten fat gentlemen were sitting round a table. At the top of the table, seated in an arm-chair rather higher than the rest, was a particularly fat gentleman with a very round, red face.

'Bow to the board,' said Bumble. Oliver brushed away two or three tears that were lingering in his eyes; and seeing no board but the table, fortunately bowed to that.

Dickens is strongly attracted by this mode of humour, and will often invent idioms for himself so that he can take them literally, if he can't find them ready made. For example, in *Little Dorrit* he decides to call Pancks the rent-collector a steam-tug, because Pancks is grimy and puffs and blows, and this dreary joke is kept alive by relentlessly talking about Pancks, whenever he appears, as if he were literally a steam-tug.

If so much of Dickens' humour depends on his seeing through conventions, whether theatrical or artistic or verbal, we may well wonder how it is that he fails to see through his own. If he is so alive to the absurdity of Mr. Wopsle reciting Collins' 'Ode to the Passions', how can he stomach the preposterous melodrama of, for instance, the interviews he arranges between Edith Dombey and Carker? Alone with the proud beauty Carker avails himself of interjections like 'Aye! How then, my queen?', while Edith's way of indicating that she has strong feelings on a subject is to clutch or pummel her person: 'her dark eyes flashing with a raging light, her broad white bosom red with the cruel grasp of the relentless hand with which she spurned it from her'. Edith spurning her bosom is no less ridiculous – and considerably harder to visualize – than Snigsworth snorting at a Corinthian column. Why, when it comes to Edith, does Dickens' sense of humour let him down? In fact we find that he supplies his novels with minor characters who ridicule the very passions that he expects us to take seriously in the big melodramatic scenes. After the elopement of Edith, Perch the messenger pretends to have been in close touch with the major actors in the catastrophe, and regales his friends in public bars with imagined incidents. 'It appears', says Dickens, 'that he met everybody concerned in the late transaction, everywhere, and said to them, "Sir", or "Madam", as the case was, "why do you look so pale?" at which each shuddered from head to foot, and said, "Oh, Perch!" and ran away.' Perch's lies are no more stagy than what actually occurred. It is as if Dickens' sense of humour has invented Perch to avenge itself on the humourless part of Dickens which writes about the passions of the main characters. Similarly while Florence is pining away for some sign of affection from Mr. Dombey, Toots is pining away for her: 'I'm getting more used up every day, and I'm proud to be so,' Toots affirms. 'If you could see my legs when I take my boots off, you'd form some idea of what unrequited affection is.' The yearning which, in Florence, is shielded from every breath of humour, is utterly fatuous in Toots.

We notice that Dickens focuses on Toots' legs, and particularly his boots, to deprive him of seriousness. For Dickens, true emotion cannot survive in the vicinity of a pair of boots. We recall how Richard III's conscience 'troubled his boots' at the Theatre Royal; and also Jingle's story in *Pickwick* of the man who committed suicide by sticking his head in a main water pipe, 'with a full confession in his right boot'. When the frigid Dombey approaches Edith, we are told, he 'betook his creaking boots towards her', and Mr. Jaggers, in *Great Expectations*, though he never laughs himself, wears 'great, bright, creaking boots' which seem to laugh for him 'in a dry and suspicious way'. At Hartford, on Dickens' first American trip, some well-wishers serenaded the famous author and his wife in the dead of night, gathering in the passage outside his bedroom to sing of 'home and absent friends'. Dickens, however, was convulsed with laughter at the thought of his boots standing in the corridor, confronting the singers, and had to muffle his cries in the bedclothes. 'I never *was* so impressed with a sense of the absurdity of boots, in all my life.' Indeed clothes and bodies, not only boots and legs, are inherently funny for Dickens. His noble characters are not visualized: they have no bodies or clothes at all. Once he starts to visualize, he starts to observe comic details. Esther Summerson's smallpox means nothing to us because, so far as we are concerned, she has no face. When Dickens considers what pimples look like, he instantly finds it amusing. George Chuzzlewit, for example:

had such an obvious disposition to pimples, that the bright spots on his cravat, the rich pattern on his waistcoat, and even his glittering trinkets, seemed to have broken out upon him, and not to have come into existence comfortably.

But legs seemed particularly preposterous to Dickens, and concentrating on them, as with Toots, is a quick way of making sentiment ridiculous. In *Great Expectations* Camilla, anxious to impress her

relatives with her grief at Miss Havisham's condition, remarks with
a sob: 'Raymond is a witness what ginger and sal volatile I am
obliged to take in the night. Raymond is a witness what nervous
jerkings I have in my legs.' To which Raymond replies: 'Camilla,
my dear, it is well known that your family feelings are gradually
undermining you to the extent of making one of your legs shorter
than the other.'

Toots and Camilla, however, who make human emotion laugh-
able, remain side by side with noble characters who are allowed to
indulge in emotion quite humourlessly. This is the characteristic
Dickens pattern. He was perfectly aware that his main characters
were made of sawdust, and defended the composition by pointing
out that the British public would put up with nothing else. He was
always hearing literary critics, he remarked, complaining that, in
English novels, the hero was 'uninteresting – too good – not natural,
etc.':

But O my smooth friend, what a shining impostor you must think your-
self and what an ass you must think me, when you suppose that by putting
a brazen face upon it you can blot out of my knowledge the fact that this
same unnatural young gentleman (if to be decent is to be necessarily
unnatural), whom you meet in those other books and in mine, *must* be
presented to you in that unnatural aspect by reason of your morality, and
is not to have, I will not say any of the indecencies you like, but not even
any of the experiences, trials, perplexities, and confusions inseparable
from the making or unmaking of all men!

Dickens, with his eye on sales, was determined not to let his smooth
friend down. Besides, there was an ample measure of smooth friend
in his own constitution. But having stuffed the novels with noble
sentiment, he retained a troop of comics to punish and deride it.
Quilp, as we have seen, threatens to wring the neck of Little Nell's
bird; and Tackleton, in *The Cricket on the Hearth*, offers to scrunch
the merry little cricket underfoot. Mr. Minns, too, in *Sketches by
Boz*, supplies a counterweight to the sentimental treatment of
animals and children. 'He was not unamiable,' says Dickens, 'but
he could, at any time, have viewed the execution of a dog, or the
assassination of an infant, with the liveliest satisfaction.' These
astringent characters are not only funny, they are also more appealing
and better written than the sentimental, elevated personages they
react against. They amount to a criticism of the work they appear in.
Scrooge, indeed, offers straightforward literary criticism to Marley's

ghost. 'Why', inquires the ghost, 'did I walk through crowds of fellow-beings with my eyes turned down, and never raise them to that blessed Star which led the Wise Men to a poor abode!' 'Don't be flowery, Jacob! Pray!' retorts Scrooge.

Dickens' humour, then, enabled him to see through not only other arts but his own as well. Nevertheless he was unable to relinquish the melodramatic excesses that Edith Dombey typifies, and though he could take a cool, literal look at the theatre he remained obsessed by the theatre and acting to the end of his life. His humour depends on the detection of falsity, but also on its invention, and he created the greatest gallery of hypocrites in fiction. The leading hypocrites are household words – Mrs. Gamp, Pecksniff, Uriah Heep, but the novels swarm with minor fakes, humbugs and charlatans. In *Little Dorrit* alone, for instance, we have Casby the fake Patriarch who contrives to appear selfless even in his bodily functions – at dinner, Dickens writes, he 'disposed of an immense quantity of solid food with the benignity of a good soul who was feeding someone else'; and Mrs. Gowan who insists on keeping alive the pretence that her son Henry, who has married the Meagles' daughter for money, has really fallen a victim to the parent Meagles' wiles; and Mrs. General, employed as companion to the Dorrit daughters, who wishes it to be understood that she is too delicate even to hear the question of remuneration hinted.

'I cannot object,' said Mrs. General – 'though even that is disagreeable to me – to Mr. Dorrit's inquiring, in confidence, of my friends here, what amount they have been accustomed, at quarterly intervals, to pay to my credit at my bankers.'

It is their superhuman ingenuity in lying that distinguishes Dickens' hypocrites. They lie with heroic energy and masterly imagination. Wishing to flatter a victim, they will turn the wildest fancies to account. Pumblechook in *Great Expectations*, entertaining his wealthy nephew, delivers an oration to the viands they are about to consume:

'Ah! poultry, poultry! You little thought', said Mr. Pumblechook, apostrophising the fowl in the dish, 'when you was a young fledgling, what was in store for you. You little thought you was to be refreshment beneath this humble roof for one as – Call it weakness, if you will,' said Mr. Pumblechook, getting up again, 'but may I? *may* I – ?'

And he advances on Pip once again to wring him by the hand.

Another arch-hypocrite, Bounderby in *Hard Times*, wishes it to be believed, despite his perfectly secure childhood, that he fought his way up from the gutter. He employs Mrs. Sparsit, a fellow hypocrite, posing as a great lady in reduced circumstances, so that he can feel superior to her fallen grandeur. Bounderby invents elaborate degradations for his own early years, and compares these with the imagined glories of the Sparsit past. In this way both hypocrites can draw satisfaction from completely fictitious accounts of themselves. 'At a time when', says Bounderby,

'to have been a tumbler in the mud of the streets, would have been a godsend to me, a prize in the lottery to me, you were at the Italian Opera. You were coming out of the Italian Opera, ma'am, in white satin and jewels, a blaze of splendour, when I hadn't a penny to buy a link to light you.' 'I certainly, sir,' returned Mrs. Sparsit, with a dignity serenely mournful, 'was familiar with the Italian Opera at a very early age.'

Adroitly Mrs. Sparsit embraces the grandeur and rejects the implication of relative seniority. Dickens' hypocrites are the prime beneficiaries of his inventive genius. The heroes and heroines have no imagination. We could scrap all the solemn parts of his novels without impairing his status as a writer. But we could not remove Mrs. Gamp or Pecksniff or Bounderby without maiming him irreparably. For Mrs. Gamp he invents a new language, complete with mispronunciations – 'sich' for 'such' and 'dispoged' for 'disposed' – to suggest her soggy, toothless mandibles. (The ear and memory for idiolect displayed take the mind back to early phases of Dickens' life. At school, already struck by idiom's pliancy, he had invented a private language, so that he and his friends might be taken for foreigners.) Mrs. Gamp's language has a strong religious flavour. From religion she has derived, it seems, no precise notions of salvation, but something far more common and far more valuable – a sense of life's ultimate desolation ('Ah! what a wale of grief!'), on which she can ruminate with perfect serenity. As an attendant upon birth and death, she has a wisdom beyond linguistic correctness.

Mrs. Gamp and Pecksniff are totally unassailable in their self-absorption, their self-dramatization, their high-handed use of poetic language. 'Rich folks may ride on camels,' says Mrs. Gamp, and Pecksniff has a habit of using any word that comes into his head if it sounds right for the occasion. True, they have no insides, or none that we can confidently penetrate. We don't even know whether Mrs. Gamp believes in Mrs. Harris. But they do not need insides.

They are whole without. Life customarily consists of physical proximity and mental distance, and this is the essence of Dickens' character creations. Pecksniff and Mrs. Gamp are so alive in themselves that we resent it when we feel the novelist steering them.

If it wasn't for the nerve a little sip of liquor gives me (I never was able to do more than taste it), I never could go through with what I sometimes has to do. 'Mrs. Harris,' I says, at the very last case as ever I acted in, which it was but a young person, 'Mrs. Harris,' I says, 'leave the bottle on the chimley-piece, and don't ask me to take none, but let me put my lips to it when I am so dispoged, and then I will do what I'm engaged to do, according to the best of my ability.' 'Mrs. Gamp,' she says, in answer, 'if ever there was a sober creetur to be got at eighteen pence a day for working people, and three and six for gentlefolks – night watching', said Mrs. Gamp, with emphasis, 'being a extra charge – you are that inwallable person.'

By this time the passage has deteriorated. Mrs. Gamp is too plainly being exhibited for some admonitory end as an extortionate and devious employee. Her language has lost its wild autonomy.

None of the heroines is ever imagined in speech or gesture with such meticulousness as Mrs. Gamp. Her living English contrasts with the impossibly good English spoken by the elevated characters and serious villains like Ralph Nickleby. When Dickens starts writing speeches for the nominally main characters, his verbal inventiveness withers. When he writes parts for his hypocrites, it bursts into rampant growth. Just as the heroes and heroines wear no clothes and have no bodies, so they do not really speak, as Mrs. Gamp really speaks.

The falsity of the hypocrite and flatterer is deliberate, but Dickens is also fascinated by the falsity of those who are quite guilelessly pretentious, who really believe in the inflated images of themselves which they project. Mr. Pott, for instance, the editor of the Eatanswill Gazette, saying to Pickwick: 'I trust, sir, that I have never abused the enormous power I wield.' Or Mrs. Wilfer in *Our Mutual Friend*, who is seriously convinced not only that she has lowered herself in marrying Mr. Wilfer, but that her parental home was a hive of brilliance and talent. 'Papa', declares Mrs. Wilfer,

also would remark to me (he possessed extraordinary humour), 'that a family of whales must not ally themselves with sprats.' His company was eagerly sought, as may be supposed, by the wits of the day, and our house was their continual resort. I have known as many as three copper-plate engravers exchanging the most exquisite sallies and retorts there, at one time.

Neither Pott nor Mrs. Wilfer is a hypocrite. Their demeanour is quite sincerely false. A related type of falsehood which Dickens exposes occurs where a character, far from being false to himself, is so fanatically true to himself that he is false to every situation into which he is introduced. An example is Mrs. Chick, Mr. Dombey's sister. Mrs. Chick honestly believes that everybody should make an effort, and this lands her in the situation of telling the first Mrs. Dombey earnestly, when she finds her in bed, that she must rouse herself and make an effort, 'and perhaps a very great and painful effort which you are not disposed to make' – a remark that acquires its full ironic flavour when we learn that Mrs. Dombey is within a few moments of death.

The exoticism to which falsehood drives its adherents is also a perpetual lure for Dickens. Mr. Filer, in *The Chimes*, expatiates on the wastefulness of tripe as a diet for the working class: 'Tripe is more expensive, properly understood, than the hothouse pineapple.' Or take Bounderby, insisting that what his workpeople want is to be set up in a coach and six and fed on turtle soup and venison, with a gold spoon. Pushed only a little further from the reality of themselves and their surroundings, Dickens' deluded figures would become demented, and the exotic potential of madness draws him on to create, for instance, the mad gentleman in *Nicholas Nickleby* who woos Mrs. Nickleby across the garden wall:

'I have estates, ma'am,' said the old gentleman, flourishing his right hand negligently, as if he made very light of such matters, and speaking very fast; 'jewels, lighthouses, fish-ponds, a whalery of my own in the North Sea, and several oyster-beds of great profit in the Pacific Ocean.'

It remains true that Dickens' hypocrites, though magnificently solid, have no insides, in that for all the opulence of voice and gesture and physical deformity with which their exteriors are fabricated, they are not allowed to have serious emotions. Real feeling is the perquisite of the solemn, nebulous characters at the centre of the novels. We are required to accept that the motives of the hypocrites and humbugs are simple and base, and that when they feel love or grief it is something different from, and something shallower than, what the main characters feel. It is not to be supposed that Pecksniff could love Mary Grant in the same way as

Martin Chuzzlewit loves her. For Uriah Heep to fall in love with
Agnes is, we are meant to agree, an impertinence. Heep's love must,
simply because he is Heep, be of some worthless and impudent
kind, and David is evidently meant to express the consensus of
decent opinion when he slaps him in the face. It is as if Heep had had
the audacity to try and scramble out of the part of the novel where
characters are comic and have no serious feelings, into the part where
they are lifeless and profound. The hypocrites are not capable of
genuine suffering. This is partly why they cannot be convincingly
punished. Pecksniff may be knocked down with a stick at the end
of the novel, but what Pecksniff in anguish would be like we have
no means of imagining, since we know Pecksniff only as a resourceful and ingenious hypocrite.

Besides, Pecksniff, Mrs. Gamp, Squeers, Bounderby and the other
great hypocrites are magnificent entertainers. It seems unjust that
they should be punished when all they have done is to amuse us.
We feel that the characters who knock Pecksniff around at the end
might instead take a lesson from him about how not to bore their
readers. The pattern of crime and retribution that Dickens seeks to
impose upon his fiction is simply blown aside by the comic vitality
of the figures we are supposed to deplore. Much the same happened
when Dickens encountered hypocrites in real life. As a wealthy
author of tender-hearted fiction he was deservedly in receipt of
numerous begging-letters. Retailing and elaborating upon the lies of
which these were compounded immensely entertained him. One
correspondent communicated his intention of joining the army, and
notified Dickens that his prospects in the regiment depended on his
possession of a Gloucester cheese. 'He does not ask for money, after
what has passed; but if he calls at nine tomorrow morning may he
hope to find a cheese?' Another, purporting to be a traveller in
crockery temporarily incommoded by the demise of his horse,
announced 'that if I would have the goodness to leave him out a
donkey, he would call for the animal before breakfast'. When
Dickens ceases to laugh at these hypocrites, and suddenly becomes
angry and virtuous about them – entitling them 'the scum of the
earth' and denouncing them in the police courts – the same sense of
inappropriateness supervenes as accompanies the spectacle of a
punished Pecksniff.

Dickens' refusal to allocate any emotions to his comic figures is
well illustrated by Bumble. Though Bumble is meant to be a

hypocrite, it is his great innocence which strikes us, for he has no inside to himself for him to be untrue to. When we see Bumble counting Mrs. Corney's tea-spoons, weighing her sugar tongs, inspecting her milk jug, and ascertaining to a nicety the exact condition of her furniture, before deciding to propose marriage to her, we are filled not with disgust but with trepidation for the wretched Bumble, foreseeing, as he cannot, what is in store for him when he wins Mrs. Corney's hand. It is not as if Bumble *could* ever feel love, or even lust, for anyone, so why should we blame him for regarding marriage as a financial venture? It is true that Bumble, within a few minutes of sealing his engagement by kissing Mrs. Corney's chaste nose, finds Noah Claypole gorging himself with oysters and kissing Charlotte Sowerberry, and expresses virtuous indignation. In anyone else this might be hypocritical, but in fact we feel sure that it never occurred to Bumble to connect the two episodes – and why should it? Noah, Charlotte and their oysters are clearly being lascivious, whereas Bumble is merely marrying Mrs. Corney's tea-spoons. But Bumble, though a far more convincing picture of innocence than Oliver, has one moment that disconcerts us. This is after one of Oliver's plaintive outbursts when they are on their way to Mr. Sowerberry the undertaker:

Mr. Bumble regarded Oliver's piteous and helpless look, with some astonishment, for a few seconds; hemmed three or four times in a husky manner; and, after muttering something about 'that troublesome cough', bade Oliver dry his eyes and be a good boy.

It is an astonishing false note. That Bumble should be brought near to tears by a puling orphan is so out of key with all we know about him, and about how he has to earn his living, that we instantly withdraw our belief. And our inability to concede Bumble the emotion Dickens tries to give him here is a measure of his emotional emptiness in the rest of the story.

Because Dickens' main comic characters are magnificent performers, but have no emotions, they provided him with no way of bringing within the scope of his comedy real suffering or real cruelty. But it is clear that he wanted to make his comedy confront and embrace the cruelty of life and that he at times felt this cruelty, even – or perhaps especially – in trivial incidents, deeply. One of his most spine-chilling bits describes watching the snakes' feeding-time at the zoo – an occasion on which the fare included live birds, rabbits and guinea-pigs. The sight appalled Dickens, and he couldn't rid his mind of it. Writing about it afterwards, he felt snakes 'coming up the legs of the table'. His account keeps trying to struggle into facetiousness, to escape the pitiful routine enacted in the cage. He watches a small snake approach a guinea-pig – 'white and yellow, and with a gentle eye – every hair upon him erect with horror' – and stretch its diminutive jaws, as if to demonstrate to the guinea-pig what its father, a huge snake coiled in the corner, will do when it wakes up.

The guinea pig backed against the side of the cage – said 'I know it, I know it!' – and his eye glared and his coat turned wiry, as he made the remark.

Five sparrows crouch together in a little trench at the back of the cage, each struggling to get into the innermost angle so as to be seized last, while the snake crawls towards them, looking back at the guinea-pig 'over about two yards and a quarter of shoulder'.

Please to imagine two small serpents, one beginning on the tail of a white mouse, and one on the head, and each pulling his own way, and the mouse very much alive all the time, with the middle of him madly writhing.

The sentence picks a situation which looks as if it might mean to be comic, but horror freezes it as it proceeds.

The black comedy in Dickens' fiction is, at the start of his career, more jocose. In *Sketches by Boz* we have the story of the baker who beat his wife, and of the baker's son who tried to intervene:

He opened the door of the parental bed-chamber. His father was dancing upon his mother. What must have been his feelings! In the agony of the minute he rushed at his male parent as he was about to plunge a knife into the side of his female. The mother shrieked. The father caught the son (who had wrested the knife from the paternal grasp) up in his arms, carried him down-stairs, shoved him into a copper of boiling water among some linen, closed the lid, and jumped upon the top of it, in which position he was found with a ferocious countenance by the mother, who arrived in the melancholy wash-house just as he had so settled himself.

A father who boils his son to death is precisely the kind of subject Sam Weller in *Pickwick* chooses for his jokes, and Weller is Dickens' most persistent purveyor of black comedy. Stabbed babies, gentlemen whose heads get knocked off, a man who gets caught in his own patent steam sausage machine, and is only discovered when a customer complains that he has found trouser buttons in his sausages – these are the materials of Sam Weller's humour. It goes only a little way towards looking death in the face, because the forms of death involved are carefully selected for their extravagant improbability. No one could be aided by this brand of humour to see everyday death and suffering as part of the human comedy. Although Sam's blood-thirsty tales are designed to show his splendidly lower-class resilience, we are supposed to take it for granted that he will be as decently moved as the next man when anyone important is in trouble. When Pickwick finds himself in the Fleet Prison, Sam becomes a model of the faithful, self-sacrificing servant, and solemnly asserts that his master is 'a reg'lar thoroughbred angel'.

Weller's joky callousness is a cover, then, for his dog-like attachment to Pickwick, and after this novel it practically disappears from Dickens' writing – from his novels at least, for Dickens remained capable of bearing up under other people's disasters with a hilarity hardly more refined than Weller's, as his letters show. He writes to Wills in 1854, for instance, about the outcome of a collision between a coal wagon and the son of one of his employees, Cooper by name, a 'steady stupid sort of highly respectable creature'. In abrupt, mocking style Dickens relates Cooper's bewilderment at his son's absence from home: 'Father conferring with Policeman on disappearance, up comes strange boy saying that how he has eerd tell as a boy is a lyin in the "Bonus", as was run over. Wretched father goes to the Bonus . . . and finds his child with his head smashed to pieces.' Seeing the comic side of lower-class death suggests a disdainful callousness already foreshadowed in the way Dickens told the story of the baker who boiled his son. 'His male parent . . . was about to plunge a knife into the side of his female.' The flippant, educated tone invites the reader to smile at the brawling of these ignoble figures. When Dickens describes the suffering of the workhouse children in *Oliver Twist*, and of the pupils at Dotheboys Hall in *Nicholas Nickleby*, this is his regular voice. Occasionally, though, he will interrupt it with a sad, lofty voice which asserts that the situation is very shocking, and there is really nothing to laugh at at all. We can observe the sad, lofty voice being discreetly exchanged for the facetious voice in this passage from *Nicholas Nickleby* which introduces us to Squeers' pupils:

Pale and haggard faces, lank and bony figures, children with the countenances of old men, deformities with irons upon their limbs, boys of stunted growth, and others whose long meagre legs would hardly bear their stooping bodies, all crowded on the view together . . . With every kindly sympathy and affection blasted in its birth, with every young and healthy feeling flogged and starved down, with every revengeful passion that can fester in swollen hearts eating its evil way to their core in silence, what an incipient Hell was breeding here!

And yet this scene, painful as it was, had its grotesque features, which, in a less interested observer than Nicholas, might have provoked a smile. Mrs. Squeers stood at one of the desks, presiding over an immense basin of brimstone and treacle, of which delicious compound she administered a large instalment to each boy in succession: using for the purpose a common wooden spoon, which might have been originally manufactured for some gigantic top, and which widened every young gentleman's mouth considerably.

The facetious voice is well in control by now, and proceeds to describe Nicholas' first day at the school. What is noticeable is that Dickens has stopped feeling, and has started to write well. The sad, lofty voice was insufferably stilted and didn't allow either his imagination or his intellect to work. Once he has laid it aside, images flood back into the writing, along with crispness and wit. At breakfast time, for example, little wooden bowls are arranged on a board in the wash-house: 'Into these bowls, Mrs. Squeers, assisted by the hungry servant, poured a brown composition which looked like diluted pincushions without the covers, and was called porridge.' Dickens is encouraging us to laugh at starving children, but we forget this and willingly co-operate with him because he is imagining with such clarity and because his mastery of ironic tone is so enjoyable. The irony of calling Mrs. Squeers' brimstone and treacle a 'delicious compound' is matched in *Oliver Twist* in the scene where the watery gruel is ladled out of its copper. 'Of this festive composition each boy had one porringer.' The result of the irony is not to make the social criticism more bitter. On the contrary the pity or anger we would normally feel at the sufferings of the little victims is extinguished in laughter. Dickens quite consciously misrepresented his subject. He did not wish to provoke anger or reform so much as to retain a large and lucrative audience. The abuses practised in the notorious Yorkshire schools could not well be exaggerated, as he remarked in a letter, but:

I have kept down the strong truth and thrown as much comicality over it as I could, rather than disgust and weary the reader with its fouler aspects.

'People', in Mr. Sleary's words, 'mutht be amuthed.' Thus the torturers become, in our eyes, genial managers of the entertainment.

Even Gamfield the sweep in *Oliver Twist* gets a laugh. Gamfield explains that he lights dry straw, rather than wet, under his climbing boys, because wet straw will only smoke and send a boy to sleep.

And that's wot he likes. Boys is wery obstinit, and wery lazy, gen'lmen, and there's nothink like a good hot blaze to make 'em come down vith a run. It's humane too, gen'lmen, acause, even if they've stuck in the chimbley, roasting their feet makes 'em struggle to hextricate theirselves.

Jonas Hanway had begun to draw attention to the sufferings of the climbing boys in the 1780s. In 1817 a Committee of the House of Commons had recommended that the use of climbing boys should be prohibited, though this recommendation was not carried into effect until 1832. Dickens, writing in 1837, is, as usual, hardly in the vanguard of protest. From Mayhew's *London Labour and the London Poor* we learn that it was common practice to light straw under the children, and also to jab pins into their feet, in order to make them climb. From clambering in the chimneys they developed sores on their thighs, knees and elbows, and soot, rubbing into these, prevented them from healing. They started climbing chimneys when they were anything from 4 to 7 years old, and frequently developed deformity of the spine, legs and arms as a result, but more frequent still was cancer of the scrotum, which was so common among them that it was known as 'chimney sweeper's cancer', and lectured upon as a separate disease at Guy's and St. Bartholomew's Hospitals. Gamfield the sweep seems suddenly less funny when we look back at him from these facts.

We end up feeling ashamed of Dickens for making us laugh, yet unable to resist the stylistic accomplishment with which he does it. It's not only that he is wonderfully resourceful at finding the inappropriate word – the device upon which irony depends – but his comic similes are highly graphic (the porridge looking like pincushion stuffing, for instance), as well as funny. In *Great Expectations* Pip, looking at his childhood with adult detachment, recalls the disgusting medicine called Tar-water which his sister used to force him to take. 'At the best of times, so much of this elixir was administered to me as a choice restorative, that I was conscious of going about, smelling like a new fence.' The fanciful leap from boy to fence is so unexpected that it has the liberating power of a poetic image, and it conveys Pip's smell exactly at the same time. The ironic words – 'elixir', 'choice restorative' – for the Tar-water lend the prose a controlled air: a sense of the writer standing back to measure the weight and tone of his vocabulary. It has an eighteenth-century feel – an offshoot of the grave hauteur first heard in Swift – and is sometimes eighteenth-century in fact (compare, say, Dickens on Squeers 'He had but one eye, and the popular prejudice runs in favour of two,' with Sheridan in *The Rivals* 'one eye may be very agreeable, yet . . . the prejudice has always run in favour of two'). By scrupulously choosing the wrong word Dickens can produce flashes of epigram. Mr. Gowan, in *Little Dorrit*, was attached to a legation abroad, and 'died at his post with his drawn salary in his hand'. More often the irony is smoother and depends upon a finer perception for its discovery. *Oliver Twist* has some beautiful examples. Oliver, on his way to London, sits down to rest by a milestone. 'The stone by which he was seated, bore, in large characters, an intimation that it was just seventy miles from that spot to London.' 'Intimation' is an absurdly discreet word for the bold announcement of a milestone. Strangely, though, it accentuates Oliver's childishness. He has always been surrounded by adults who have disguised their cruelty under polite forms and official language. Here, in the milestone, is another one: a stonehearted flunkey who gravely informs the child that he has 70 miles to walk. Again, when Oliver arrives at Fagin's den, he washes himself, 'and made everything tidy, by emptying the basin out of the window, agreeably to the Jew's directions'. 'Agreeably to', which looks an innocent adverbial construction, makes a disdainful comment, in passing, about people who pour dirty water out of windows.

This skill easily degenerates into sarcasm. Dickens is particularly apt to indulge himself in the heavy humour which results from rephrasing what one of his lower-class characters has said in portentously literate language. Similarly he will contrive to be funny by giving a stuffily decorous description of lower-class manners. Mrs. Gamp, for instance:

stopped between her sips of tea to favour the circle with a smile; and at those periods her countenance was lighted up with a degree of intelligence and vivacity, which it was almost impossible to separate from the benignant influence of distilled waters.

The superciliousness, marshalled to communicate the fact that Mrs. Gamp has been drinking gin, invites the reader to join the author on an elevated platform of language, to watch Mrs. Gamp at tea. He will feel that he can afford to patronize Mrs. Gamp, because Dickens, in describing her, has adopted that smiling over-politeness which we reserve for social inferiors.

The disdainful and supercilious note in Dickens' humour is not confined to his fiction. On his frequent visits to workhouses, lunatic asylums, and other haunts of the poor and suffering, we find that he derives a surprising amount of amusement from contemplating the inferior creatures they contain. In Wapping workhouse he is struck by the way the old women sit in a line, 'silently working their mouths like a sort of poor old Cows'. The superintendent of another ward, whom Dickens describes as 'an elderly, able-bodied pauperess, with a large upper lip' is in charge of a number of women who are subject to fits. 'This civil personage', he writes, '(in whom I regretted to identify a reduced member of my honourable friend Mrs. Gamp's family) said, "They has 'em continiwal, sir. They drops with no more notice than if they was coach-horses dropped from the moon." '
That the women have fits, and that their nurse has not an educated voice, are both sources of comedy for Dickens. His mock courtesy – 'This civil personage' – is knowingly offensive. He looks the woman over – 'an elderly, able-bodied pauperess, with a large upper lip' – with as much fellow-feeling as if he were sizing up a purchase at a horse-fair.

The composure and aloofness link Dickens with four of his own characters – three of them villains: Sir John Chester in *Barnaby Rudge*, Skimpole in *Bleak House*, the Marquis de St. Evremonde in *A Tale of Two Cities* and Eugene Wrayburn in *Our Mutual Friend*. These characters project and drive to an extreme the contempt Dickens felt for those who were not successful, not gentlemen, and not Dickens. The fact that he kept repeating the character with slight variations – Steerforth in *David Copperfield* is another offshoot of the type – indicates how captivated he was by superciliousness. Sir John Chester is a prodigiously languid character. He calmly picks his teeth or sips tea in the middle of other people's disasters. He finds the lower classes offensive, and regards them, if at all, with humourous disdain, through his eye-glass. When his son wants to marry Emma Haredale, whose father was found stabbed to death, the prospect is too much for Sir John's delicate sensibility: 'The very idea of marrying a girl whose father was killed, like meat! Good God, Ned, how disagreeable!' Harold Skimpole, in *Bleak House*, shares this fastidiousness. He regards tradespeople as half comic figures who absurdly expect him to pay for the little elegancies of life without which his existence would be intolerable. He tells Jarndyce and Esther about a baker – 'a rough kind of fellow, a sort of human hedgehog rolled up' – who loaned him two armchairs and complained when they were damaged. Skimpole explains how he tried to draw the baker's attention to the beauties of nature. 'I said, "Now my good man . . . I entreat you, by our common brotherhood, not to interpose between me and a subject so sublime, the absurd figure of an angry baker." But he did,' said Mr. Skimpole, raising his laughing eyes in playful astonishment; 'he did interpose that ridiculous figure, and he does, and he will again.' The Marquis, in *A Tale of Two Cities*, is more outrageous still, and doesn't even try to be funny. He flouts decent, Christian humbug about the brotherhood of mankind in a perfectly shameful way in the scene where his coach runs over and kills a pauper child. The howling of the child's father over the little corpse is distateful to the Marquis. 'Why does he make that abominable noise? . . . It is extraordinary to me', said he, 'that you people cannot take care of yourselves and your children. One or the other of you is for ever in the way. How do I know what injury you have done my horses?' The thrill of this magnificent inhumanity is plainly considerable for Dickens – appalling and exciting at the same time. Other manifestations of the Marquis' elegant barbarity are enthusiastically fabricated. Significantly the disdainful monster – the apotheosis of the raised eyebrow – has become the hero in *Our Mutual Friend*. Eugene Wrayburn's 'lazily arrogant air' with the lower classes, particularly Bradley Headstone, has Bradley perspiring with impotent rage. 'Composedly smoking, he leaned an elbow on the chimney-piece . . . and looked at the schoolmaster. It was a cruel look, in its cold disdain of him, as a creature of no worth.' Eugene's cigar – a permanent companion – is the equivalent of Sir John Chester's toothpick. He calmly blows the ash off it while Bradley boils and bubbles. He is unscrupulous in his pursuit of a lower-class girl whom he has no intention of marrying. When he finds her walking home with Riah, he contemptuously draws attention to the fact that Riah is a Jew. 'If Mr. Aaron', said Eugene, 'will be good enough to relinquish his charge to me, he will be quite free for any engagement he may have at the Synagogue.' Eugene also bribes the alcoholic Mr. Wren with rum to worm out of him Lizzie Hexam's whereabouts. While the drunkard sits soaking up the spirit, which is shortly to be the death of him, Eugene, 'with great composure', fumigates him, using a shovel of coals and some scented pastilles, so that he does not have to smell his guest as well as talk to him. Mortimer Lightwood, Eugene's ex-public-school chum, finds this deliciously funny, and it testifies to the lasting appeal of this type of humour that Pamela Hansford Johnson should pronounce Eugene 'an attractive and wholly adult character'. It has been suggested that Eugene's taking ways reflect Dickens' response to the young Etonians who were his son's schoolfellows. But, as we've seen, disdain had corrupted him long before this, and it is the seed of much of his humour.

The irony and facetiousness which Dickens developed so that he could face the cruelty of Oliver Twist's workhouse or Squeers' Yorkshire school has eventually produced Eugene Wrayburn. Being cool and detached, it has inevitably turned vicious in the long run. It still leaves Dickens with no comic method that can express sympathy for the object of his humour, and yet see its humour. The sympathy has to be pronounced by the sad, lofty voice which occasionally breaks in on the facetious one. But in *Little Dorrit* the depiction of Mr. Dorrit does – and it is a unique achievement – demonstrate a comic method where humour and depth of sympathy combine. Dorrit, in some sense a portrait of Dickens' father, who was also imprisoned in the Marshalsea, never gets detached from his creator enough to be treated with disdain. His great scenes – like that at the grand banquet in Rome where he forgets where he is and addresses the guests as if they were newcomers to the Marshalsea – are both funny and painful. The occasion is not sentimentalized. Dorrit's speech is presented with acute comic accuracy. But we wince with embarrassment, and also, as Amy Dorrit does, with pity at her father's breakdown.

Ladies and gentlemen, the duty – ha – devolves upon me of – hum – welcoming you to the Marshalsea! The space is – ha – limited – limited – the parade might be wider; but you will find it apparently grow larger after a time – a time, ladies and gentlemen – and the air is, all things considered, very good. It blows over the – ha – Surrey hills. Blows over the Surrey hills. This is the Snuggery. Hum. Supported by a small subscription of the – ha – Collegiate body.

Dorrit letting out his guilty secret would naturally move Dickens, since he harboured one himself. He had never been able to tell even his own wife and children of the months he spent working in Warren's Blacking warehouse as a boy or of his father's confinement in the Marshalsea. But the identification of Dorrit with himself as well as his father might easily have led to a sentimentalized figure like Oliver in Fagin's den. Instead Dorrit's vanities and his baseness are scrupulously observed: the pathetic pride, for instance, with which, when in the Marshalsea, he treats Old Nandy from the workhouse to tea; patronizing him; commenting sadly and with evident relish on the old man's infirmities; arranging for Nandy to consume his shrimps and bread and butter at a little distance from himself and his family.

'If Maggy will spread that newspaper on the window-sill, my dear,' remarked the Father complacently and in a half whisper to Little Dorrit, 'my old pensioner can have his tea there, while we are having ours.'

When it is time for Nandy to depart, he is dismissed with a final burst of patronage from Dorrit: 'We don't call this a shilling, Nandy, you know,' he said, putting one in his hand. 'We call it tobacco.' But the finest of Dorrit's scenes, and also Dickens' greatest piece of comic writing, occurs earlier in the novel when Amy Dorrit has just discouraged the attentions of John Chivery, son of the Marshalsea gate-keeper, with the result that her father finds old Chivery treating him with less indulgence than usual. Dorrit is too ashamed to ask Amy to encourage John so that her father will get better treatment. He is almost, but not quite, too ashamed to broach the subject at all. He pretends to feel unwell, to gain Amy's sympathy, and begins to fabricate a devious story about a man called Jackson who used to be turnkey at the prison:

and – hem! – and he had a – brother, and this – young brother paid his addresses to – at least, did not go so far as to pay his addresses to – but admired – respectfully admired – the – not the daughter, the sister – of one of us; a rather distinguished Collegian; I may say, very much so. His name was Captain Martin.

Dorrit rambles on about the fictitious Captain Martin – 'highly respected in the army' – who opined that his sister might well tolerate the young man's advances 'on her father's – I should say, brother's – account'. But at last even he grows ashamed of the shabby pretence, and dwindles into silence.

His voice died away, as if she could not bear the pain of hearing him, and her hand had gradually crept to his lips. For a while, there was a dead silence and stillness; and he remained shrunk in his chair.

The silence continues. He starts eating his dinner. Father and daughter avoid each other's eyes.

By little and little he began; laying down his knife and fork with a noise, taking things up sharply, biting at his bread as if he were offended with it, and in other similar ways showing that he was out of sorts.

This is a prelude to a pettish outburst; he calls himself a 'squalid, disgraced wretch', and eventually bursts into tears of self-pity. Weeping he tells his daughter how proud she would have been of him had she known him before he lost his fortune:

and how (at which he cried again) she should . . . have ridden at his fatherly side on her own horse, and how the crowd (by which he meant in effect the people who had given him the twelve shillings he then had in his pocket) should have trudged the dusty roads respectfully.

That last sardonic parenthesis retrieves the scene from mawkishness just as it was about to slip out of the sharp comic perspective. Of course, it is a very different brand of comedy from that of Squeers' school or Mrs. Gamp. There is no touch of facetiousness and no touch of condescension. Dickens has too much respect for his victim to suggest that he can be smilingly indulged, as Mrs. Gamp can. The respect is shown in the unerring attention that is paid to the shifts of Dorrit's mood, his exact psychological lineaments.

As if Dorrit himself were not a remarkable enough attainment for one novel, the book contains, we should notice, a second comic figure whose presentation is also cleansed of that genial humour which Dickens exudes over the Gamps and the Pecksniffs. This is Merdle, the mighty financier. The portrait consists of a few bare but masterly strokes. We see little of Merdle, and know almost nothing of what goes on in his head. He is an intriguing blank. He feels nervous of his own butler, and when he sticks his finger into his parrot's cage to assert the fact that he is master of the house, the parrot bites it. Eventually he pays a desultory call on his son's wife, and asks to borrow a penknife. She offers him a mother of pearl one.

'Thank you,' said Mr. Merdle; 'but if you have got one with a darker handle, I think I should prefer one with a darker handle.'
  'Tortoise-shell?'
  'Thank you,' said Mr. Merdle; 'Yes. I think I should prefer tortoise-shell.'

Merdle's drab phrasing (carefully drab: both manuscript and proof corrections show Dickens angling here for the flat note), conceals, we later discover, a curious aestheticism. For Mr. Merdle wishes to borrow the penknife in order to cut his throat. When he is found dead that night in a bath full of blood and water, we recall the scene at the end of the previous chapter when his daughter-in-law, who had been bored to tears by his visit, saw him and her penknife off:

Waters of vexation filled her eyes; and they had the effect of making the famous Mr. Merdle, in going down the street, appear to leap, and waltz, and gyrate, as if he were possessed by several Devils.

This bland aside, which seems to look forward to the Conrad of *The Secret Agent*, is all we have to suggest any internal tumult in the doomed man. Merdle's mind is closed to us, and this distinguishes him from Mr. Dorrit. But they are alike in the respect Dickens shows them. Not moral respect, of course. Morally he despises both. But he respects them as creations. Neither is subjected to the jovial condescension with which he regards comic characters in other novels. With Dorrit Dickens' respect takes the form of acute scrutiny; with Merdle, of reticence. When Merdle's butler hears of the suicide, he is not surprised: 'erect and calm', says Dickens, he greets the news with 'these memorable words. "Sir, Mr. Merdle never was the gentleman, and no ungentlemanly act on Mr. Merdle's part would surprise me."' That we deprecate this comment, and are at once inclined to take Merdle's side, is a testimony to the respect with which Dickens has treated him.

4

CORPSES AND EFFIGIES

When Mrs. Gamp, in the sick room contemplates her patient, Dickens tells us in what direction her thoughts are straying:

By degrees, a horrible remembrance of one branch of her calling took possession of the woman; and stooping down, she pinned his wandering arms against his sides, to see how he would look if laid out like a dead man. Hideous as it may appear, her fingers itched to compose his limbs in that last marble attitude.

Dickens' virtuous indignation here is decidedly overdone. He was just as intrigued by dead bodies as Mrs. Gamp, and they wonderfully stimulated his imagination. His undertakers – Mr. Sowerberry in *Oliver Twist*, Mr. Mould in *Martin Chuzzlewit*, Mr. Omer in *David Copperfield* – are conceived with genial interest. Dickens goes happily to work to illustrate their familiarity with the routines of death. Mr. Mould beams lovingly at Mrs. Mould across the chest full of shrouds and winding sheets, and Mr. Sowerberry uses as a snuff box 'an ingenious little model of a patent coffin'. Snuff was one of the things which dead bodies might well turn into in Dickens' estimation, and maybe we're to assume that Mr. Sowerberry came by his in the way of trade. Writing on his visits to London churches Dickens remarks how the congregation is always convulsed with coughs and sneezes because of the snuff compounded of pulverized dead citizens which rises from the floor in clouds and chokes up even the organ bellows. He was fascinated by coffins. When Captain Hawdon dies in *Bleak House*, Dickens makes the coffin stand all night beside Hawdon's old portmanteau, to encourage a comparison of the two receptacles (in *The Holly Tree* a portmanteau is carried in from a coach 'stiff, like a frozen body'), and later when Krook blows up, leaving only some soot and a little puddle, a full-sized coffin is solemnly constructed and buried although there's nothing to put in it. At his sister's interment Pip is astonished to see that the six coffin-bearers are half hidden by a black velvet housing that hangs down, so that the whole contraption resembles 'a blind monster with twelve human legs, shuffling and blundering along'. But Dickens' best walking coffin is the one which gives Jerry Cruncher junior in *A Tale of Two Cities* a nightmare after he has seen his father digging up corpses in the graveyard:

He had a strong idea that the coffin he had seen was running after him; and, pictured as hopping on behind him, bolt upright, upon its narrow end, always on the point of overtaking him and hopping on at his side – perhaps taking his arm – it was a pursuer to shun . . . It hid in doorways too, rubbing its horrible shoulders against doors, and drawing them up to its ears, as if it were laughing. It got into shadows on the road, and lay cunningly on its back to trip him up. All this time it was incessantly hopping on behind and gaining on him, so that when the boy got to his own door he had reason for being half dead. And even then it would not leave him, but followed him upstairs with a bump on every stair, scrambled into bed with him, and bumped down, dead and heavy, on his breast when he fell asleep.

The vivacity of this imaginative play with coffins is thoroughly typical of Dickens, who never missed a human carcass if he could help it. 'Whenever I am in Paris, I am dragged by invisible force into the Morgue,' he confesses. He even goes there on Christmas Day, to see the corpse of an old grey-haired man with a tap running over him, and water dripping off the corner of his mouth, making him look sly. Other corpses he met there are meticulously described: the flaxen-haired boy with a bullet through his forehead; the swollen, saturated corpse in a corner 'like a heap of crushed over-ripe figs'; the large, dark man whose disfigurement by the water was, Dickens recalls, 'in a frightful manner comic'. This last cadaver haunted Dickens for several days. When he went swimming in the river he seemed to be drinking him, and food on his plate would suddenly look like part of the dead man and cause Dickens to leave the restaurant. Dickens confesses too that he was drawn back to the Morgue after the man was put underground to inspect his clothes, and 'I found them frightfully like him – particularly his boots.' In the absence of a drowned corpse, Dickens would make do with imitations. Once, in Lausanne, a girl perished in the lake while he was at dinner. Though arriving too late to view her remains, Dickens secured a boatman who had been more fortunate, and persuaded him to act out the whole scene, 'depositing himself finally on a heap of stones, to represent the body'. A paper in *The Uncommercial*

Traveller entitled 'Some Recollections of Mortality' might easily be
called 'Mortuaries I Have Known'. One of the bodies described is
that of a baby. 'It had been opened, and neatly sewn up', Dickens
relates, 'and regarded from that point of view, it looked like a stuffed
creature.' He had a taste, in his fiction, for bottled babies. Mrs.
Harris' sister's child travels the fairgrounds preserved in spirits in a
bottle. It is a shock for Mrs. Harris to come upon this relation at
Greenwich Fair, as Mrs. Gamp explains, 'the same not bein'
expected from the outside picter, where it was painted quite con-
trairy in a livin' state, a many sizes larger, and performing beautiful
upon the Arp.' A child with three heads in a bottle confronts Tom
in *The Lamplighter*. Bottled parts were similarly intriguing. As a
boy Dickens used to visit a shop in Long Acre which displayed, in
tall jars, preparations which had the appearance of 'unhealthy
macaroni', but proved on closer inspection to be tapeworms 'extracted
from the internal mechanism of certain ladies and gentlemen' who
were delicately referred to, on the receptacles, by initial letters.

With several corpses in 'Some Recollections', what Dickens
particularly observes is the way the spectators regard them, 'like
looking at waxwork, without a catalogue, and not knowing what to
make of it'. The varying expressions of the crowd possess, he notes,
the 'one underlying expression of *looking at something that could not
return a look*'. The concept is important to him, or so his italics
suggest.

Perhaps it was this property which interested Dickens in blind
people. Blind Stagg in *Barnaby Rudge* is a 'pale and unwholesome'
creature, living underground, and has an uncannily attentive expression on his face when people are about. Mr. Dombey's blurred
impressions as he rushes across France after his wife and Carker are
of 'blind men with quivering eyelids, led by old women holding
candles to their faces; idiot girls; the lame, the epileptic, and the
palsied' – all the benighted, misshapen creatures, in fact, that
Dickens energetically pursued. *American Notes* describes his visit to
the Institute for the Blind at Boston. In the kindred Institute at
Lausanne he found two patients – girl and boy – who were deaf and
dumb as well as blind. Their expressions, antics and affinity to
corpses deeply engrossed him. The girl, he was appalled to relate,
'*laughs sometimes* (good God! conceive what at!)'. When she felt
with her hand the vibrations from a piano 'her breath quickened, her
colour deepened – and I can compare it to nothing but returning

animation in a person nearly dead.' The boy, taught to speak, recounted his sleeping experiences, and on learning that these were called dreams, 'asked whether dead people ever dreamed when they were lying in the ground'. Dickens supplied him with cigars, and facetiously reports his gratitude: 'I don't know whether he thinks I grow them, or make them, or produce them by winking, or what.' Like the dead, the handicapped can often be counted on for a little humour.

But to return to corpses: in the novels, too, they are objects of interested scrutiny. Quilp's, lying on a swamp in the glare of flames, with its hair 'stirred by the damp breeze'; Lord Frederick's 'pressing down the grass whose every blade bore twenty tiny lives', and staring 'stark and rigid' at the sky; Merdle's lying in the marble bath as in a 'sarcophagus', with his blood draining down the plughole. Jerry Cruncher digs up corpses; Gaffer Hexam fishes them from the Thames; in London they are crammed into graveyards already bulging with dead flesh – Jo the crossing sweeper announces that they put Hawdon 'wery nigh the top. They was obliged to stamp upon it to git it in. I could unkiver it for you with my broom, if the gate was open.' The monks of the Great St. Bernard in *Little Dorrit* stack frozen travellers in a grated house outside – 'The mother, storm-belated many winters ago, still standing in the corner with her baby at her breast; the man who had frozen with his arm raised to his mouth in fear or hunger, still pressing it with his dry lips after years and years.' (Dickens had visited this set of corpses on his Swiss trip, and dispatched an appreciative account to Forster.) Bill Sikes is pursued by Nancy's body after he has murdered her – 'If he ran, it followed – not running too: that would have been a relief: but like a corpse endowed with the mere machinery of life, and borne on one slow melancholy wind that never rose or fell'; and when Pip watches Magwitch stumbling across the churchyard it seems to him 'as if he were eluding the hands of the dead people, stretching up cautiously out of their graves, to get a twist upon his ankle and pull him in'. The corpses are as fanciful in their postures as the live characters in Dickens and their inclination to remain dead is by no means firm. It gave him a nasty turn one day at the Paris Morgue to see the keeper moving about among the bodies, looking 'more ghastly and intolerable' than the other exhibits, what with the bleak overhead lighting and the clammy air: 'I think that with the first start of seeing him must have come the impression that the bodies were all getting up!'

We've seen Dickens likening the occupants of mortuaries with their intent, blind look and rigid stance to waxworks, and waxworks intrigued him almost as much as corpses. Indeed he recognized no very clear boundary between them. 'Waxen babies with their limbs more or less mutilated, appealing on one leg to the parental affections from under little cupping glasses' figure in his account of boarding-house nick-nacks. Corpse-hue he typifies as 'the colour of impure wax'. Mrs. Jarley's waxworks are all 'looking intensely nowhere, and staring with extraordinary earnestness at nothing', and their 'death-like faces' and 'great glassy eyes' so terrifying Little Nell as they stand about her bed in the caravan that she has to get up and light a candle. When Pip first sets eyes on Miss Havisham, she seems like a waxwork and a corpse as well:

Once, I had been taken to see some ghastly waxwork at the Fair, representing I know not what impossible personage lying in state. Once, I had been taken to one of our old marsh churches to see a skeleton in the ashes of a rich dress, that had been dug out of a vault under the church pavement. Now, waxwork and skeleton seemed to have dark eyes that moved and looked at me.

Waxworks staring at people and people who appear to be waxworks are regular inhabitants of the novels. Hairdressers used wax dummies for display, and Sam Weller tells a story about one of these with 'wery large whiskers' and 'uncommon clear eyes' whose owner melts it down at the parlour fire because his girl friend has fallen in love with it. Mr. Dombey, when he sits in his office, is 'stared at' through a dome-shaped window in the leads by a waxen effigy in a hair-cutting saloon on the first floor. Typically, when Dickens visited Florence he was deeply impressed by the waxworks of dead children in the Museum of Natural History, 'admonitions of our frail mortality' as he calls them, 'counterfeits of Youth and Beauty . . . lying there, upon their beds, in their last sleep' – much as if the waxworks had actually been alive until shortly before he came along.

Dickens' dead figures who subject the living to their alarmed and alarming gaze are made of wood and stone and metal and painted canvas as well as wax. The mingled terror and hilarity they cause harks back to Dickens' toddler days. His nursery contained a monstrous collection of effigies, who pretended to be dead with alarming ill-success. Prominent among them was a tumbler, who came upright whenever pushed down, bringing his 'lobster eyes' to bear on the aggressor – 'I affected to laugh very much, but in my heart of hearts was extremely doubtful of him.' Assisting the tumbler in his work of mental derangement was a 'demoniacal Counsellor in a black gown', given to springing out of a snuff-box with 'a red-cloth mouth, wide open'. 'Not to be endured on any terms', the counsellor could yet not be put away, for he insisted on flying out of mammoth boxes in nightmares. A frog, adept at landing unexpectedly on one's palm – 'horrible' – and a hanged cardboard man with a 'sinister expression' about his nose were other playthings. Most dreadful, though, was the comic mask. Who wore it, Dickens can't recall; but he was 'so frightened that the sight of it is an era in my life'. Its 'stolid features' were intolerable – like death coating a live face. In vain did the adults show him it was only paper, and lock it up. 'The mere recollection of that fixed face, the mere knowledge of its existence anywhere, was sufficient to awake me in the night all perspiration and horror, with, "O I know it's coming! O the mask!" ' Some of Dickens' fictional children inherit this trauma – made semi-comic for adult consumption. As little Kitty Kimmeens searches the empty house in *Tom Tiddler's Ground* 'the disagreeable thought came into her young head, What a very alarming thing it would be to find somebody with a mask on like Guy Fawkes, hiding bolt upright in a corner and pretending not to be alive!' Young Jackson in *Mugby Junction*, whose joyless education resembles Clennam's, has visions of his repressive step-parents permanently sporting wax masks. Effigies, and their kinship with corpses that have somehow eluded the normal burial arrangements, attracted little Dickens' notice outside the nursery too. Rochester cathedral, for instance, had a tomb with a 'staring' effigy 'bursting out' of it, 'like a ship's figure-head'. In the novels the effigies distinguish themselves from the living by their abnormally attentive gaze. The wooden midshipman in *Dombey* peers through a piece of optical equipment, and the wooden figurehead of a 'goggle-eyed' admiral which Quilp drives red-hot pokers through thrusts itself forward, says Dickens, 'with that excessively wide-awake aspect, and air of somewhat obtrusive politeness, by which figureheads are usually characterised'. The stone effigies of men and lions which cover the chateau in *A Tale of Two Cities* seem to the villagers to change their expressions when the Marquis is killed, and his dead face becomes like theirs – 'there was one stone face too many, up at the chateau,' says Dickens, announcing the murder. *Sketches by Boz* has an investigation into the expressions of the faces on street door-knockers, and when Scrooge fits his key into his front door, he sees the knocker change into Marley's face. Nell and her grandfather meet a Punch and Judy man in a graveyard, and Punch is perched on a tombstone where, Dickens notes, he retains his imperturbable smile, although his body is hanging loose and limp. Even without the tombstone it would be hard to miss Punch's resemblance to a corpse. Wemmick shows Pip in Mr. Jaggers' office two casts of hanged criminals, made just after they were taken down from the gallows. The curious twitchy leer they have about their noses is the result of hanging, he explains; 'much as if one nostril was caught up with a horsehair and a little fish-hook'. The hanged man who figures in *The Lazy Tour of Two Idle Apprentices* exhibits the same nasal peculiarity, 'immovably hitched up on one side, as if by a little hook inserted in that nostril'. This corpse's stare is like an effigy, just as the effigies are like corpses: it is unblinking, 'as if his eyelids had been nailed to his forehead', and perfectly still – the eyes apparently 'connected with the back of his skull by screws driven through it, and riveted and bolted outside, among his grey hair'. The same book contains a reanimated corpse called Mr. Lorn, now in the medical line of business, who gives unsuspecting visitors the impression that 'a stone figure' has looked round at them.

The effigies which crowd into the novels remind one of the corpses. But they have something in common with the living, too. An expression and a characteristic gesture is enough to mark out a Dickens' character, even a relatively important one like Blandois in *Little Dorrit*, who is mainly occupied in drawing his moustache up under his nose. An effigy can be counted on to repeat its gesture each time it appears, just like a person, and it has the advantage of the strangeness and intensity that naturally adhere to something which only *looks* alive. Dickens had that primitive response to painted figures which attributes to them a kind of paralysed life. Tulkinghorn in *Bleak House* has an allegorical figure in Roman helmet and celestial linen sprawling on his ceiling. When he comes into the room it stares down at his intrusion 'as if it meant to swoop upon him'. Each time we revisit Tulkinghorn's room we are reminded of this silent witness: when he leaves the window open, it looks cool, and when there is a draught, dust blows in its eyes. At the end of Chapter 42, when Hortense pays her angry call on Tulkinghorn, Dickens silently alters the position of the Roman. Instead of merely staring, he is now actually pointing down from the ceiling. Later, when

Tulkinghorn arrives home for his last evening on earth, he glances up at the painted watcher, but no message passes between them:

There is no new significance in the Roman's hand tonight, or in the flutter of the attendant groups, to give him the late warning, 'Don't come here!'

But next morning the Roman who has been pointing unavailingly from the ceiling for so many years takes on a new significance, since he is pointing at Tulkinghorn's corpse.

The Roman pointed at the murderous hand uplifted against his life, and pointed helplessly at him, from night to morning, lying face downward on the floor, shot through the heart.

Everyone who comes into the room looks up at the Roman and, says Dickens, 'he is invested in all eyes with mystery and awe, as if he were a paralysed dumb witness.' The Roman is in the same predicament as Pip's sister in *Great Expectations*, the only witness of her own murder by Orlick, who lingers for a while, dumb and paralysed. Besides Tulkinghorn's Roman, and also reminiscent of the frozen corpses in the Great St. Bernard, there are the Dedlock portraits in *Bleak House*, who seem like frozen watchers, and 'thaw' when the light of a sunset plays on them. As Tulkinghorn is watched by his Roman so, in *Dombey*, Miss Tox is watched by the portrait of an ancestor with a powdered head and pigtail which adorns her room. Giving a fictional character an effigy to keep him company is a way of packing twice as many sets of curious physical features into a novel as it would otherwise hold. For Dickens this is important, since the rich proliferation of physical peculiarities is one of the effects on which his art depends. It takes the place of the conventional novelistic 'inner life', much in the same way as the invention of odd speech habits atones for the rarity of dialogue. The dialogues between Carker and Edith Dombey are terrible failures, but Dickens arranges for Carker to get hold – by some unexplained means – of a picture that resembles Edith. With this on his wall he can sneer and look wicked, and she can look haughty, which is as close a contact as Dickens can manage between them even when Edith is there in the flesh. Substituting a picture for Edith does away with the embarrassment of making her talk. When the plot requires her to be present, there is a tendency to freeze her into a work of art. She looks 'like a handsome statue'. Her face is said to have a 'marble stillness and severity', and Dombey, coming into her room, sees her features reflected in the mirror in front of her 'as in a picture frame'. On the

other hand Amy Dorrit, with all the qualities of humility and goodness that Edith lacks, is taken along by her admiring uncle and
exhibited to the portraits at Venice as a kind of example. Frederick
Dorrit would, writes Dickens, 'carry a chair about for her from
picture to picture, and stand behind it, in spite of all her remon-
strances, silently presenting her to the noble Venetians'. As a matter
of fact Edith Dombey, besides resembling an effigy, marries one.
Her husband's rigidity attracts much notice: he looks 'like a man of
wood, without a hinge or joint in him', and turns his head in his
neckcloth 'as if it were a socket'. Critics have taken this as a sign that
he lacks human affection. Of course, he does. But the more pressing
reason for his woodenness is that Dickens likes wooden men. It is
perfectly possible to find in his work men who are both wooden and
richly affectionate – the exemplary old sailors in 'Our English
Watering-Place', for instance, who 'seem to be carved out of hard-
grained wood', and occupy themselves tending toy boats for
toddlers.

The effigy, the picture, the thing with human lineaments which
watches, paralysed and dumb – this supplies a major imaginative
level in Dickens' novels which interacts with the human beings just
as importantly as the human beings react to each other. It wasn't
until his last completed novel that Dickens produced his great set
piece of dumb witnesses, and dumb witnesses who are real corpses as
well as effigies. This is Mr. Venus' shop in *Our Mutual Friend* (based
on an actual shop in St. Giles' which Marcus Stone, knowing
Dickens' tastes, took him to), crammed with the stuffed animals and
preserved babies and articulated human skeletons which make up
Mr. Venus' stock in trade, together with the various skulls and
skeletal limbs which are waiting to be fitted into a marketable
skeleton. When Wegg slams the street door of the shop the whole
grisly population is shaken into momentary life:

the babies – Hindoo, African and British – the 'human warious', the
French gentleman, the green-glass-eyed cats, the dogs, the ducks, and all
the rest of the collection, show for an instant as if paralytically animated.

Mr. Venus, as a dealer in preserved corpses, is rather a speciality in
the novels, but there are dealers in imitation corpses as well. Jenny
Wren, the doll's dressmaker, watches society ladies going to balls
and receptions, and then reproduces them, in effigy, for sale. The
situation is complicated because Jenny, who makes the perfect little

replicas, is herself a cripple, and hates healthy children. In a sense she's more like a doll herself than a child, being partly paralysed, and there's something puppet-like about her way of throwing up her eyes and her chin at once, as if, Dickens says, 'her eyes and her chin worked together on the same wires'. The same sort of irony occurs in *The Cricket on the Hearth* where Caleb Plummer's daughter, who stitches eyes onto dolls, is herself blind. Their workroom is full of 'imperturbably calm dolls' and 'agitated rocking horses with distended eyes and nostrils' who seem, Dickens notes, 'to be stricken motionless with fantastic wonder' at the goings on of the human occupants.

Effigies grip Dickens' imagination not only because of their silent watching, but because they ape human gestures, and in this sense empty clothes are the commonest effigies of all. Looking at Kate's empty clothes in *Nicholas Nickleby* Dickens muses on the way in which each article of dress partakes 'of that indescribable air of jauntiness and individuality which empty garments – whether by association, or that they become moulded, as it were, to the owner's form – will take'. This mimicry, practised by worn clothes, had engaged his imagination early on. *Sketches by Boz* has a chapter called 'Meditations in Monmouth Street' where Dickens describes how he spends hours peering into the windows of old clothes shops, fitting the clothes to wearers, 'until whole rows of coats have started from their pegs, and buttoned up, of their own accord, round the waists of imaginary wearers'. The novels spend more time describing clothes than describing people. People are, largely, their clothes; and the clothes keep the shape and personality of the character when they're taken off. Captain Cuttle in *Dombey* is so forcibly a broad blue coat and waistcoat that when Walter calls on him he's astonished to see these garments hanging out of the window to air:

It appeared incredible that the coat and waistcoat could be seen by mortal eyes without the Captain: but he certainly was not in them, otherwise his legs – the houses in Brig Place not being lofty – would have obstructed the street door.

Mr. Vholes in *Bleak House*, another man compounded largely of clothing, takes off his black gloves, Dickens writes, 'as if he were skinning his hands' and 'lifts off his tight hat as if he were scalping himself'. Mrs. Gamp is in the habit of wearing particularly tattered clothes when called upon to lay out a deceased patient, in the hope

that the bereaved relatives will be moved to present her with a new
outfit – 'an appeal so frequently successful,' says Dickens, 'that the
very fetch and ghost of Mrs. Gamp, bonnet and all, might be seen
hanging up, any hour of the day, in at least a dozen of the second-
hand clothes shops about Holburn'. One of Barnaby Rudge's mad
fancies, we recall, is that the clothes hanging on clothes lines are
alive, and talk to each other as they whirl and plunge in the wind.
Mr. Pecksniff, opening a vestry cupboard, is rather similarly startled
by the sight of 'a black and white surplice dangling against the wall;
which had very much the appearance of two curates who had committed suicide by hanging themselves'. What it all amounts to is that
the second-hand clothes shop is a good substitute, from Dickens'
point of view, if the mortuary doesn't happen to be open. In either
place you will find supplies of effigies which intriguingly populate
the shadow-land that lies between objects and people. Indeed an
advantage of the Paris Morgue was that it incorporated a mortuary
for clothes as well. The raiment of the dead hung from pegs and
hooks, that from the drowning cases performing a particularly
heartless mimicry of its owners' sodden disfigurement: 'such awful
boots,' noted Dickens, 'such slimy garments with puffed arms and
legs'.

   With old clothes retaining so much of their owners, it's no wonder
that wearing a dead man's garments should be an especially gruesome proposition for Dickens. Dennis, the loathsome hangman in
Barnaby Rudge, is totally arrayed in his victims' cast-offs, and
proudly explains how each article has been bequeathed to him. To
complete his association with effigy and corpse, Dennis carries
round with him a little effigy-Dennis, carved on a stick by a prisoner
whom he shortly afterwards hanged. Outside Newgate Pip, in *Great
Expectations*, meets a man dressed from head to foot in 'mildewed
clothes', which, comments Pip, 'had evidently not belonged to him
originally, and which, I took it into my head, he had bought cheap
of the executioner'. It's a nice example of Dickens forcing one of his
imaginative obsessions into the novel without any help from the
plot. The man is not encountered again, and there's no evidence,
anyway, that Pip's fancy about his clothes is correct. Dickens' plots
are his most discardable properties, and often have to be pushed
aside to let the strange poetry of his imagination emerge.

   Besides effigies and pictures and clothes, other creatures which
inhabit this hinterland between life and non-life are people made up

from inanimate bits and pieces – wooden legs, wigs, artificial hands and so forth. The prize performers in this section are Mrs. Skewton in *Dombey*, Smallweed in *Bleak House*, and Lady Tippins in *Our Mutual Friend*. Mrs. Skewton has false curls, false eyebrows, false teeth and a false complexion. When her maid comes to prepare her for bed, a fearful transformation takes place:

The painted object shrivelled underneath her hand; the form collapsed, the hair dropped off, the arched dark eyebrows changed to scanty tufts of grey; the pale lips shrunk, the skin became cadaverous and loose; an old, worn, yellow, nodding woman, with red eyes, alone remained . . . huddled up, like a slovenly bundle, in a greasy flannel gown.

Mrs. Skewton is now just a corpse and some old clothes. The maid's touch, Dickens says, is as 'the touch of Death', and the brilliance of the writing as he describes her bedtime decomposition shows his imagination involved as the able-bodied heroes and heroines can never involve it. He pursues the hideous old woman through the book with keen attention, until she is converted into a genuine effigy by a paralytic stroke: Edith hurries to her mother's room to find her:

arrayed in full dress, with the diamonds, short sleeves, rouge, curls, teeth, and other juvenility all complete; but Paralysis was not to be deceived, had known her for the object of its errand, and had struck her at her glass, where she lay like a horrible doll which had tumbled down.

The elder Turveydrop in *Bleak House* has 'a false complexion, false teeth, false whiskers, and a wig', too, and the paralysed old Smallweed, who has to be carried round in a chair, is reduced, says Dickens, to 'a broken puppet', a 'mere clothes-bag with a black skull-cap on the top of it'. The same mutation into old clothes and an effigy as Mrs. Skewton performed. *Our Mutual Friend* has the grisly Lady Tippins, who has to be dyed and varnished each morning before she's presentable, and is so entirely composed of cosmetic and false hair that, we are told, 'you might scalp her, and peel her, and scrape her, and make two Lady Tippinses out of her, and yet not penetrate to the genuine article.' As to her face and neck she is a 'diurnal species of lobster – throwing off a shell every forenoon, and needing to keep into a retired spot until the new crust hardens'. She is a work of art, an effigy, made up of lifeless bits.

Dickens' most popular lifeless bit is the wooden leg, about which he has a positive obsession. The things you can do with a wooden leg, the damage it is subject to, its relations with its owner, are endlessly fascinating to him. Thomas Burton in *Pickwick* finds his second-hand wooden legs split and rot very quickly, and believes their constitution is undermined by his drinking gin and water. Mr. Vuffin the freak-manager in *The Old Curiosity Shop* envisages staging Shakespeare with an entire cast of wooden-legged actors. Tungay, Mr. Creakle's cruel accomplice in *David Copperfield*, has a wooden leg, and so has Silas Wegg, the villain of *Our Mutual Friend*. Pecksniff, drunken, amorous, half-clothed, desires suggestively 'to see Mrs. Todger's notion of a wooden leg, if perfectly agreeable to herself'. Mrs. Gamp's husband has a wooden leg and, when desperate for liquor, sends his son out with it to try and sell it for matchwood. Mrs. Gamp blames the wooden leg for dragging her husband into public houses against his will – 'quite as weak as flesh, if not weaker', is her opinion of it. Eventually it accompanies Mr. Gamp to the grave: his widow takes her last farewell of him at Guy's Hospital 'with a penny piece on each eye, and his wooden leg under his left arm'. Wooden legs are introduced into the novels as chance spectators quite without justification in the plot. Florence Dombey's wedding is watched by 'a man with a wooden leg, chewing a faint apple and carrying a blue bag in his hand', and when Bella Wilfer gets married a pensioner with two wooden legs is the sole bystander. A variation on the wooden leg is Captain Cuttle's right hand in *Dombey and Son*, in the shape of an iron hook. When leaving the company of ladies he kisses his hook to them 'with great elegance and gallantry', and at mealtimes can screw bits of cutlery into the socket. Legs, though, as we noted in relation to Dickens' humour, are his particular fancy, and even when not wooden they are likely to strike him as irrational and separable appurtenances. Sir Leicester Dedlock in *Bleak House* has not so much his own legs as the legs of the Dedlock family, with the Dedlock family gout in them. 'Sir Leicester', Dickens relates, 'yields up his family legs to the family disorder, as if he held his name and fortune on that feudal tenure.' Simon Tappertit's legs are his pride and joy in *Barnaby Rudge*, and at the end of the book his special retribution is to have them amputated. 'Shorn of his graceful limbs', he is discharged from hospital on two wooden legs, and in marital upsets thereafter his wife punishes him by taking off his wooden legs and leaving him exposed to the derision of the street urchins. Mr. Merdle, in *Little Dorrit*, stands up suddenly, 'as if he had been waiting in the interval for his legs, and they had just come'. Like most of Dickens' imaginative

ideas, the idea of separable legs is kept going by minor figures who
have really no claim to be in the novel at all. In *Nicholas Nickleby*,
for instance, Sir Mulberry's footman has legs which, Dickens writes,
'although somewhat large for his body, might, as mere abstract legs,
have set themselves up for models at the Royal Academy'. And in
Bleak House Esther dances with a melancholy child who does
'wonders with his lower extremities, in which there appeared to be
some sense of enjoyment though it never rose above his waist'. But
the most separable leg of all is Silas Wegg's in *Our Mutual Friend*
which is still hanging around in Mr. Venus' shop waiting to be fitted
to a skeleton, while Wegg makes do with his wooden one. Wegg
displays a lively interest in his detached limb, and complains about
its being kept waiting so long for a situation, though Mr. Venus
explains that the peculiarities of its bone structure make it difficult to
fit into one of his marketable skeletons. The problem of what pro-
noun to use when referring to his separated member is a delicate
one for Wegg, and he settles on the first person: 'Am I still at
home?' he inquires, and Venus tells him, 'You're somewhere in the
back shop across the yard, sir; and speaking quite candidly, I wish
I'd never bought you of the hospital porter.' Eventually Wegg tires
of having his leg insulted in this way. For one thing, his prospects
have improved, and he feels that a gentleman shouldn't leave his
limbs scattered about. 'I tell you openly,' he says, 'I should *not* like –
under such circumstances, to be what I may call dispersed, a part of
me here, and a part of me there, but should wish to collect myself
like a genteel person.' Accordingly he buys the leg back. He is
particularly offended when Mr. Venus turns up with it in a brown
paper parcel, instead of bringing it in a cab. Oddly enough, Dickens'
first extant letter – to a schoolfellow – begins 'Tom, I am quite
ashamed I have not returned your Leg' (slang, apparently, for
lexicon), and ends, 'I suppose all this time you have had a *wooden*
leg. I have weighed yours every Saturday night.' So he had played
Venus to a Wegg early on.

Wegg's tender feelings for his wandering portion are rather like
David Copperfield's for his caul. A caul is a membrane which
encloses the foetus, some of which is occasionally found on the
child's head at birth. David is born in a caul, and cauls were believed
to protect the owner from drowning, a factor linking thematically
with the drowning of Ham and Steerforth later in the novel. David's
caul is advertised for sale in the newspapers at 15 guineas, but there

are no buyers, and ten years later it is put up for raffle and won by an old lady with a hand basket. 'I was present myself,' says David, 'and I remember to have felt quite uncomfortable and confused, at a part of myself being disposed of in that way.'

Admittedly, Dickens' people don't usually have bodies so spectacularly separable that they can buy and sell bits of them, but it is a deeply ingrained imaginative habit to see bits of people's bodies as if they have come adrift from the rest, or to make them handle parts of themselves as if they belonged to someone else. Maybe this habit has its root in the childhood experience of seeing an adult's feet and legs closely and separately, or its face closely when it lifts the child up. The little boy in *George Silverman's Explanation* recalls how he used to wait for his mother to come down the cellar steps: 'I used tremblingly to speculate on her feet having a good or an ill-tempered look, – on her knees, – on her waist, – until finally her face came into view and settled the question.' A similar process occurs in *Dombey*, when Captain Bunsby appears on deck:

Immediately there appeared, coming slowly up above the bulkhead of the cabin, another bulkhead – human, and very large – with one stationary eye in the mahogany face, and one revolving one, on the principle of some lighthouses. This head was decorated with shaggy hair, like oakum . . . The head was followed by a perfect desert of chin, and by a shirt-collar and neckerchief, and by a dreadnought pilot coat, and by a pair of dreadnought pilot trousers . . . As the lower portions of these pantaloons became revealed, Bunsby stood confessed.

Likewise, when Kate Nickleby hears a strange man's voice in a room in Mrs. Mantalini's shop, we aren't told that she looks round and sees a bailiff but that 'she . . . started . . . to observe, on looking round, that a white hat, and a red neckerchief, and a broad round face, and a large head, and part of a green coat were in the room.' So, too, the French child in *Somebody's Luggage*, arrayed in a shapeless blue frock, looks from behind 'as if she had been cut off at her natural waist and had had her head neatly fitted on it'. People become articles of clothing and pieces of body, loosely assembled, and they strike the observer as a set of barely connected impressions. Frequently their bodies have one portion out of harmony with the rest. Bunsby, with one stationary and one revolving eye, resembles Newman Noggs in *Nicholas Nickleby* – 'a tall man of middle-age, with two goggle eyes whereof one was a fixture'; and Miss Podsnap's dancing partner in *Our Mutual Friend* belongs to the same coterie –

'an ambling stranger, with one eye screwed up into extinction, and the other framed and glazed'. Zephaniah Scadder, the evil land-agent in *Martin Chuzzlewit*, has a face which divides exactly down the middle: one half paralysed, with a blind eye in it, always looking coldly attentive, and one half shifting according to mood. When he has cheated Martin, he turns his blighted profile towards him so as to look serious, while in the mobile side 'every little wiry vein' is 'twisted up into a grin'. Phil, the shooting gallery attendant in *Bleak House*, though a benevolent character, suffers from the same afflic-tion. Owing to some explosion, one half of his face is blue and speckled, and lacks an eyebrow, while the other half sprouts a bushy black one. Mrs. Merdle, in *Little Dorrit*, has odd hands, 'the left being much the whiter and plumper of the two'.

With this inclination to break his characters into fragments it's not surprising that Dickens' first success, *Pickwick Papers*, already contains two medical students, Bob Sawyer and Ben Allen, whose function is to exchange anecdotes about the dissection of corpses, particularly at meal times. Characters often treat themselves as if they were dissectable. Pecksniff, when striving to impress the elder Chuzzlewit with his sincerity, keeps his hand in his waistcoat as though, says Dickens 'he were ready, on the shortest notice, to produce his heart for Martin Chuzzlewit's inspection'. Spottletoe, enraged, holds his clenched fist under Pecksniff's nose, 'as if it were some natural curiosity from the near inspection whereof he was likely to derive high gratification and improvement'. Scadder sits with one leg doubled up under him, 'as if he were hatching his foot'. Magwitch on the marshes shudders with cold and hugs himself 'as if to hold himself together'. Inspector Bucket has a fat forefinger which he shakes threateningly at suspects, and presses to his ear as if it were whispering information. Jaggers in *Great Expectations* also treats his forefinger as a foreign body, biting it constantly. Wemmick, his assistant, has a mouth like a letter-box, and at lunch time throws pieces of biscuit into it impersonally, as if he were posting them. Mr. Fips, in abstracted moments, takes up a metal stamp and stamps capital F's all over his legs. Mr. Pocket pulls at his own hair as if he were trying to lift himself out of his seat. On one occasion he does lift himself several inches. Vholes fingers the pimples on his face as if they were ornaments. It's not only comic figures who treat pieces of themselves as foreign bodies. Mr. Dombey, contemplating suicide, sees a 'spectral, haggard, wasted likeness of himself' in a mirror. He watches it brooding and stalking to and fro, and going into the next room to fetch a weapon:

it got up again, and walked to and fro with its hand in its breast. He glanced at it occasionally, very curious to watch its motions, and he marked how wicked and murderous that hand looked.

The sense of depersonalization which makes Dombey watch his reflection in the glass settles finally on the single bit of body which looks too evil to be his own. The severed hand, a comic property with Captain Cuttle, is still a part of the way Dickens' imagination works at this tragic climax. So is the severed head. The leering casts of hanged clients exhibited to Pip by Wemmick suggest a head going about without its body, and when Bradley Headstone pursues Wrayburn, this is what seems actually to happen. Wild with hate and anger, Bradley passes Wrayburn and Lightwood in the street at night:

white-lipped, wild-eyed, draggle-haired, seamed with jealousy and anger, and torturing himself with the conviction that he showed it all and they exulted in it, he went by them in the dark, like a haggard head suspended in the air: so completely did the force of his expression conceal his figure.

Later, when Bradley spies on Wrayburn: 'the haggard head floated up the dark staircase, and softly descended nearer to the floor outside the outer door of the chambers.' The severed head flitting about in the darkness resembles, Dickens notes, the spectre of one of the heads that used to be hoisted on Temple Bar. At the height of the drama in *Dombey* there is a magnificent moment when not even Carker's head but just his teeth glide through the darkness towards his victim. Gleaming teeth have been Carker's ensign from the start – his 'two rows' of 'bristling' teeth, Dickens calls them, almost as if he had one row too many. *Dombey* comes near to being a novel with a set of dentures as its villain. And when, finally, Edith is waiting for Carker in their rooms at the French hotel, she sees the teeth coming towards her, and goes faint with terror. He 'came', writes Dickens, 'with his gleaming teeth, through the dark rooms, like a mouth'. The walking mouth – perfectly faithful to Dickens' imaginative habits: the imagination which pulls apart human bodies like dolls, and grasps at amputated members.

A power of observation that gives distinct and individual attention to each part of a body, and watches it moving as something apart from the mass, is capable of creating a fresh imaginative vision because it contradicts the accepted view of what constitutes a unity.

Only habit determines that a man is a unity, rather than his hand or his head or his teeth. Only habit determines that when we look at a man we should think of him as wearing clothes instead of the clothes constituting the man. Dickens refuses allegiance to either habit, and this makes him capable of visual and imaginative breakthroughs. Humans treating parts of their bodies as excrescences immediately attracted his attention in real life as well as in the novels. When travelling in Switzerland he noticed that the women who sat by the roadside suckling their children had 'such enormous goitres (or glandular swellings in the throat) that it became a science to know where the nurse ended and the child began'. When a woman was summoned she would approach hastily, 'throwing a child over one of her shoulders and her goitre over the other'. Dickens' obsession with deformity combines here with his habit of separating the body into inanimate bits. The two are closely related. Tiny Tim's crutch is a variant of the wooden leg fixation. When a person is maimed or crippled or has a growth, attention naturally fixes on a particular limb, in the way Dickens' imagination is always requiring that it should. This separating out of a single feature has a startling effect. The feature stands in sharp relief, and its normal, reassuring accompaniment sinks from view. It has an element of nightmare, as Bradley's head and Carker's teeth show. Pip, in *Great Expectations*, is tormented by guilt for taking the file to Magwitch on the marshes. It turns into a nightmare: 'I was haunted by the file . . . A dread possessed me that when I least expected it, the file would reappear . . . In my sleep I saw the file coming at me out of a door, without seeing who held it, and I screamed myself awake.' The file has become an autonomous thing, with all the horror of its weird and separate being – like Carker's teeth or, for that matter, like Mr. Gamp's wooden leg, dragging him into public houses of its own accord. The fragmented vision results in both nightmare and farce. Naturally enough since farce is only nightmare of which we are no longer afraid. Reducing the body to a collection of spare parts can also revive everyday actions which have fossilized into figures of speech – shaking hands, for instance. Dickens watches the hands as they shake, and sees that shaking hands is by no means what happens. Mr. Chick:

gave Mr. Dombey his hand, as if he feared it might electrify him. Mr. Dombey took it as if it were a fish, or seaweed, or some such clammy substance, and immediately returned it to him with exalted politeness.

Chick treats his own hand as if there's no knowing what it will do when Dombey gets hold of it, and Dombey receives it as an unpleasant specimen, quite detached from Mr. Chick. David Copperfield, recalling Miss Murdstone's greeting, reports: 'Miss Murdstone gave me her chilly fingernails, and sat severely rigid.' Mr. Merdle in *Little Dorrit* seems to have no more hand to shake his daughter-in-law's with than a maimed war veteran:

> The illustrious visitor then put out his coat cuff, and for a moment entombed Mrs. Sparkler's hand: wrist, bracelet, and all. Where his own hand had shrunk to, was not made manifest, but it was as remote from Mrs. Sparkler's sense of touch as if he had been a highly meritorious Chelsea Veteran or Greenwich Pensioner.

And Mr. Vholes in *Bleak House*, Esther remembers, 'put his dead glove, which scarcely seemed to have any hand in it, on my fingers, and then on my guardian's fingers, and took his long thin shadow away'. These examples show us, in miniature, why Dickens is a creative genius. He is intransigent. He won't accept that what's normally thought to be seen is what he sees. And so he revives, and releases into endless variety, experiences which language has killed and petrified in a figure of speech like 'shaking hands'.

The peculiarity of Dickens' imaginative vision which draws him to limbs or features cut away from their normal accompaniments, also alerts him to human actions which have come adrift from their contexts. The way different people laugh supplies him with a particularly rich field, and especially the laugh from which has been subtracted any of the noise which the word 'laughter' usually implies. The silent laugh, like the wooden leg, is a Dickensian obsession.

In *Pickwick Papers* Serjeant Snubbin's laugh is 'a silent, internal chuckle' which repels Mr. Pickwick. 'When a man bleeds inwardly', Dickens comments, 'it is a dangerous thing for himself; but when he laughs inwardly, it bodes no good to other people.' Job Trotter, Jingle's accomplice, also gives vent to 'a low noiseless chuckle, which seemed to intimate that he enjoyed his laugh too much, to let any of it escape in sound'. The silent laugh, though, like the amputated limb, has its farcical as well as its horrifying side. The elder Mr. Weller's laugh 'working like an earthquake, below the surface, produced various extraordinary appearances in his face, chest, and shoulders, – the more alarming because unaccompanied by any noise whatever'; and the meritorious Newman Noggs in *Nicholas Nickleby* also seems to be convulsed with silent laughter:

Newman fell a little behind his master, and his face was curiously twisted as by a spasm; but whether of paralysis, or grief, or inward laughter, nobody but himself could possibly explain.

The mention of paralysis, common when Dickens is describing effigies or pictures, helps us to relate the silent laugh to that branch of his imagination. A dumb laugh is an effigy's laugh. Despite Weller and Noggs, it usually strikes Dickens as sinister or imbecile. The mother of the fatuous Mr. Guppy in *Bleak House*, for instance, is hugely diverted when she believes her son is about to propose to Esther and that she and Caddy Jellyby must leave the lovers together:

Anything like the jocoseness of Mr. Guppy's mother just now, I think I never saw. She made no sound of laughter; but she rolled her head, and shook it, and put her handkerchief to her mouth, and appealed to Caddy with her elbow, and her hand, and her shoulder, and was so unspeakably entertained altogether that it was with some difficulty she could marshal Caddy through the little folding door.

Blandois, the villain of *Little Dorrit*, repeatedly laughs a 'diabolically silent laugh'; and the silent laugh is also numbered among Uriah Heep's disgusting propensities:

Uriah stopped short, put his hands between his great knobs of knees, and doubled himself up with laughter. With perfectly silent laughter. Not a sound escaped from him. I was so repelled by his odious behaviour, particularly by this concluding instance, that I turned away without any ceremony; and left him doubled up in the middle of the garden, like a scarecrow in want of support.

Here the connection between the silent laugh and the effigy is deliberately made. Most spectacular of the silent laughers, however, is the odious Major Bagstock, Mr. Dombey's evil genius. The obese Bagstock laughs hideously, and quite without noise. His whole form dilates till he resembles 'a heavy mass of indigo'; the tips of his ears and the veins in his head vibrate; he rolls, gasps and has paroxysms. Practically his only other activity is charging himself with food, and this coincides with the laughter alarmingly:

The Major being by this time in a state of repletion, with essence of savoury pie oozing out at the corners of his eyes, and devilled grill and kidneys tightening his cravat . . . sat for a long time afterwards, leering, and choking, like an over-fed Mephistopheles.

Bagstock does for the amputated laugh what Silas Wegg did for the amputated limb. With him it becomes a drama.

With the silent laugh, the sound has got lost. The body's antics and the noise that ought to accompany them have somehow drifted apart. Another lost noise occurs in *Mugby Junction*. The heroine, who has an amputated head, plays amputated music. Approaching a cottage, Mr. Jackson is startled to descry 'a very bright face, lying on one cheek on the window sill'. Though he passes and repasses, the face remains bodiless, but a pair of hands appears beside it 'performing on some musical instrument' yet producing no sound. Solution: a crippled, horizontal girl making lace – 'a poor little broken doll', as she styles herself, to secure her inclusion among the effigies. Noises which, though audible, have been broken off from their context continually intrigue Dickens also. When Mrs. Jarley's caravan takes to the road, for instance, it is a thoroughly Dickensian touch to draw our attention to 'the bright brass knocker, which nobody ever knocked at, knocking one perpetual double knock of its own accord as they jolted heavily along'. The doorknocker knocking itself, like the head or the teeth which walk without their bodies, is a product of the fragmented vision, only we have now passed from the area of sight into that of sound. Speech which has got detached from its normal office of communication takes up much of Dickens' imaginative energy. Talking birds – Mrs. Merdle's parrot which breaks into a violent fit of laughter when she claims she is a child of nature, and Barnaby Rudge's raven constantly pretending it's a devil – have the fascination of a human characteristic grafted onto a dumb creature, like wooden legs in reverse, so to speak. Characters who repeat senseless or wildly inappropriate phrases have the same appeal. Dickens' comic nonconformist ministers, churning out their scraps of biblical phraseology, are akin to his talking birds. So is the embarrassing Mr. F's aunt bequeathed to Flora Finching in *Little Dorrit*, who brings conversation to a halt with insane announcements like 'When we lived at Henley, Barnes's gander was stole by tinkers.' In some situation or other in Mr. F.'s aunt's past this remark would have been reasonable, but it has got amputated, and wanders strangely in the realm of language like Silas Wegg's leg in Mr. Venus' shop. Similarly old John Willet in *Barnaby Rudge*, after his stroke, is quite unable to get his mind to cope with the fact that his son has lost an arm on military service. In a daze he repeats the phrases 'My son's arm – was took off – at the defence of the – Salwanners – in America – where the war is.' And repeating this pathetic creed, much as a talking bird would, is as near as he gets to understanding. He dies with the words 'I'm a-going . . . to the

Salwanners.' Not surprisingly, Grip the talking raven is much affected by his death. Bunsby, whose brain-power is the wonder of Captain Cuttle, communicates his profundities in a comparably dismembered idiom: ' "For why?" growled Bunsby, looking at his friend for the first time. "Which way? If so, why not? Therefore." ' When Old Chuffey in *Martin Chuzzlewit* tries to pray, out come the strings of arithmetical figures which his years in the counting-house have ingrained; and Paul Dombey, lying awake in the dormitory, hears his fellow pupils talking 'unknown tongues, or scraps of Greek and Latin', which, Dickens writes, 'in the silence of the night, had an inexpressibly wicked and guilty effect'. The dislocated fragment of language has the same sinister potential as the severed limb. A similar absorption, on Dickens' part, in dislocated language produces the situation of Mr. Boffin, in *Our Mutual Friend*, paying Silas Wegg to read to him from Gibbon's *Decline and Fall of the Roman Empire*, which neither he nor Wegg understands. In *Great Expectations* Magwitch implores Pip to read foreign languages to him:

While I complied, he, not comprehending a single word, would stand before the fire surveying me with the air of an Exhibitor, and I would see him, between the fingers of the hand with which I shaded my face, appealing in dumb show to the furniture to take notice of my proficiency. The imaginary student pursued by the misshapen creature he had impiously made, was not more wretched than I, pursued by the creature who had made me.

The allusion in the last sentence is to Mary Shelley's Frankenstein, creator of an effigy that comes to life. Pip, and all the speakers of dislocated language in Dickens, have this in common with his effigies that, though they seem bent on communication, they are cut off from the creatures around.

Corpses, coffins, waxworks, portraits, clothes, wooden legs, speakers of strange tongues and suchlike inhabitants of Dickens' imagination, are related in that they are neither impersonal objects nor fully human. They may be almost human, or like coffins, just disturbingly crude approximations to the human shape; but they aren't any of them things which human beings can feel entirely estranged from or entirely identified with. They populate the border country between people and things, where Dickens' imagination is mostly engaged. One way to increase the population of this region is to liken inanimate objects to people. Another is to to liken people to inanimate objects. Dickens does both incessantly. Stilled life, and the

still enlivened are the hallmarks of his imagination. Houses and
furniture are particularly apt to be living things in his novels. Gaffer
Hexam's house in *Our Mutual Friend* has once been a mill, and the
place where the sails were fixed on is described as 'a rotten wart of
wood upon its forehead'. The Clennam house in *Little Dorrit* 'had
had it in its mind to slide down sideways' many years ago, and now
leans on gigantic crutches. Flintwinch, who lives in it, leans to one
side like the house; and Mrs. Clennam, disabled in her chair, has
disabled furniture in her room – 'a maimed table, a crippled ward-
robe, a lean set of fire-irons'. The prison ship in *Great Expectations*,
'barred and moored by massive rusty chains', seems to Pip to wear
irons like the prisoners. The story of Tom Smart in *Pickwick Papers*
features a chair which actually turns into an old man and carries on a
conversation; and in *Nicholas Nickleby* the miser Arthur Gride's
house, which seems 'to have withered, like himself, and to have grown
yellow and shrivelled in hoarding him from the light of day', contains an animated collection of chairs, some of them cocking their
arms suspiciously and looking uneasy in their minds, some of them
drawing themselves up to their full heights and putting on their
fiercest expressions, and others leaning weakly against the wall –
'somewhat ostentatiously', says Dickens, as if to prove to a likely
thief that they're not worth the taking. Nothing is more usual in
Dickens' imaginative arena than for a miser's furniture to behave like
a miser or a cripple's like a cripple. His novels are stacked with living
furniture – gesticulating wooden legs and arms. In *A Tale of Two
Cities* when Mr. Lorry hacks to pieces Dr. Manette's old shoemaker's
bench, the deed, we are told, is performed at night 'in a mysterious
and guilty manner', and Miss Pross stands by with a candle 'as if she
were assisting at a murder'. So she is, in a world of living furniture,
and from contact with humans Dickens' furniture, like his clothes,
derives life, if only the life of an effigy.

People transfigured by Dickensian similes into furniture or other
impedimenta inhabit the novels almost as thickly as animated
furniture. Mrs. Rouncewell's corseted bosom in *Bleak House* suggests 'a broad old-fashioned family firegrate', and watermen with their
brass plates and numbers round their necks look like exhibits in a
'collection of rarities'. In a sense the wooden-legged men are at an
intermediate stage of turning into wood, and with Silas Wegg the
process has gone further. He is described as 'knotty' and 'close-
grained', altogether so wooden that he seems to have grown his

wooden leg naturally, and may be expected to develop a second one, Dickens conjectures, in about six months. Half way to being a chair. And in *Hard Times* we almost see the metamorphosis of a woman into a wooden fence. Mrs. Sparsit, spying on Louisa Gradgrind out in the wood in the drenching downpour, turns slimy and sodden, prickly things stick to her, caterpillars swing from her, and gradually she gathers a stagnant verdure, 'such as accumulates', says Dickens, 'on an old park fence in a mouldy lane'. The plot doesn't demand this spectacular transformation scene at all; but Dickens' imagination does.

But to end, where we began, with Dickens in the mortuary. What struck him, we recall, as the onlookers viewed the corpses, was the expression in their eyes – the expression of '*looking at something that could not return a look*'. The blank stare, not baleful but utterly impersonal, is the optic counterpart of dislocated language. It achieves no human communication. Staring eyes haunt Dickens. This is the final element in the spell which effigies cast over him. Their eyes stare intently, but there is no personality behind them to communicate with. They turn you to an object, because their stare acknowledges nothing human in you. 'Widely staring eyes', 'lustreless' and 'glassy', drive Sikes to his death in *Oliver Twist*, and Fagin at his trial is surrounded by a 'firmament' of 'gleaming eyes', in none of which can he discover 'the faintest sympathy with himself'. Defending a digression in *The Old Curiosity Shop* about 'dead mankind, a million fathoms deep' (casualties from Noah's Flood), Dickens explained that he was fascinated by the thought 'of the dreadful silence down there, and of the stars shining through upon their drowned eyes'. Likewise, reading Tennyson, the submarine poems – *Merman, Mermaid, Kraken* and so forth – gripped him because they raised images of fungoid sea-creatures 'staring in with their great dull eyes at every open nook and loophole'. Two holes in the shutters of Captain Hawdon's room like look eyes, and he lies on the bed, a corpse, with, writes Dickens, 'the gaunt eyes in the shutters staring down upon the bed'.

Being looked down on by unknown eyes while asleep – even effigy-eyes – was one of Dickens' dreads. The bedroom of a house he rented in Italy had an altar, with a mark on the wall above where a religious picture used to hang, and he upset himself as he lay in bed by worrying about 'what the subject might have been, *and what the face was like*'. He complains that Italian hotel rooms have several doors which will not lock, and round apertures high in the walls, with scraping noises in the night, suggesting that someone is trying to climb up to them and look in. Oliver Twist, cosily ensconced at the Maylies, awakes from a doze to find Fagin at the window 'with his eyes peering into the room', and the scowling Monks beside him. Gone in a flash, the pair have time to resemble effigies before they disappear: 'their look was as firmly impressed upon his memory, as if it had been deeply carved in stone.' In *Martin Chuzzlewit* Montague Tigg awakes from a fearful dream about trying to nail iron plates across a mysterious extra door in his bedroom wall, and finds that Jonas, his murderer, has come through this door and is staring down at him. (This dream reflects a recent fright: in America Dickens, benighted at a hamlet called Lower Sandusky, had occupied in the ramshackle inn 'the queerest sleeping-room' with two unlockable doors giving directly onto 'wild black country', and had spent much of the night frantically blockading them with portmanteaux lest he should be murdered.)

Dombey, in his disgrace, 'feels that the world is looking at him out of their eyes' – Dickens' odd phrasing captures the blankness of the stare – 'looking at something that could not return a look'. Paul Dombey remembers Dr. Blimber's academy as 'a dream, full of eyes', 'heaped up, as faces are at a crowded theatre'. The dying clown's nightmare in *Pickwick* is of wandering through a maze of low-arched, dark rooms, alive with insects, 'hideous crawling things with eyes that stared upon him'. We know that this was one of Dickens' own recurrent nightmares. In *American Notes* he describes being driven through a wooden tunnel on a bridge crossing a river. It is dark, with great cross-beams, and innumerable crevices through which the river below gleams, he says, 'like a legion of eyes'. And he adds, 'I have often dreamed of toiling through such places.' The beams, the dark rooms, and the vermin all suggest that this nightmare can be traced to his days at Warren's blacking factory. And in fact at Warren's he was made an exhibit. When the warehouse moved to Chandos Street, he and Bob Fagin had to work at a window looking out on Bedford Street, and a crowd would often gather to watch them. It was this disgrace which finally made his father decide to remove him from the warehouse. But by that time the experience of being looked at as something that can't return a look, the crowd of glassy eyes, the blank stare as of an effigy, had been indelibly inscribed upon Dickens' imagination.

5

SYMBOLS

Dickens' earliest attempt to pull a novel together by repeating a 'symbol' seems to be *Dombey and Son*. The symbol is the sea. Mrs. Dombey dies at the end of Chapter 1 with Florence in attendance. 'Clinging fast to that slight spar within her arms, the mother drifted out upon the dark and unknown sea that rolls round all the world.' Later Dombey remembers his wife and daughter as two figures 'at the bottom of . . . clear depths', while he stands isolated 'on the bank above them'. Little Paul asks what the waves are saying with an innocent insistence designed to wring the adult reader's heart, and on his deathbed imagines himself being borne out to sea while the sunbeams play like 'golden water' on the bedroom wall. Mrs. Skewton, the next casualty, passes away to the accompaniment of lofty talk from Dickens about how her friends remain deaf to what the waves are saying. 'All goes on', Dickens intones,

as it was wont, upon the margin of the unknown sea; and Edith standing there alone, and listening to its waves, has dank weed cast up at her feet, to strew her path in life withal.

The same vague and elevated language sends Walter and Florence off on their trip to China:

The voices in the waves are always whispering to Florence, in their cease-less murmuring, of love – of love, eternal and illimitable, not bounded by the confines of this world, or by the end of time, but ranging still beyond the sea, beyond the sky, to the invisible country far away!

The novel ends with a regenerate Mr. Dombey walking his grand-children along the beach, and with a final report from the waves about 'the invisible country far away' which happily had to be cut in proof as the number was too long.

One trouble with this symbol is the disastrous effect it has on Dickens' style. The religiosity, which can only survive in the absence of imaginative precision, encourages stilted archaisms like 'as it was wont' and 'withal'. The phrases are strung together in the hope of some approximation to transcendental effect, but whether the sea represents death or love or eternity or God is neither clear nor of much moment. Moreover this nebulous, symbolic sea collides curiously in the novel with the real sea of ships and tar and tackling. Captain Cuttle with his hook hand and salty language, Sol Gills' nautical instrument shop, the wooden midshipman, and the old sailor in battered oilskins who pushes Paul's wheelchair and smells like a weedy beach at low tide, simply refuse to combine with the shadowy symbolic sea. Their sea is geographic and commercial, solid with detail from Dickens' childhood memories – mast and oar and block makers, docks and coalyards and ships' chandlers. A comic encounter occurs between Paul and Mr. Toots which shows the two seas in sharp opposition. Paul, as usual, is rhapsodizing about death:

'Don't you think you would rather die on a moonlight night when the sky was quite clear, and the wind blowing, as it did last night?'

Mr. Toots said, looking doubtfully at Paul, and shaking his head, that he didn't know about that.

'Not blowing, at least,' said Paul, 'but sounding in the air like the sea sounds in the shells. It was a beautiful night. When I had listened to the water for a long time, I got up and looked out. There was a boat over there, in the full light of the moon; a boat with a sail.'

The child looked at him so steadfastly, and spoke so earnestly, that Mr. Toots, feeling himself called upon to say something about this boat, said, 'Smugglers.'

. . . 'A boat with a sail,' repeated Paul, 'in the full light of the moon. The sail like an arm, all silver. It went away into the distance, and what do you think it seemed to do as it moved with the waves?'

'Pitch,' said Mr. Toots.

'It seemed to beckon,' said the child.

The dialogue doesn't make Mr. Toots' notion of the sea seem comic or substandard. It makes Paul's seem weakheaded. Probably the two seas should be related to two different bits of Dickens' boyhood. He had an uncle, a Mr. Christopher Huffam, who was a rigger and mast, oar and block maker, residing in Limehouse. Visits to him and his nautical acquaintances – among them an admiring boat-builder who pronounced the little lad a 'prodigy' – were among the high spots of young Dickens' London life. On the other hand, he remembered the sea he had left at Chatham in dreamy terms – 'the ships floating out in the Medway, with their far visions of sea'. And

because he had led an 'ailing little life' there – not strong enough to
play with the other boys – he connected this marine vagueness with
languishing infants of the Paul Dombey class.

A similar duality, though not so drastic, can be felt about the
novel's other symbol – the railway. It's not easy to correlate the
railway being built through Staggs' Garden, which earns Mr.
Toodle the engine stoker his bread and butter, with the fiery monster
which wreaks vengeance upon Carker in the last act. As with the sea,
there's a sense of one of the novel's well-grounded properties being
inflated into something apocalyptic.

Likewise with *A Tale of Two Cities*. Taking resurrection as his
central theme, Dickens provides on the one hand thoroughly
imagined, earthbound illustrations of it, while on the other hand he
insists on a transcendental meaning. Seventeen years before, when
writing *American Notes*, Dickens had described with horror the
system of solitary confinement at the Eastern Penitentiary in
Philadelphia. Occasionally in the corridors of the prison, he says,
one may hear the sound of a shoemaker's last, but no prisoner ever
sees a human face except those of the warders. 'He is a man buried
alive', Dickens writes, 'to be dug out in the slow round of years.'
This is the germ of *A Tale of Two Cities* (*Buried Alive* was one of the
titles proposed for it). At the start of the book Dr. Manette has been
in solitary confinement for eighteen years, making shoes. Crossing to
France to bring him back Jarvis Lorry is, we are told, 'on his way to
dig some one out of the grave' – someone who has been 'buried alive
for eighteen years'. In his dreams on the journey Lorry keeps
enacting different versions of this resurrection. He:

would dig, and dig, dig – now with a spade, now with a great key, now
with his hands – to dig this wretched creature out. Got out at last, with
earth hanging about his face and hair, he would suddenly fall away to dust.

Jerry Cruncher is a resurrection man. He digs bodies from graveyards to sell as anatomical specimens. Another contributor to the
resurrection theme is the secret agent Roger Cly who feigns death
and comes to life again. He arranges an elaborate funeral for himself,
but the coffin contains only paving-stones and earth. As Carton
prepares to sacrifice himself, and again on the scaffold, Dickens
chants from the burial service: 'I am the resurrection and the life,
saith the Lord: he that believeth in me, though he were dead, yet
shall he live: and whosoever liveth and believeth in me, shall never

die.' The quotation, inserted into the narrative with no explanation of who in the novel it's supposed to be occurring to, represents a stout effort on Dickens' part to shove his readers onto a higher plane so that they won't mind too much the injustice of Carton's death. And it works. But when we look back from this to Jerry Cruncher exemplifying the resurrection theme by digging up a coffin full of paving-stones, we sense the same gap between a solid event and the attachment of 'symbolic' import to it that we felt between Captain Cuttle's sea and Paul Dombey's.

In both cases the desire to lead his readers in public worship has betrayed Dickens into making metaphysical noises about his stage properties, instead of letting the objects – the sea, or the grave – exist for themselves. A similar, and similarly unfortunate bid for religious significance occurs in *Our Mutual Friend*. The idea of being submerged in water and hauled out of water is ingrained from the start, as we watch Gaffer Hexam at his daily task of fishing bodies out of the Thames. The hero of the novel, John Harmon, is believed drowned but has risen from the water a new man with a new name, while Radfoot, the man who tried to murder him, has actually been drowned and his body retrieved. Gaffer Hexam and Rogue Riderhood and Bradley Headstone are all eventually drowned and retrieved, but before this Riderhood has been run down by a river steamer and resuscitated in the Six Jolly Fellowship Porters, and Headstone has thrown his false identity – the clothes he wore to attack Wrayburn – into the river, and they have been retrieved by Riderhood. Gaffer's corpse is fished out during a hailstorm, and Dickens inserts some rhetorical questions evidently supposed to be passing through Lizzie Hexam's mind:

Father, was that you calling me? Was it you, the voiceless and the dead? Was it you, thus buffeted as you lie here in a heap? Was it you, thus baptized unto Death, with these flying impurities now flung upon your face?

Lizzie, we notice, though she has never been to school, can turn an elegant phrase with the best. Few daughters of Thames scavengers could refer to hail as 'flying impurities'. 'Baptized unto Death' is apparently a misremembrance of Paul's phrase in *Romans* about being baptized into Christ's death. Lizzie's version, while missing the point of Paul's remark, preserves a religious ring and vaguely links all the drowned villains of the novel to some kind of false baptism. The true baptism is reserved for Eugene Wrayburn, whom Dickens tries to depict as a basically good-natured wastrel. Knocked into the river by Headstone, he is fished out a changed man, ready to have the wedding service read over him by the Rev. Frank Milvey. Lest we should miss the exalted significance of Wrayburn's wetting, Bella, in the chapter immediately before, breaks the news to her husband that she is pregnant, and playfully recites with him the section of the catechism which deals with godfathers and god-mothers giving the child a name at baptism. As in *Dombey* and *A Tale of Two Cities* we seem to have drifted away from the solidly imagined scene – Gaffer dragging his carrion out of the Thames – into a vague, religious area. Muddled, as well as vague. How, we wonder, can baptism be so important in a novel where Riah the Jew is almost the only consistently good character?

Jenny Wren, the tough, industrious cripple, regularly seen giving her drunken father the rough side of her tongue, has some wistful religious experience foisted onto her by Dickens as well. She tells Lizzie of the visions of angelic children, 'all in white dresses', which she used to have:

They used to come down in long bright slanting rows, and say altogether, 'Who is this in pain! Who is this in pain!' When I told them who it was, they answered 'Come and play with us!'

This maudlin vision, worthy of Paul Dombey himself, incites Jenny to play her game of being dead in the garden on the roof of Riah's house. As Riah climbs the stairs, we are told:

he saw the face of the little creature looking down out of a Glory of her long bright radiant hair, and musically repeating to him, like a vision: 'Come up and be dead! Come up and be dead!'

It evidently doesn't occur to Jenny that her host's religion holds out an expectation of a heaven rather unlike her own. Little differences of opinion over the divinity of Christ disappear in the wash of Dickensian religious sentiment.

Happily Dickens refrains from cumbering his other big central property in *Our Mutual Friend* – the dust heaps – with any elevated significance, indeed with any distinct significance at all. In *Hard Times*, ten years before, 'the national cinder heap' was a name for the House of Commons, and Members of Parliament were 'national dustmen'. But Mr. Boffin's heaps clearly don't represent parliament. Some critics have thought that they are meant to make a moralizing connection between money and dirt; and Humphry House has helped to make the heaps seem dirtier by pointing out, as Dickens does not, that Victorian dust heaps regularly contained human excrement. Dr. Daleski assures us that 'Money is dust' constitutes the book's message, and Dr. Sucksmith applauds Dickens for 'intuitively' equating wealth with excrement – 'a genuine correspondence (as we know today) since the acquisition of gold is partly motivated by an anal complex'. Dickens himself was a highly successful businessman who amassed a fortune of £93,000. Presumably his understanding of the anal complex was first-hand. Be that as it may, there can be no question of his presenting money as dirt in *Our Mutual Friend*. Money buys John and Bella Harmon at the end their beautiful house with its aviary of tropical birds and its fountain and waterlilies and gold and silver fish, not to mention the ivory casket of jewels on Bella's 'exquisite toilette table'. The other financial arrangements at the end of the novel also bespeak a keen approval of the value of money. The feeble Mr. Sampson, Lavinia Wilfer's betrothed, has to make do, we are told, with a 'moderate salary', and the detested Mr. Veneering is punished with bankruptcy which, if money were dirt, would be a positive benefit. John Harmon, the hero, goes out of his way to inform his wife that people 'are not the worse for riches' – and considering the size of his fortune it's as well for him they aren't. We can dismiss the notion that the dust heaps are charged with any moral message about the worthlessness of material wealth. Nor are the mounds repulsive, as Humphry House's suggestion would make them. They are the site of Boffin's Bower, and the High Mound is decorated with a lattice-work arbour in which the amiable Boffin sits of a summer evening. They relate less to human excrement than to Dickens' genial interest in the resourceful use of junk, illustrated by Wemmick or the Staggs' gardeners. His early memories of dust heaps were romantic. He connected them with the bits of struggling countryside islanded in London's urban sprawl. To walk to the top of Bayham Street as a child and gaze 'over the dust-heaps and dock-leaves and fields' towards the dome of St. Paul's looming through the smoke was, he told Forster, 'a treat that served him for hours of vague reflection afterwards'. Similarly the first volume of *Household Words* has a story about some dust heaps in which, far from appearing sinister or filthy, they are the venue of a warm-hearted, meritoriously dilapidated trio, wooden-legged Peg Dotting, deformed Jem Clinker, and Gaffer Doubleyear whose eye-patch neatly contrived from oyster-shell and string relates him to the Peggottys' mirror. Pigs, geese, thistles, groundsel and snug cottages complete the tumbledown idyll, and the three friends demonstrate their heap's life-enhancing qualities by burying a drowned man up to the neck in it, with the result that its heat revives him. Heaps were not horrible for Dickens, nor was money, and the presence of the dust heaps in *Our Mutual Friend* is the richer because they won't submit to be catalogued under any moral platitude.

The fog in *Bleak House* is another large-scale Dickensian property. It is said to represent the obscurity of the legal system, and it also relates to the ignorance which hides characters in the novel from the people around them. Esther remains ignorant of her parenthood for much of the time, and thinks till almost the end that she is to marry Jarndyce not Woodcourt. Woodcourt is a fog disperser. Just before Esther runs into him unexpectedly in Deal she notes 'the fog began to rise like a curtain.' So, in the end, is Jarndyce. The summer morning on which he hands Esther over to Woodcourt is innocent of the least vestige of mist – the 'water sparkling away into the distance', Esther observes; and as for Jarndyce himself:

As I sat looking fixedly at him, and the sun's rays descended, softly shining through the leaves, upon his bare head, I felt as if the brightness on him must be like the brightness of the Angels.

Once more, as we contemplate the angelic Jarndyce, we have an uneasy feeling that the 'symbolism' depends on falsity and inflation. The fog as Dickens originally imagined it – hovering in the rigging of ships, blearing the London gas lamps, making the loungers on Thames bridges feel they are up in a balloon among misty clouds – this fog, inventively depicted, had its own reality and value. It strikes us as a mechanical addition, not in itself damaging to the Lord Chancellor, that he should have 'a foggy glory round his head' to contrast with Jarndyce's glowing pate at the end. What little a London fog can tell us about the Court of Chancery or Esther Summerson's family relationships is really irrelevant to its poetic force.

Likewise with the rain, falling in torrents on the Dedlock house in Lincolnshire:

An arch of the bridge in the park has been sapped and sopped away. The adjacent low lying ground, for half a mile in breadth, is a stagnant river, with melancholy trees for islands in it, and a surface punctured all over,

all day long, with falling rain . . . The weather, for many a day and night,
has been so wet that the trees seem wet through, and the soft loppings and
prunings of the woodman's axe can make no crash or crackle as they fall.
The deer, looking soaked, leave quagmires, where they pass. The shot of a
rifle loses its sharpness in the moist air, and its smoke moves in a tardy
little cloud towards the green rise, coppice-topped, that makes a background
for the falling rain.

The observation, notably of sounds, and the drear rhythms of the
prose, increasing the desolation, place this passage among Dickens'
finest achievements. It is not improved, though its 'meaning' is
certainly made firmer in one particular direction, if we connect it, as
we are probably meant to, with a speech of Sir Leicester's later in the
book. 'Upon my honour, upon my life, upon my reputation and
principles,' says Sir Leicester, 'the floodgates of society are burst
open, and the waters have – a – obliterated the landmarks of the frame-
work of the cohesion by which things are held together!' The
Lincolnshire floods and the breaking bridge now look sociological
for a moment. But they have been too firmly established in the novel
in their own right to be replaced by an interpretation, least of all one
supplied by Sir Leicester. The 'symbolism' is best forgotten.

The smaller 'symbols' in *Bleak House*, which simply establish
connections between people and objects, are safe from religious or
moral interpretation. There is no danger here of observation getting
twisted so as to provide Jarndyce with a halo of sunbeams. For
example, Dickens notices a parallel between the elderly Volumnia
Dedlock, with her attempts at girlish vivacity, and some little old-
fashioned glass chandeliers which, he writes, 'with their meagre
stems, their spare little drops, their disappointing knobs where no
drops are, their bare little stalks from which knobs and drops have
both departed, and their little feeble prismatic twinkling, all seem
Volumnia'. This works like metaphor. Without being able to point
to any definite visual similarities, we recognize that Volumnia's
quality has been caught in the little chandelier. Less overt is the
connection suggested between Volumnia's friends and the contents
of the Dedlock conservatory. Elderly like Volumnia, but eager to
retain their girlish charms, the friends are described several times as
'peachy-cheeked charmers' with 'skeleton throats'. In the conservatory of the Dedlock town house, when snow is falling thick outside,
peach blossom can be seen, says Dickens, 'turning itself exotically to
the great hall fire from the nipping weather out of doors'. The
comparison – or contrast – between the women and the winter

blossom is not direct; they are merely placed near enough to intimate a relationship. And more striking than the comparison is the physical evocation of the conservatory itself. Dickens loved conservatories, and long planned one at Gadshill: in the event it proved his last addition, finished four days before his death. The appeal of the micro-summer, a pane's thickness from snow, fits in understandably with his other imaginative traits. Odd contiguities, nearness in space masked by a wall or ceiling, always caught his attention. Passing Newgate at night, he would touch its rough stone, and think of the prisoners asleep near his hand. Tulkinghorn, abed in his turret at Chesney Wold, has a creaky flagstaff sticking into the air just above his forehead. Such juxtapositions, like conservatories, provided tangible evidence for Dickens' favourite theory about the smallness of the world – 'how things and persons apparently the most unlikely to meet were continually knocking up against each other'.

Dickens' symbolic writing is best, then, when it sticks closest to physical objects and doesn't break out into abstract – and especially religious – annotation. *Little Dorrit* is a novel which describes for its readers several instances of physical imprisonment. Opening in the prison at Marseilles, where Blandois and John Baptist are incarcerated, and on a quarantine island where Mr. Meagles refers to his fellow-travellers as 'jail-birds', it moves to the Marshalsea prison in which much of it is set. When the Dorrits escape from there, we first see them imprisoned by darkness and weather in the convent of the Great St. Bernard. Figurative examples of imprisonment are multiplied relentlessly. Mrs. Clennam announces herself 'in prison' in her room; her Bible is bound with a 'chain'; Arthur recalls being marched to chapel 'morally handcuffed' to another boy; even his bed has spikes like the Marshalsea wall; Miss Wade sits behind the 'bars' of a lattice, avoided by the rest of the company; on the London Sunday all amusements are 'bolted and barred'; Mr. Merdle is said to have a nervous habit of taking 'himself into custody by the wrists . . . as if he were his own Police Officer'; the Barnacle house off Grosvenor Square is called a 'coop' and a 'hutch'. The landscape, too, is made to conform to a strict segregation, as of a prison wall. The water in Marseilles harbour, we are told at the start, is foul; the sea outside, beautiful. 'The line of demarcation between the two colours, black and blue, showed the point which the pure sea would not pass.' Likewise at the beginning of the second part, it is vintage time on the Swiss side of the Alps, and the warm air is full of the scent of gathered grapes, while snow and ice cover the mountain, and the only vegetation is scrubby moss 'freezing in the chinks of rock'. This theme of segregation, to which so much of the novel's figurative language contributes, is evidently meant to lend 'significance' to otherwise innocuous details, like the fact that Clennam and Little Dorrit have their first private meeting on a bridge. 'Will you go by the Iron Bridge?' asks Clennam. And later, we learn, 'they emerged upon the Iron Bridge, which was as quiet after the roaring streets, as though it had been open country.'

The proliferation of so-called 'prison-images' in *Little Dorrit* is often much admired. We're told that the repetition unifies the novel, and that it reveals a deeper meaning. This deep meaning is represented by maxims like 'Society is a prison' or 'All the world's a prison,' which you will find people seriously prepared to accept as the lesson the novel is intended to convey. A little thought, however, will tell us that if the novel is really designed to pass on such messages it fails in a very remarkable way. The scenes in the Marshalsea demonstrate with great imaginative conviction how being in prison corrodes the personality of a prisoner. We are shown in numerous scenes how the taint of prison has entered Dorrit's soul. We observe his desperate selfishness, the erosion of his self-respect, his pathetic attempts to keep up appearances. The prisoner becomes, by long incarceration, a separate species of human being. Even the ragged messengers who run errands for the prisoners are, we're told, a race apart:

Their walk was the walk of a race apart. They had a peculiar way of doggedly slinking round the corner, as if they were eternally going to the pawnbroker's. When they coughed, they coughed like people accustomed to be forgotten on door-steps and in draughty passages, waiting for answers to letters in faded ink, which gave the recipients of those manuscripts great mental disturbance and no satisfaction.

A special walk. Even a special way of coughing. But if the prison produces a 'race apart', there can be very little meaning in such assertions as 'Society is a prison' or 'All the world's a prison.' These can be using the word 'prison', we realize, only in some enfeebled figurative sense – a sense which no one who had ever really been in prison would condone. If society is a prison, then there's no great difference between being in prison and out of it. Dorrit would have been much the same had he never been in prison. Such suppositions run counter to everything the novel has shown us. However, it is not

the critics who are to be blamed for introducing these trite formulations about the world and society, and brandishing them as the
'meaning' of *Little Dorrit*. Dickens, when he abandons his firm
imaginative task of presenting what it's like inside the Marshalsea,
can be found endorsing similar trite formulations himself. Apart
from all the figurative language in the novel which, as we've seen,
insinuates that being outside the prison is really like being in it, there
are some quite blatant assertions of the idea. Little Dorrit, who has
not the slightest appreciation of the cultural riches of Italy, and who,
we are given to understand, is somehow the better for this obtuseness,
is struck by a similarity between the devotees of culture in Venice
and the Marshalsea prisoners.

It appeared on the whole, to Little Dorrit herself, that this same society in
which they lived, greatly resembled a superior sort of Marshalsea.
Numbers of people seemed to come abroad, pretty much as people had
come into the prison; through debt, through idleness, relationship,
curiosity, and general unfitness for getting on at home. They were brought
into these foreign towns in the custody of couriers and local followers, just
as the debtors had been brought into the prison. They prowled around the
churches and picture galleries, much in the old, dreary, prison-yard,
manner . . . They had precisely the same incapacity for settling down to
anything, as the prisoners used to have; they rather deteriorated one
another, as the prisoners used to do; and they wore untidy dresses, and
fell into a slouching way of life: still always like the people in the
Marshalsea.

The vague phrases with which the analogy is recommended – 'on
the whole', 'pretty much as' – warn us that we have drifted into a
looser part of the book. In the Marshalsea scenes we were not told
'on the whole' but precisely and distinctly what it was like to be in
prison. But there's no hint that we're meant to think less of Amy
Dorrit for her dull-witted philistine fancy. On the contrary, the
deeply-entrenched middle-class antagonism with which she watches
people in picture galleries – bored herself, and convinced that
everyone else's enthusiasm must be affected – is precisely Dickens'
own. Visitors to picture galleries are an untidy, pretentious lot who
ought to be doing a job of work. We may recall his complaint on
visiting the untidy Thompsons at Nervi, a year or so before he began
Little Dorrit, that they were allowing music and oil-painting to take
precedence over 'household affairs'. These are the assumptions we
encounter when the book leaves off its dark figurative intimations
and actually spells out why it considers society is like a prison.

Similarly, while the sight of Miss Wade sitting behind the 'bars' of a lattice seems a firm imaginative moment, routine phrases like 'the prison of the self' with which critics gloss it, have a hollow sound. And here too the critics are not solely to blame. Dickens himself presents Miss Wade arguing with Meagles about imprisonment, and claiming that she knows by experience that a prisoner never forgives his prison. The figurative prison which Miss Wade is in is further explained by the clumsy artifice of her manuscript autobiography which she hands over to Clennam, and which is supposed to show her cut off from her fellow human beings by arrogance and hypersensitivity. In fact Miss Wade's fiery defiance bears no relation to the state which, as we know from Mr. Dorrit, real prisons reduce their inmates to. Her experience of prison, like that of the visitors to the picture gallery, is a mere figure of speech.

As the novel approaches its climax, a further extension of the prison 'symbol' is attempted. 'The last day of the appointed week touched the bars of the Marshalsea' Dickens writes:

Black, all night, since the gate had clashed upon Little Dorrit, its iron stripes were turned by the early-glowing sun into stripes of gold. For aslant across the city, over its jumbled roofs, and through the open tracery of its church towers, struck the long bright rays, bars of the prison of this lower world.

Now, it appears, not just society or the self but the whole world is a prison. Not that Dickens supports his hackneyed whim with any documentation. The presentation of the Marshalsea prison was dense with detail and actuality. Here the writing is just slipshod. A portion of religious verbiage is hopefully dropped into the narrative, along with a mention of church towers. The sense that a physical object – a prison – which was scrupulously investigated earlier in the novel is now being allowed to float out of focus in the interests of religion, is similar to the feeling one had on seeing Captain Cuttle's ocean becoming a sign of eternal love, or on watching the sunlight glorifying Jarndyce's hair.

It is habitual in *Little Dorrit* to refer to prisoners as birds. The Marseilles gaoler tells his daughter 'Look at the birds, my pretty' when indicating his charges. Clennam takes leave of Little Dorrit outside the Marshalsea: 'The cage door opened, and when the small bird, reared in captivity, had tamely fluttered in, he saw it shut again.' The Marshalsea veterans are called 'seasoned birds', and when Dorrit, after his breakdown, forgets everything but the Marshalsea, his spirit, we're told, remembered only 'the place where it had broken its wings'. John Chivery offers Clennam watercress in the Marshalsea, like someone putting food 'into the cage of a dull imprisoned bird'. The metaphor is made to cover other types of inmate too. Mr. Plornish's father, inmate of the workhouse, is 'a poor little reedy piping old gentleman, like a worn-out bird'. Prisoners in the hypothetical prison of society are also birds. At Mr. Merdle's party Lord Decimus Tite Barnacle urges 'his noble pinions' and soars up to the drawing-room, and the 'smaller birds . . . flutter up-stairs' after him. The bird metaphor, like the prison images, tends to confuse the issue. Why should our sympathy be specially canvassed for Little Dorrit, a 'small bird, reared in captivity', if in fact everyone is reared in captivity, whether in the Marshalsea or the grand houses of the upper middle class?

Dickens wishes to emphasize that society itself is like a caged bird by his odd positioning of Mrs. Merdle's parrot: 'a parrot on the outside of a golden cage holding on by its beak with its scaly legs in the air'. The parrot is on the same side of the bars as Mrs. Merdle and her guests. The caged bird is a well established Dickensian property, representing either a protected favourite or a prisoner or both. Sam Weller points out a caged bird to Mr. Pickwick in the Fleet, with the sage remark 'a prison in a prison'; but Tim Linkinwater in *Nicholas Nickleby* keeps a blind blackbird in 'a large snug cage' who is said to be the picture of happiness. In *The Old Curiosity Shop* Dickens describes how, at dawn, 'birds in hot rooms, covered up close and dark . . . chafed and grew restless in their little cells'; yet Nell herself keeps a bird in a cage, evidently with no suggestion of cruelty, and Kit Nubbles, who has been looking after it, takes it along to be an attendant at her deathbed. Cruelty to caged birds is one of the melancholy results of popular uprising. The mob wrecking houses in *Barnaby Rudge* find some caged canaries and throw them into the fire alive – 'the poor little creatures screamed', Dickens relates, 'like infants.' The scene was authentic, as it happens, like most of *Barnaby*'s mob antics. Dickens carefully imported it from the accounts of the Gordon Riots he consulted. Poll Sweedlepipe the barber in *Martin Chuzzlewit* is another bird fancier, and when we first see his birds the cruelty of their imprisonment is stressed. They hop their 'little ballet of despair' in tiny cages, and one goldfinch, looking at his drinking water, 'mutely appealed to some good man to drop a farthing's worth of poison into it'. Later, though, we receive an altogether cosier picture of the establishment, 'one great bird's nest', Dickens calls it, and Poll himself, it turns out, is a kindly figure, like a sparrow, but without its quarrelsome nature, and with 'no more wickedness' in him than a robin.

By the time Dickens came to write *Dombey* he had a large collection of caged birds, variously pampered or tormented, behind him. In that novel Walter, returning from his first day's work at Dombey and Son, enumerates the contents of the office to his eager Uncle Sol. 'Nothing else?' asks Sol, when he's finished. 'No, nothing else', says Walter, 'except an old bird-cage (I wonder how *that* ever came there).' We have less excuse for wondering than Walter. We are supposed to realize that this is one of the sad, not the happy, cages, and take against Dombey's office accordingly. Dickens invokes a favourite symbol, and the office is instantly established as a place of incarceration which cramps the spirit. The symbolic method seems, in this instance, to be somewhat shallow. We don't even know what Mr. Dombey's business is, so are precluded from making an intelligent estimate of why it should cramp the spirit. Dickens has done nothing but hang a bird-cage in it, and assure us that Mr. Dombey sits 'as if he were a lone prisoner in a cell'.

A less objectionable bird-cage is Miss Tox's. When she deludes herself with hopes of marrying Dombey, she provides 'a new cage with gilded wires' for her 'ancient little canary bird'. The bird and Miss Tox are presumably meant to be interchangeable to some degree, and the gilded wires relate to her false hopes. The symbol works better because it isn't just a symbol. It is a perfectly credible instance of a character revealing thought through action. Miss Tox expects her new suitor to be impressed by, and eventually defray the cost of, her smart new cage. In her place, we might do the same. Whereas taking an empty bird-cage to the office to indicate one's spiritual incarceration is a mode of behaviour found only among characters in symbolic novels. Besides, Miss Tox's cage merges into a wealth of other information about her furniture and daily routine, while the Dombey office is practically empty except for its bird-cage.

Carker, though, has the novel's best bird:

A gaudy parrot in a burnished cage upon the table tears at the wires with her beak, and goes walking, upside down, in its dome top, shaking her house and screeching.

Carker, meanwhile, gazes 'with a musing smile' at the picture of

Edith Dombey on the wall. With a gesture at the picture suggestive, says Dickens, of 'an insolent salute wafted from his lips', he:

calls to the chafing and imprisoned bird, who, coming down into a pendant gilded hoop within the cage, like a great wedding ring, swings in it, for his delight.

The obedient female prisoner with its wedding ring is evidently a projection of Carker's hopes concerning Edith, and the gilded ring, like Miss Tox's gilded wires, introduces the note of falsity. Once more, the caged bird is a way of telling us about a character's state of mind by looking at the things he surrounds himself with. Dombey's strange office-equipment, on the other hand, was there simply to condemn an institution we know nothing about.

Besides the bird-cage, another object which, through Dickens' obsession with imprisonment, takes on an imaginative prominence is the lock. A padlock and a gate in a high fence feature among David Copperfield's earliest memories. On the other side lies the garden, where, David recalls:

the fruit clusters on the trees, riper and richer than fruit has ever been since, in any other garden, and where my mother gathers some in a basket.

Garden, tree, fruit, the woman picking it: Eden seems deliberately invoked as a frame to the theoretically innocent sexuality which David and his mother enjoy. Between this and the present stands the lock. A lock attracts careful attention too in *Sketches by Boz*. When Watkins Tottle is taken to the debtors' lock-up, a sallow-faced boy, relates Dickens:

applied a large key to an immense wooden excrescence, which was in reality a lock, but which, taken in conjunction with the iron nails with which the panels were studded, gave the door the appearance of being subject to warts.

A locksmith is a central character in *Barnaby Rudge* (originally entitled *Gabriel Varden, the Locksmith of London*). Gabriel's shop, blackened by the smoke of its forge, has 'great bunches of rusty keys, fragments of iron, half-finished locks' which cover the walls and hang in clusters from the ceiling. His trade sorts weirdly with his cheeriness and sociability: 'the easiest, freest, happiest man in all the world', busy making locks. Varden's moment of heroism comes when he refuses despite the threats of the mob to open the lock on Newgate Prison. A recruit in the Royal East London Volunteers, he

stands for law and order – and prisons – in a novel which is torn
between the glamour of anarchy and the terror of it. The book has its
evil locksmith too in Simon Tappertit, who carries a lock around
with him like a badge. When he visits Mr. Chester, for instance: 'in
he came . . . and a great lock in his hand, which he put down on the
floor in the middle of the chamber as if he were about to go through
some performances in which it was a necessary agent.' Mr. Chester
inquires about 'that complicated piece of ironmongery which you
have done me the favour to bring with you', and is informed by
Tappertit that 'It's going to be fitted on a ware'us-door in Thames-
street.' We sense that Dickens' imagination has run together the
blacking warehouse by the Thames in which he was incarcerated,
and the prison in which his father was. The contrast between the
evil locksmith, and the good locksmith who is in favour of prisons,
repeats itself in *Great Expectations*, where Joe Gargery is put to
work by the soldiers hunting Magwitch to mend the lock on a pair of
handcuffs – 'I find the lock of one of them goes wrong,' says the
sergeant – whereas Orlick murders Pip's sister with the leg iron
which was locked on Magwitch's leg. The strange fascination of
smiths, and their business with locks, accounts too for the scene at
the climax of *Barnaby Rudge* when the prisoners are led to execution.
In the final room beside the gallows they find not an executioner but:
'two smiths, with hammers, stood beside an anvil.' They are there
to take off the leg irons. Hugh sets his foot on the anvil with a sound
'as though it had been struck with a heavy weapon'. We recall the
heavy weapon that struck down Mrs. Joe. In order to commit his
murder in *Martin Chuzzlewit* Jonas has to get through a door with a
rusty lock: 'He had a little bottle of oil,' writes Dickens, 'and the
feather of a pen, with which he lubricated the key and the lock too,
carefully.' The lock plays a leading role in *Little Dorrit*, naturally.
Chapter 8, in which Clennam first sets eyes on the Marshalsea, is
entitled 'The Lock'. The gaoler on duty is said to be 'on the lock'.
Amy, my dear . . . Will you go and see if Bob is on the lock,' asks
Dorrit, when he breaks down at the Roman banquet.

The ambivalent quality of the lock – insignia of order and of
oppression – is brought out in *Bleak House*. 'Mr. Tulkinghorn', we
learn:

takes a small key from his pocket, unlocks a drawer in which there is
another key, which unlocks a chest in which there is another key, and so
comes to the cellar key.

When Tulkinghorn shows this key to Hortense, the prison is invoked:

'Look, mistress, this is the key of my wine-cellar. It is a large key, but the keys of prisons are larger. In this city, there are houses of correction (where the treadmills are for women) the gates of which are very strong and heavy and no doubt the keys too.'

But the orderly Esther carries the symbol of the lock too – 'jingling about with my basket of keys', as she puts it, while our first visit to the irresponsible Skimpole's house tells us of his careless way with locks. A 'slatternly' girl lets Esther in: 'The lock of the door being in a disabled condition, she then applied herself to securing it with the chain, which was not in good condition either.' The word 'lock' itself assumes a menacing quality in *Our Mutual Friend*. Old Betty Higden, near to death, and running away from the threat of the workhouse, loses consciousness, and when she comes to a man she has never seen before is holding a candle to her face:

'I am the Lock,' said the man.
    'The Lock?'
    'I am the Deputy Lock, on job, and this is the Lockhouse. (Lock or Deputy Lock, it's all one.)'

This Kafkaesque conversation resolves itself when we discover that the man is Rogue Riderhood, currently employed on one of the locks on the Thames.

The lock is never preached over, as Dickens is inclined to preach over the occupants of the bird-cage. It is a 'symbol' only in the sense of being a strangely potent object, recurrently invoked. A third stage property which seems to be associated with the prison in Dickens' mind is the graveyard. It is always the same graveyard, whichever novel it happens to be moved into: iron railings round it, a locked iron gate, rank grass and weeds inside, bloated with corpses. It radiates gloom and taint. In *Pickwick* Grub the sexton goes into it to dig a grave, carefully locking the gate behind him first, and inside he meets the goblin king with whom he has a horror-comic dialogue. This scene is rewritten much more intensely in *Nicholas Nickleby* when Ralph is on his way home to commit suicide. Coming to the graveyard he is peering through the iron railings when a crowd of drunken passers-by arrives, with a 'little, weazen, hump-backed man' among them who performs a dance. Ralph is fleetingly reminded of a goblin he saw chalked on a door as a child. The lurid moment has all the arbitrariness of real experience. Indeed, it is real experience. Dickens, ever effigy-obsessed, writes elsewhere about a figure that habitually stalks into his mind as he lies awake at night:

> It is a figure that I once saw, just after dark, chalked upon a door in a little back lane near a country church – my first church. How young a child I may have been at the time, I don't know, but it horrified me so intensely – in connection with the churchyard, I suppose, for it smokes a pipe, and has a big hat with each of its ears sticking out in a horizontal line under the brim, and is not in itself more oppressive than a mouth from ear to ear, a pair of goggle eyes, and hands like two bunches of carrots, five in each, can make it – that it is still vaguely alarming to me to recall (as I have often done before, lying awake) the running home, the looking behind, the horror, of its following me; though whether disconnected from the door, or door and all, I can't say, and perhaps never could.

The eye of childhood that fears a painted devil: of childhood, and of adults who cannot forget it.

The iron-barred graveyard has a small part in *A Christmas Carol*, too, where the ghost shows Scrooge his own grave in it, and Jerry Cruncher digs for corpses in it in *A Tale of Two Cities* (young Jerry, coffin-pursued, is plainly Dickens running from his door-man), but its biggest role is in *Bleak House*. There Captain Hawdon gets buried in it and Lady Dedlock comes to look at his grave through its bars, accompanied by Jo the crossing sweeper, who tells her 'It's always locked.' Jo wishes to be put in it beside Hawdon, and reiterates, when dying: 'They'll have to get the key of the gate afore they can take me in, for it's allus locked.' In the big scene at the end Esther finds her mother dead on its step. The novel dwells heavily on the idea of contamination – Esther gets smallpox from Jo, and when Richard gets the law on the brain Jarndyce informs Esther that it's the fault of Chancery spreading contagion:

> It is in the subtle poison of such abuses to breed such diseases. His blood is infected.

Accordingly the graveyard is turned to account as a symbol of contamination. When Hawdon is buried in it, Dickens delivers a funeral oration on the subject of sanitary reform:

> a hemmed-in churchyard, pestiferous and obscene, whence malignant diseases are communicated to the bodies of our dear brothers and sisters who have not departed . . . With every villainy of life in action close on death, and every poisonous element of death in action close on life – here, they lower our dear brother down a foot or two, sow him in corrup-

tion, to be raised in corruption: an avenging ghost at many a sick bedside: a shameful testimony to future ages, how civilisation and barbarism walked this boastful island together.

Hygienic cemetries are a perfectly sensible requirement, but the bitterly ironic tone seems deliberately to merge together religion and sanitation. Essentially Dickens is saying that we ought to give paupers a decent burial, because otherwise their corpses will only spread disease among the middle class. The message needs some rhetorical clothing to make it look less self-interested, and Dickens' fervour is able to present the graveyard as an outrage to religion as well as health. We sense again that a powerfully-apprehended physical object is being preached about, not left to speak for itself. Once preached about, it loses some of its power and becomes a teaching aid. The poet, who has evoked it, gives place to the didactic author wagging his finger. By contrast, when Lady Dedlock goes to the graveyard, to see Hawdon's burial place, its contagious influence is impressed on the reader by a single physical detail. She stands in the archway, Dickens writes, 'with its deadly stains contaminating her dress'. The suggestion that the corpses are a soluble deposit smeared on the very railings of the place, like the black fat which smears the neighbourhood where Krook blows up, stirs the reader's imagination. The graveyard repels without any prompting from the author. The difference between the two ways of communicating is that between imagination and reason. That graveyard railings stain ladies' dresses is from a reasonable viewpoint a trivial objection, but it has more power over the imagination that any amount of sanitary argument. Reason is circumspect, and can enlarge the issue with religious considerations. Imagination is direct.

Another 'symbolic' device in Dickens is the use of objects as portents, heralds of momentous happenings. They are naturally apt to appear planted. It seems unduly convenient that there should be a huge storm on the night Magwitch comes blundering back into Pip's life, and especially that, even before the convict has appeared, the noise of the wind should remind Pip of 'discharges of cannon' – echoes of the cannon which fired to signal Magwitch's escape. Another suspiciously appropriate storm occurs on the night of Edwin Drood's murder. In Elizabethan drama the turmoil in the elements which accompanies human misdeeds like the murder of Duncan relates to a system of belief binding man to his universe. By the nineteenth century this kind of sympathetic weather has dwindled to a poetic convenience. Flashes of chance memory from childhood, like Ralph Nickleby's chalked goblin, are more likely companions than thunder and lightning for the modern murderer. But objects which foreshadow future events can be naturalistic, because they can be projections of the fears of the character who notices them. When Nancy, in *Oliver Twist*, is about to turn informer, she tells Brownlow that a coffin was carried past her in the street on her way to their meeting place. 'There is nothing unusual in that,' says Brownlow, 'They have passed me often.' '*Real* ones,' Nancy replies. 'This was not.' Nancy knows her fear is making her see things. Dorrit has less self knowledge when he meets a symbolic coffin on his way back to Rome and death:

a funeral procession . . . came mechanically chaunting by, with an indistinct show of dirty vestments, lurid torches, swinging censers, and a great cross borne before a priest. He was an ugly priest by torch-light; of a lowering aspect, with an overhanging brow; and as his eyes met those of Mr. Dorrit, looking bare-headed out of the carriage, his lips, moving as they chaunted, seemed to threaten that important traveller; likewise the action of his hand, which was in fact his manner of returning the traveller's salutation, seemed to come in aid of that menace. So thought Mr. Dorrit, made fanciful by the weariness of building and travelling, as the priest drifted past him, and the procession straggled away.

Actually Dickens himself had met this funeral, 'about midway between Rome and Genoa', but, lacking Mr. Dorrit's jumpiness, had been struck only by the badness of the priest's chanting and the lively appearance of the corpse – a woman's, and uncoffined. The threatening symbol is invented by the character's own unease. It becomes, like Carker's parrot, a way of imparting his state of mind to the reader.

There is a more complicated version of the same thing in *David Copperfield*. David and Little Em'ly are playing on the beach when she tells him how much she wants to be a lady, and, immediately afterwards, runs along a piece of jagged timber sticking out over some deep water. David says the incident so impressed itself on his memory that, even though it was years ago, he could still draw an accurate sketch of it. The image of the child poised over water reflects David's worries about where her ambition will lead, and it evolves naturally out of Em'ly's taste for dangerous games, which makes her run off with Steerforth. It is like a photograph, because it tells you something about the person who took it as well as the person taken. At the other end of the scale of naturalism from David's snapshot belongs the theatrical thunderstorm which rages around Bradley Headstone shortly before he tries to finish off Eugene Wrayburn. Red, white, and blue lightning flicker over the sleeping schoolmaster, and the wind bursts in at the door as if, declares Dickens, 'invisible messengers were come around the bed to carry him away.' As usual, a desire to inject religion into the narrative is at the root of the trouble. Anxious to assure his readers that Bradley will go to Hell, Dickens arranges some supernatural manifestations. The method is self-defeating as well as puerile. A character who has such an unfortunate effect on the weather even when he's asleep can't, we feel, be getting a fair chance.

An incident can also acquire an unusual feel, which might, though misleadingly, be called 'symbolic', from being repeated later in the novel with a different set of actors. For example, *A Tale of Two Cities* opens with a coach containing Mr. Jarvis Lorry toiling up a steep hill on the Dover road and being pursued by what is at first thought to be a highwayman, but turns out to be a friendly messenger. A garish re-enactment of the scene comes about when a coach containing the Marquis toils up a steep hill on the way out of Paris, pursued by a man whom the Marquis takes to be a thief, but who turns out to be his murderer. This second scene is steeped in portentous colours, as well as being weirdly anticipated by Lorry. The Marquis is bathed in the blood-red glow of the setting sun; his pursuer white with the dust of the road: 'whiter than a miller,' says an onlooker, 'white as a spectre, tall as a spectre'. Another mirrored episode occurs in *Great Expectations*. At Miss Havisham's house Pip has a fight with the pale young gentleman, whom we later find to be Herbert Pocket, while Estella looks on. Back at the forge, Joe has a fight with Orlick, incited by Mrs. Gargery. A comparison of the two fights is enjoined, since Pip remarks that Joe knocked Orlick down 'as if he had been of no more account than the pale young gentleman'. This isn't just a Technicolor play-back like the second stage-coach episode. It provides new information, because it relates Estella's excitement over the fight to Mrs. Gargery's. Estella is sexually stirred by the spectacle of the battling males. Years later she says to Pip: 'I must have been a singular little creature to hide and see that fight that day: but I did, and I enjoyed it very much.' Nothing appears more singular to us than the sexual instincts we have in common with everyone else. Dickens' insight is beautifully sharp. After the fight Pip notices the flush of delight on Estella's face, and she imperiously gives him permission to kiss her. The presence of this sprouting puberty in the first scene naturally makes us wonder what was going on behind Mrs. Gargery's coarse apron when her infuriatingly submissive husband was asserting himself for once. After defeating Orlick, Pip recalls:

Joe unlocked the door and picked up my sister, who had dropped insensible at the window (but who had seen the fight first, I think) and who was carried into the house and laid down, and who was recommended to revive, and would do nothing but struggle and clench her hands in Joe's hair.

Poor Mrs. Gargery is obviously in dire need, but whether her obtuse husband realizes it and takes appropriate steps we are not told. All Pip can remember is that the uproar is followed by a 'singular calm and silence', as if someone had died. Perhaps Mrs. Gargery was lucky after all. Few of the examples of mirroring are as suggestive as this, and sometimes they seem to be there only to establish a neat moral. In *Hard Times* a horse figures prominently in the class-room scene at the start when the tyranny of fact is being demonstrated. Cissy Jupe can't define a horse, though she belongs to Sleary's horse-riders, whereas Bitzer knows it's a gramnivorous quadruped with forty teeth. But in the end a dancing horse of Sleary's is instrumental in defeating Bitzer and rescuing Tom Gradgrind from justice. More in the tradition of Carker's parrot is the scene where Tom Gradgrind sits on the terrace with Harthouse, picking roses and tearing them to pieces with his teeth. The sorry state of Tom's soul, implied by such behaviour, is fully explained in the later interview between Louisa Gradgrind and her father, when she strikes herself on the bosom and asks 'What have you done, O father, what have you done, with the garden that should have bloomed once, in this great wilderness here!'

Gardens frequently symbolize their owners as tellingly as the little chandelier symbolized Volumnia Dedlock. The garden belonging to sterile, elderly Dr. Strong and his excessively young wife, in *David Copperfield*, is occupied, so far as we can gather, only by peaches ripening against a sunny south wall and, on the other hand, two great aloes, in tubs, 'the broad hard leaves of which plant', says David:

(looking as if they were made of painted tin) have ever since, by association, been symbolical to me of silence and retirement.

As Estella sheds light on Mrs. Gargery's cravings, so Dr. and Mrs.

Strong are revealed as the ripening peach in bed with the tin aloe. Miss Wade's garden in *Little Dorrit* is a dull yard with a dead wall:

> where an attempt had been made to train some creeping shrubs, which were dead; and to make a little fountain in a grotto, which was dry; and to decorate that with a little statue, which was gone.

The dry fountain in a grotto could scarcely be more specific about the withered condition of Miss Wade's natural instincts, and the vanished statue which used to decorate it would be a broad hint that she had been disappointed in love, even if we did not have the later revelation that it was Gowan who let her down. A garden symbolizing an emptiness occurs in David Copperfield too. When David's father dies, David and his mother are left to develop their ingrown relationship, and the loss of the male presence is reflected in the garden. The ragged old rooks' nests in the elm trees are empty of rooks, and the dog kennel in the yard has no dog in it – not, anyway, until the new male, Murdstone, arrives and puts his there.

Whereas Dickens' symbolic gardens are adapted to suit the particular owner, there are one or two objects which carry a permanent aura with them whoever they belong to. It is typical of Dickens' philistinism, for example, that people who play musical instruments are regularly ineffective, half-comic characters, and their playing seldom amounts to much more than making a painful noise. Dickens had no musical talent. At school his music master reported that it 'was robbing his parents to continue giving him lessons'. But his sister Fanny was a concert pianist, and as a boy he was desperately jealous of her. When she won a scholarship to the Royal Academy of Music, it was 'a stab to his heart'. Perhaps this nourished his contempt for music. The flute, particularly, is the sign of the underdog. The feeble Felix Nixon in *Sketches by Boz* plays the flute. So does the lowly schoolmaster Mr. Mell in *David Copperfield*, and Jack Redburn, another failure with a heart of gold, in *Master Humphrey's Clock*. In *No Thoroughfare*, the clerk, Mr. Jarvis, executes a duet on the flute alongside 'an odd man with a violin'. Dick Swiveller plays a flute mournfully in bed in *The Old Curiosity Shop*, and a miserable, shoeless personage arrested for playing the flute features among the victims of Mr. Fang the magistrate in *Oliver Twist*. Of these seedy flautists, Mr. Mell perhaps derives from the humble usher whom Dickens remembers at his own school:

He was rather musical, and on some remote quarter-day had bought an old trombone; but a bit of it was lost, and it made the most extraordinary sounds when he sometimes tried to play it of an evening . . . Poor fellow!

This was Mr. Taylor, English master at the Wellington House Classical and Commercial Academy, and in real life his instrument was apparently the flute not the trombone. The downtrodden Frederick Dorrit plays the clarinet in a small theatre orchestra. So improbable is it, apparently, for a performer on a wind instrument to be dishonest that when David Copperfield's thieving page is taken to Bow Street we're specifically told he doesn't know how to play the second-hand fife found on his person, and Bradley Headstone, though he has learnt to 'blow various wind instruments', does so only 'mechanically'. Another kindly backnumber, Mr. Morfin in *Dombey*, plays the 'cello, and Miss Tox, the pathetic spinster, plays the harpsichord. Tom Pinch, an inveterate loser, is an organist. The shabby neighbourhood called Golden Square where Ralph Nickleby lives shelters 'two or three violins and a wind instrument from the opera' and:

the notes of pianos and harps float in the evening time round the head of the mournful statue, the guardian genius of a little wilderness of shrubs in the centre of the square.

Dickens' musicians, in fact, are a moth-eaten lot and they make a melancholy noise. The exceptions are Rosa Dartle on the harp and John Jasper the cathedral organist, both of whom play better than average and are positively evil.

Umbrellas as well as musical instruments deserve a place among Dickens' symbolic fixtures. Elaborately undignified, they immediately locate their owner in the lower class. Silas Wegg has one which looks, when furled, 'like an unwholesomely-forced lettuce', and the simile is picked up when Mrs. Gamp's friend Betsey Prig produces from her pocket a lettuce 'of such magnificent proportions that', says Dickens, 'she was obliged to shut it up like an umbrella before she could pull it out.' An 'old Frenchman with an umbrella like a faded tropical leaf' is among the odd types Dickens meets in Naples. Mrs. Gamp's umbrella, responsible for immortalizing her name in the English language, is a vast affair, 'in colour like a faded leaf, except where a circular patch of lively blue had been dexterously let in at the top', and Mrs. Bagnet in *Bleak House* carries a similar flabby article which she uses as a carpet-bag on journeys. Having both an umbrella and a husband who plays the bassoon, Mrs. Bagnet is doubly disadvantaged socially. Miss Mowcher's umbrella in *David Copperfield* completely shrouds its dwarfish owner from view, and goes bobbing down the street 'like an immense bird'. Even the smell of umbrellas seems to have had a special quality for Dickens. The prison at New York smelled, he thought, 'like a thousand mildewed umbrellas', and when Pecksniff collides with Tigg in the dark he finds himself 'collared by something which smelt like several damp umbrellas'.

Grindstones, too, have a peculiar imaginative value, sinister and violent. (*The Grindstone* appears among possible novel-titles in Dickens' memo book.) In *Barnaby Rudge* Simon Tappertit, furious with jealousy, sets about grinding up all the tools in his master's workshop, and the terrible grindstone on which the revolutionaries sharpen their weapons in *A Tale of Two Cities* is a focus for fantastic energies. The men who turn it have faces of hideous cruelty, covered in blood, with false eyebrows and false moustaches stuck on them, awry with howling. The crowd fighting to get its hatchets, knives and bayonets sharpened, includes men dressed in women's lace and silks and ribbons, drenched in blood. Mr. Jarvis Lorry watches this spectacular grindstone from the safety of Tellson's Bank which has orange-trees in its courtyard and a whitewashed Cupid – suggesting dispassionate respectability – on the ceiling. (Compare the ill-matched Dombeys' dining-table 'whereon frosted Cupids offered scentless flowers' – 'allegorical to see', says Dickens.) Another clerkly figure shut off from the rough men who use the grindstone is Clennam in *Little Dorrit*. In his glass-screened counting-house at Doyce's factory, he is secluded from the big grindstone in the outer yard and from the workshop machines, geared to a steam-engine, which tear round, we're told, 'as though they had a suicidal mission to grind the business to dust'. Dickens, then, relates people to objects, and gives people objects which immediately colour them – flutes, umbrellas, grindstones. The process is congenial to his imagination, since viewing people as objects is one of his main occupations.

But the sort of symbolism that issues in protracted allegories has no place in Dickens – or not when he's writing well. Critics devoted to extracting these from the novels seldom conclude with anything but catchwords and platitudes. The insight, for instance, which Mr. Daleski offers as the fruit of his investigation of *Martin Chuzzlewit* is that 'Business precepts corrupt moral values.' Why should one read a novel, to enter into possession of something so trite? Likewise, when Edmund Wilson tells us that the coal pit into which Stephen Blackpool tumbles is a symbol for 'the industrial system', we can only reply that, if it were, it would be sadly unequal to the complexity of what it symbolized. Perhaps Dr. Lucas has stretched credulity farthest in this direction by asking us to accept the vivacious Quilp as an 'emblem of business affairs'. Symbolism, by its nature, blurs objects into abstractions, whereas imagination is sharp-edged – Dickens' imagination, anyway. He fills his novels with objects that vividly loom – locks, graveyards, cages – intensely themselves, not signs for something else.

Apart from this, simile not symbolism is his strength. His similes, however fantastic, have the power of conveying instant visual truth. Writing of a visit to his old school, for instance, he relates that a railway line has pared off one corner, so that the house faces 'profile-wise towards the road, like a forlorn flat-iron without a handle, standing on end'. The lopped appearance comes across as blankly as in Tennyson's 'Half of the gold stack stared over the pales in the yard' (and without the copybook assonance). Or Dickens meets a flock of sheep in a gale, 'with the wool about their necks blown into such great ruffs that they looked like fleecy owls'. Or, travelling by train in the States, he observes that passengers in front, engaged in the national pastime of expectoration, cause incessant flashes of saliva past his window, 'as though they were ripping open feather beds', while the floor 'looks as if it were paved with open oysters'. Through simile, too, his violent imagination can thrust unguessed energies into the most somnolent of objects – ledgers, for instance. In *Martin Chuzzlewit* they have 'red backs, like strong cricket-balls beaten flat'. The exuberance of the similes is equalled only by their precision. 'It is my infirmity', wrote Dickens, 'to fancy or perceive relations in things which are not apparent generally.' The infirmity indispensable to poets. His similes remake the world – his similes, and the symbols that work through similitude, like Volumnia Dedlock's chandelier or Miss Wade's garden.

6

DICKENS' CHILDREN

Reminiscing about his childhood in Rochester Dickens relates how he was frequently taken by his nurse, who evidently had a large circle of married acquaintances, to visit ladies who were in various stages of parturition.

At one little green-grocer's shop, down certain steps from the street, I remember to have waited on a lady who had had four children (I am afraid to write five, though I fully believe it was five) at a birth. This meritorious woman held quite a reception in her room on the morning when I was introduced there, and . . . the four (five) deceased young people lay, side by side, on a clean cloth on a chest of drawers; reminding me by a homely association, which I suspect their complexion to have assisted, of pig's feet as they are usually displayed at a neat tripe shop.

Hot caudle is handed round, and a subscription is got up among those present on behalf of the bereaved mother. Young Dickens remembers with alarm that he has pocket money on his person, and that this fact is known to his nurse. Sure enough he is earnestly exhorted to contribute, but declines, much to the disgust of the company, who warn him that he will not go to Heaven.

We think of Dickens as a manufacturer of model children, pious little monsters, moribund and adult. In this context the Rochester scene is refreshing. The caustic view of adult company, the imperturbable attitude to death, the heartless, graphic image of pig's feet, the resolute meanness over money on such an occasion, conspire to remind us how unlike human beings children are. Dickens' manufactured children, by contrast, gratify the ideals of the adult reader. So far as the novels are concerned, most of the pieces of real childhood Dickens was able to remember turn up in *David Copperfield* and *Great Expectations*. The extreme tenderness of a child's skin, plus the fact that he is always being handled by gigantic anthropoids, makes him discriminate between people by touch as much as by sight. David Copperfield has a hard and a soft handler in Peggotty and his mother, and retains an impression, he says, 'of the touch of Peggotty's forefinger, as she used to hold it out to me, and of its being roughened by needlework, like a pocket nutmeg grater'. The nutmeg-grater recurs in Pip's description of Mrs. Joe, his sister:

Mrs. Joe . . . had such a prevailing redness of skin, that I sometimes used to wonder whether it was possible she washed herself with a nutmeg-grater instead of soap. She was tall and bony, and almost always wore a coarse apron, fastened over her figure behind with two loops, and having a square impregnable bib in front, that was stuck full of pins and needles.

Mrs. Joe is catalogued by the child as an uncomfortable texture, a kind of biped hedgehog, rather than an appearance. So is Miss Murdstone by little David Copperfield. He notices her 'hard black boxes' when she arrives, with her initials on the lids in 'hard brass nails'. She pays the coachman from a 'hard steel purse' which 'shuts up like a bite', and the child notes the heaviness of the chain which connects her handbag to her arm. He can relate Miss Murdstone to nothing in his experience of female texture. 'I had never', he says, 'seen such a metallic lady.' Similarly the purse Peggotty gives him when he goes off to school is described as 'a stiff, leather purse, with a snap' – experienced through the fingers, not the eyes.

The child's sense of smell is also inordinately sensitive, and having his nose two or three times nearer the ground than an adult he takes in the smells of floor coverings, plants and furniture much more readily. Dickens says that he never forgot the smell of the damp straw on the floor of the stage-coach in which he was sent, as a child, from Rochester to London. To David Copperfield Peggotty's store-room is a dark and frightening doorway out of which issues 'the smell of soap, pickles, pepper, candles, and coffee, all at one whiff', and the Salem House schoolroom has a smell 'like mildewed corduroys, sweet apples wanting air, and rotten books'. 'A breathless smell of warm black crape' permeates Mr. Omer's undertaking establishment, as David recollects, and on the morning of his mother's funeral the parlour is suffused with 'the faint, sweet smell of cake, the odour of Miss Murdstone's dress, and our black clothes'. The smell of cement used on blacking corks during his days in the warehouse stayed with Dickens so long that as a grown man he would always cross over when going down the Strand towards Warren's in order to avoid it, and the smell of hat-making, 'encountered anywhere or under any circumstances' always recalled the little shops in the Blackfriars Road where he used to loiter on his way home from Warren's at night. Smell is often a factor in the child's first observation of a difference between the sexes, particularly as adults tend to hug the child to their clothes or bend down close to talk to him, giving him ample opportunity to smell their breath. Sartre, in his reminiscences of childhood, lists among his pleasures:

kissing my mother's soft, scented skin; but I attached greater value to the complex, studious pleasures which I experienced in the company of grown men: the repulsion with which they filled me was part of their glamour: I confused disgust with seriousness. I was a snob. When Monsieur Barrault leant over me, his breath caused me delicious agony, and I eagerly inhaled the unpleasant odour of his virtues.

Dickens is never as good on sex-smells as this. Perhaps he thought them indecorous. Pip smells the scented soap on Mr. Jaggers' hands, but when Mr. Murdstone lifts David Copperfield up David doesn't say he smelt him, as he surely must have. Instead another adult curiosity catches his attention – hair growing out of Mr. Murdstone's face:

His hair and whiskers were blacker and thicker, looked at so near, than ever I had given them credit for being. A squareness about the lower part of his face, and the dotted indication of the strong black beard he shaved close every day, reminded me of a wax-work that had travelled into our neighbourhood some half-a-year before.

When Jaggers peers at Pip, Pip similarly observes the 'strong black dots' left by his shaving. Getting so close a look at the black vestiges of a man's bristles is the kind of ordeal a child is subjected to. From its vantage point on the ground, too, it is vouchsafed strange glimpses of bits of the human being generally overlooked. Dickens remembers how at church he used to look up the preacher's outstretched coat-sleeve 'as if it were a telescope with the stopper on'. The size of adults, the vast articles of clothing they require to cover themselves, and the metal curiosities with which they decorate their bodies – watches, rings, spectacles – lead the child to confuse them with inanimate objects. David Copperfield notices opposite him in the coach 'an elderly lady in a great fur cloak, who looked in the dark more like a haystack than a lady'. Florence Dombey's idea of her father is a 'blue coat and stiff white cravat . . . with a pair of creaking boots and a very loud ticking watch'. Though watchless, the convict on the marshes also sounds like a clock to Pip: 'Something clicked in his throat as if he had works in him like a clock, and was going to strike.'

It is particularly difficult for the child to rule watches and clocks out of the list of animate creatures. Paul Dombey is aware that the great clock in Dr. Blimber's hall goes on repeating the Doctor's stately welcome, 'How is my little friend?' When workmen come to repair it, the face is taken off, and leans against the wall all askew, ogling Paul. The mix-up between clocks and people, though Dickens links it with childhood in these instances, stays on, like most of his childish perceptions, as a regular imaginative habit in his writing. A man's relationship with a timepiece, which appears to smile and talk to him, forms the basis of *Master Humphrey's Clock*. Todger's boarding house has a gigantic clock with a coronet of three brass balls on its head, which stands in a dark corner of the staircase heavily ticking to warn people not to run into it. 'Bilious-faced clocks, supported on sickly white crutches, with their pendulums dangling like lame legs', feature at the annual auction of china-goods in 'Our English Watering-Place'. Conversely when Anthony Chuzzlewit has a stroke, and grunts painfully on the floor, Jonas, who has not noticed his father's plight, remarks, 'Something wrong in the clock, I suppose.'

The child's mind incompletely distinguishes people from their clocks and watches and clothes, then, and it associates them closely with the animals they own. David Copperfield, coming home to find his new stepfather Murdstone in command, wanders down for comfort to the old dog kennel in the yard:

I very soon started back from there, for the empty dog kennel was filled up with a great dog – deep-mouthed and black-haired like Him – and he was very angry at the sight of me, and sprang out to get at me.

This childish instinct is carried over into Dickens' normal imaginative vision too. Carker, for instance, the villain with the gleaming teeth, rides a white-legged horse – as if some of the master's whiteness had spilled over onto the mount.

As, for the child, the adult's being can stretch into his accoutrements and beasts, so it can pervade the atmosphere. The child's apprehension and his sharpened senses alone will tell him when the adult he dreads is close by. David, going up to bed, feels the Murdstones coming into the house like 'a cold blast of air'. Adults might find it hard to believe that they are accompanied by personal climates. But young David's conviction is supported by Dickens in other novels. Scrooge 'carried his own low temperature always about with him; he iced his office in the dog-days, and didn't thaw it one degree at Christmas.' Mrs. Pardiggle, in *Bleak House*, 'seemed to come in like cold weather, and to make the little Pardiggles blue as they followed', and Mr. Vholes rides along on top of a stage-ocach, with his thin shadow 'passing over all the sunny landscape . . . chilling the seed in the ground as it glided along'. Mr. Dombey has an even more unfortunate effect on agriculture. 'As cold and hard as the weather', he has only to look out of the window for the leaves on the trees outside to come 'fluttering down, as if he blighted them'. The deathly aura these characters possess perhaps connects with magical ideas about the potency of breath. One of Uriah Heep's more gratuitous nastinesses is breathing into a pony's nostrils, 'and immediately covering them with his hand, as if he were putting some spell upon him'. And with the impure Carker's 'daily breath', it is suggested, 'there issues forth some subtle portion of himself' which taints his books and furniture.

In these various ways the child's view of grown-ups is not just unflattering but alien, barbaric. The child's response to death also dismays adult sensibilities. Gorky, in his book *My Childhood*, recalls attending his father's funeral. Standing at the graveside he sees a lot of water and some frogs, two of which have succeeded in climbing onto the yellow coffin lid. When the gravediggers start to pile the earth in, the frogs jump off the coffin, and try to escape up the sides. However, they are thrown back by clods of earth. Coming away from the cemetery Gorky is reprimanded by his grandmother for not crying at his father's burial. In fact his mind is totally occupied with the frogs, and he proceeds to consult various acquaintances about their likely fate. The incident shows that little Gorky has not yet mastered the strange adult theory that human life is more important than other forms. It also shows his hostility to mourning. He is disgusted by his mother's grief, since she is usually neat, and grief makes her look unpleasantly swollen and dishevelled. It seems to him that she is being perverse, deliberately destroying by her ugly howls of woe the clean, secure image of her he depends on. As with Sartre, we feel that Gorky's resurrection of childhood is more accurate even than Dickens' best; but Dickens, in naturalistic moments, can also recapture the freakishness of the normal child's

opinion of death. Pip entertains the eccentric idea that the tomb-
stones which cover various members of his family have a close
resemblance to their owners. His mother's tombstone has spindly,
italic script, and from this he deduces that she was 'freckled and
sickly'. Beside her stone are 'five little stone lozenges' marking five
brothers of Pip's who, as he puts it, 'gave up trying to get a living
exceedingly early in that universal struggle'. To the shape of these
lozenges Pip is indebted for a belief that his brothers had all been
born and died with their hands in their trouser pockets. The weird,
emotionless curiosity with which Pip contemplates the family
resting-place is instantly credible. Contrast it with the behaviour, in
a parallel situation, of one of Dickens' plastic children. This occurs in
The Old Curiosity Shop, when Nell wanders into a churchyard.

Some young children sported among the tombs, and hid from each other,
with laughing faces. They had an infant with them, and had laid it down
asleep upon a child's grave, in a little bed of leaves. It was a new grave –
the resting place, perhaps, of some little creature, who, meek and patient
in its illness, had often sat and watched them; and now seemed to their
minds scarcely changed.
She drew near and asked one of them whose grave it was. The child
answered that that was not its name; it was a garden – his brother's. It
was greener, he said, than all the other gardens, and the birds loved it
better because he had been used to feed them. When he had done speaking,
he looked at her with a smile, and kneeling down and nestling for a
moment with his cheek against the turf, bounded merrily away.

It is evident that something has horribly corroded Dickens' intelli-
gence here. Partly, no doubt, we may put it down to the influence of
Wordsworth's foolish verses in *Lyrical Ballads* entitled 'We Are
Seven', which Dickens is known to have admired. But the trouble
lies deeper. Dickens is pretending that children are small adults.
Their thoughts, he makes out, are like those of adults, only purer.
They still believe the things which adults would find it comforting
to believe, if only they could bring themselves to be fatuous enough.
Such plastic children bring tears to the grown-up eye, because they
represent an innocence which the grown-up wrongly imagines he
once possessed himself. Tears of this kind are especially enjoyable
because they are tears of self-pity without seeming to be so. To the
shedder they appear magnanimous. Fictional children thus constructed are purely an adult amenity. Being small but adult they are
strictly dwarfs – antiseptic, expurgated dwarfs, purged of all the
features which make child psychology offensive to the adult mind.

We recall Dickens' affection for dwarfs like Little Dorrit, who has a child's body but is really a woman. As dwarfs, they have close affinities with the modern garden gnome. The gnome has no psychology at all, so can be a perfectly trouble-free recipient of an adult's love. Like Dickens' plastic children, the gnome is a cheery, middle-class version of an alien and menacing species of being – the race of deities, who used to be worshipped in churches, but are now stuck in gardens, as they were before churches were thought of.

The child's reaction to an adult's death frequently seems monstrous to an adult. To re-establish our faith in Dickens after the Little Nell encounter, we should remember what David Copperfield feels when he receives news of his mother's death:

I am sensible of having felt that a dignity attached to me among the rest of the boys, and that I was important in my affliction . . . I remember that this importance was a kind of satisfaction to me, when I walked in the playground that afternoon while the boys were in school. When I saw them glancing at me out of the windows, as they went up to their classes, I felt distinguished, and looked more melancholy, and walked slower. When school was over, and they came out and spoke to me, I felt it rather good in myself not to be proud of any of them, and to take exactly the same notice of them all, as before.

We acknowledge that this is keenly imagined, because it is faithful to the human child's desperate selfishness and its hunger for prestige. In the battle for recognition the child naturally turns a bereavement to account. A Dickensian dwarf would never entertain such disgraceful notions. Feeling no grief himself, the child is in an advantageous position for detecting the falsity in adult displays of grief. He smiles maliciously at funerals. Dickens, in *The Uncommercial Traveller*, recalls his first funeral, which he attended when he was 7 or 8. He thought it absurd that they should be there consuming sherry and plum cake, and that the undertaker should hand round black gloves on a tea-tray as if they were muffins. He felt they all looked ridiculous in their black cloaks. His own was too long, and he kept disarranging the procession by tripping up the people behind him with it, and by falling onto the people in front because he was blinded by his handkerchief, which he had been instructed to hold before his eyes as an indication that his feelings had overcome him. He was astonished to see grown-up people chewing their plum cake mournfully and trying to keep in step with the undertaker. 'I felt', he recalls, 'that we were all making game.'

It never occurred to little Dickens that the ceremony he was attending had a religious significance. This leads us to another discrepancy between his natural children and his dwarfs. His natural children are utterly unstirred by religion. Dickens recalls how he used to be carried off to religious services as a child, and how their effect was to induce gradual unconsciousness.

I felt the fatal sleep stealing, stealing over me, and . . . I gradually heard the orator in possession, spinning and humming like a great top, until he rolled, collapsed, and tumbled over, and I discovered to my burning shame and fear, that as to that last stage it was not he, but I.

Similarly when Pip goes to the Wopsle school, the only thing that intrigues him about the Bibles which are handed out is the iron-mould with which they are speckled all over, and the 'various specimens of the insect world smashed between their leaves'. The unlikely tales with which religion cheers its followers are received with incredulity or terror by the normal child. Little David Copper-field remembers how one Sunday night his mother read to him about Lazarus being raised from the dead, and he was so frightened that they had to take him to the bedroom window and show him the churchyard where his father's grave was, to reassure him that there was nothing sticking out of the ground. Even so, the horrible story lingers in his mind, and when Peggotty comes to tell him 'Master Davy . . . You have got a Pa!', meaning that his mother has married again, he trembles and turns white. 'Something . . . connected with the grave in the churchyard, and the raising of the dead, seemed to strike me like an unwholesome wind.' Like Dickens, little David is so bored by church services that after desperately trying to amuse himself by reading monumental tablets and making faces at a boy in the aisle, he goes to sleep and falls off his pew with a crash.

The dwarfs, on the other hand, are all convinced Christians, as their dying speeches proclaim. Lucie Manette's little boy dies with its golden hair carefully arranged in a halo on the pillow, and politely explains: 'Dear papa and mamma, I am very sorry to leave you both; and to leave my pretty sister; but I am called, and I must go!' Little Dick in *Oliver Twist* also feels that he is bound for a better place, he dreams so much, he says, 'of Heaven, and Angels'. Dickens was quite ready to wring sympathy from his readers by pretending that he had been just such a dwarf himself when young. In one of his Christmas stories he casts himself as a seraphic tot mulling over

favourite biblical stories in bed – among them the raising of Lazarus·
David Copperfield's reaction is instantly the more credible, but
plainly it was important to the Victorians to believe that God still
showed Himself to someone, and children, with their legendary
purity, seemed the obvious candidates. The seventeenth century
would have found this odd, since then faith was still connected with
the intellect, and a child's mind could not be expected to grasp the
truths of religion. Milton, like many others, believed children unfit
for baptism on this account. But as theology became discredited,
and the intellect drained out of Christianity, it came to be felt that
those with least brain were best able to cope with it. Here was a ready
opening for Dickens' dwarfs. They could reassure the worried adult
with glimpses of eternity. Paul Dombey, a thoroughgoing dwarf,
has a sort of mystic vision just before he expires, in which his dead
mother and the print of Christ on the wall at school both figure.
Folding his hands in prayer, he remarks to his sister:

Mama is like you, Floy. I know her by her face! But tell them that the
print upon the stairs at school is not divine enough. The light about the
head is shining on me as I go!

The tears to which Dickens reduced his grown-up readers by these
means were in some measure tears of relief, for the dying dwarf had
given them something with which to bolster their century's waning
faith in immortality. Little Nell, similarly, hears beautiful music in
the air before she dies, and Dickens says firmly over her serene
corpse, 'So shall we know the angels in their majesty, after death.'
Many of his readers broke down when they came to the passage.
Lord Jeffrey was found with his head on his library table, weeping.
Daniel O'Connell, the Irish M.P., burst into tears and threw the
volume, in anguish, out of the window of the train in which he was
travelling. Such scenes became part of the established Dickens
appeal, and Dickens himself was as much affected as any. He wrote
to Forster that he had had a 'real good cry' over the ending of *The
Chimes*. When Forster read this story to one of the staff of *Punch*, he
told Dickens that the man 'cried so much and so painfully' that he
did not know whether to go on or stop. Dickens' own rendering of
the tale was no less successful. 'If you could have seen Macready
last night,' he wrote to his wife, 'undisguisedly sobbing, and crying
on the sofa as I read, you would have felt, as I did, what a thing it is
to have power.'

The assimilation of Nell to an angel is meant literally, and this is another way in which the Dickensian dwarfs offer a debased religion to their customers. We are given to understand that they actually become angels after death. 'They say that you will be an Angel, before the birds sing again,' a child considerately informs Nell; and Lucie Manette's little boy departs from life with a rustle of angel's wings. This, too, would have seemed preposterous to Milton or Donne. For the seventeenth century the angels were all created long before the first man, and immensely excelled man in power and intellect. They were not remotely like a dead child. In *Paradise Lost* they wear armour and hurl mountains about. The deterioration of the angel is a further sign of Victorian religion ebbing into sentiment. The other myth about childhood which Nell fosters is that children are extremely attached to adults, particularly their relations. In this she contrasts with the naturalistic Pip, who has few qualms about deserting the Gargerys. But Nell's fidelity to her disgraceful grandfather is as sanctimonious as it is improbable. There are several references to *King Lear* in the novel, and we are evidently invited to regard Nell as an improved Victorian version of Cordelia, without Cordelia's regrettable impoliteness in the first Act. In an age without Social Security, when the elderly depended upon the strength of the family bond for their survival, Nell's unnatural concern about her grandfather's welfare would particularly endear her to the adult world. For parents with every intention of becoming a burden to their children, she is the ideal heroine. She is a dwarf who brings not only intimations of immortality but a superannuation scheme as well. Dickens was enchanted by her. The antics she performs to cheer her elderly companion are an indication of the effect his infatuation had on his writing.

When they rose up from the ground, and took the shady track which led them through the wood, she bounded on before, printing her tiny footsteps in the moss, which rose elastic from so light a pressure and gave it back as mirrors throw off breath; and thus she lured the old man on, with many a backward look and merry beck, now pointing stealthily to some lone bird as it perched and twittered on a branch that strayed across their path, now stopping to listen to the songs that broke the happy silence.

This sickly scene carries the usual indications that Dickens is becoming besotted. The prose breaks down into numerous monosyllables in order to signify the writer's childlike innocence. An air of antiquity, distantly biblical, is instilled by expressions like 'When they rose up from the ground'. Dickens' alarming gift of comic observation is hastily stuffed out of sight, and hackneyed charms like the elastic moss and the merry beck are imported to take its place. When in full possession of his faculties, Dickens could easily see through such stuff, and use it for comic purposes. His sardonic account of Mercy Pecksniff's winsome ways uses the same woodland material as the Little Nell passage, only here Dickens reckons on his reader perceiving what nonsense it is:

Oh, the gay simplicity of Mercy: so charming, innocent, and infant-like that if she had gone out walking by herself, and it had been a little earlier in the season, the robin redbreasts might have covered her with leaves against her will, believing her to be one of the sweet children in the wood, come out of it, and issuing forth once more to look for blackberries in the young freshness of her heart.

Nell's willingness to be exploited by her grandfather is the reverse of the natural pattern. It is natural for children to exploit adults. To this end they will do their best to gratify adult expectations. If, for example, they observe that an adult enjoys reading them childish stories, they will, if anything is to be gained by it, encourage this taste by acting the part of a delighted audience. If it is a common joke with the adults of a family that a child likes eating cake, say, he will stuff himself with cake, even when he doesn't want it, rather than lose his status as a popular entertainer. The more precocious a child is, the more adept he becomes at this hypocrisy. Naturally if the adults detect the falsity of the performance and complain, the child will be enraged, since it is only for their sake that he is putting it on. Sartre recalls how, as a child in the France of 1915, he was asked by a lady what his dearest wish was. After spending some time selecting the most acceptable wish, he replied 'To be a soldier and avenge the dead.' The lady was unkindly sceptical, his mother went pink, and little Sartre felt he would die of shame. Dickens, too, recollects his hypocrisy as a child. At church there was one preacher who made a point of addressing the infants in the congregation. 'At this present writing', says Dickens, 'I hear his lumbering jocularity (which never amused us, though we basely pretended that it did).' This trait passes into David Copperfield, who recollects the sadistic Creakle's jokes and the prompt amusement of his pupils: 'we laugh at it, – miserable little dogs, we laugh, with our visages as white as ashes, and our hearts sinking into our boots.' Pip, in deference to the fear-some Magwitch, develops an extreme politeness, calls him 'Sir', and elaborately refrains from mentioning his leg-iron. He reveals that he has seen another convict on the marshes:

'Dressed like you, you know, only without a hat,' I explained, trembling; 'and – and' – I was very anxious to put this delicately – 'and with – the same reason for wanting to borrow a file.'

The Dickensian dwarfs have none of this hypocritical ingenuity. They are there solely to comfort the adult, and it would be unpleasant for him to believe that they were hypocritical. Oliver Twist could not tell a lie. Paul Dombey, with his improbable enquiries about what the waves are saying, is improbable too in his studied discourtesy to adults. On his first day at Mrs. Pipchin's school he announces to her that her house is 'a very nasty one'. Sitting by the fire watching her, he is asked what he is thinking of.

'I'm thinking how old you must be,' said Paul.
'You musn't say such things as that, young gentleman,' returned the dame. 'That'll never do.'
'Why not?' asked Paul.
'Because it's not polite,' said Mrs. Pipchin, snappishly.
'Not polite?' said Paul.
'No.'
'It's not polite', said Paul innocently, 'to eat all the mutton-chops and toast, Wickam says.'
'Wickam', retorted Mrs. Pipchin, colouring, 'is a wicked, impudent, bold-faced hussy.'
'What's that?' inquired Paul.
'Never you mind, Sir,' retorted Mrs. Pipchin, 'Remember the story of the little boy that was gored to death by a mad bull for asking questions.'
'If the bull was mad,' said Paul, 'how did *he* know that the boy had asked questions?'

It would take a mentally subnormal child to make these retorts 'innocently', as Dickens claims Paul made them. Yet Paul is supposed to be exceptionally intelligent, as his response to Mrs. Pipchin's bull story shows. Very little observation of the adult world is needed to inform a child that it is not innocent to carry back to adults in authority servants' criticisms of them. The word 'innocently' stamps Paul as a dwarf, not a child, at once. A pert, amusing dwarf, whose function is to regale the adult with his rude replies to a person who is, after all, only a schoolmistress hired by his father, and therefore a suitable laughing stock. Dwarfs of Paul Dombey's calibre wouldn't dream of laughing obediently at a preacher's or schoolmaster's jokes. A real child – David Copperfield or Pip or little Dickens for that matter – would have had the sense to invent a sycophantic reply to Mrs. Pipchin, even if he *had* been thinking how old she was. And he would have understood that Wickam's dietary observations were not for Mrs. Pipchin's ears. Dickens, of course, had encountered Mrs. Pipchin. She was the lady he lodged with as a boy in Little College Street, Camden Town. 'I hope you will like Mrs. Pipchin's establishment,' he wrote to Forster:

It is from the life, and I was there – I don't suppose I was eight years old; but I remember it all as well, and certainly understood it as well, as I do now. We should be devilish sharp in what we do to children.

To make Paul answer 'innocently', as one who does not comprehend adult proprieties, involves a suppression of Dickens' real experience of childish shrewdness.

Dickens has other brands of comic child besides Paul. Lower-class children are laughed at quite openly and warm-heartedly for their old clothes and deformed bodies. When Mr. and Mrs. Boffin in *Our Mutual Friend* visit Betty Higden's cottage, with the intention of adopting a child, they find a boy called Sloppy turning the mangle. Sloppy is grotesquely shaped: he has a very little head and a huge mouth, and his body is too long, too thin and too full of sharp angles; his clothes seem to be covered in buttons, and they make his wrists and ankles unduly prominent. He stares and grins in what Dickens presents as a comic fashion. On the other hand, he works hard, and is apparently intelligent. 'Sloppy is a beautiful reader of a newspaper,' testifies Betty Higden, 'He do the Police in different voices.' Also in the cottage is a pretty child with blue eyes and dimpled hands called Johnny, who is naturally selected for adoption. Before long, however, Johnny is taken to hospital and dies, having first made the customary speech about God to one of the nurses. It now occurs to Mrs. Boffin that they should adopt Sloppy instead. Accordingly she tells Sloppy he'll always be taken care of, provided that he's 'industrious and deserving'. The proviso is significant. Sloppy is taken on as an employee, rather than a son. Because he is a misshapen, lower-class, Dickensian comic, he is not fit to be properly adopted. Admittedly, he is also older than Johnny. But a decent Dickensian dwarf like Oliver Twist would be fit to adopt at any age. Sloppy forfeits his right to be treated as a human being, because he is there to make adults laugh and feel generous.

Healthy, happy children of the lower orders regularly bring a
smile to Dickens' prose as well. Being juveniles and social inferiors
they obviously invite harmless merriment. Consider, for instance,
Dickens' account of Mr. Toodle the railway stoker at tea in *Dombey
and Son*:

> In satisfying himself . . . Mr. Toodle was not regardless of the younger
> branches around him, who, although they had made their own evening
> repast, were on the look-out for irregular morsels, as possessing a relish.
> These he distributed now and then to the expectant circle, by holding out
> great wedges of bread and butter, to be bitten at by the family in lawful
> succession, and by serving out small doses of tea in like manner with a
> spoon; which snacks had such a relish in the mouths of these young
> Toodles, that, after partaking of the same, they performed private dances
> of ecstasy among themselves, and stood on one leg apiece, and hopped,
> and indulged in other saltatory tokens of gladness.

Dickens makes the children seem funny by talking of them in words
of several syllables. It is the prose equivalent of the fixed smile
which some adults assume when addressing children. The purpose
is to register adult superiority from the outset, under the guise of
being ingratiating. Once this is established, almost anything the
children do will seem endearing, because it will be seen through a
determined adult smile. Pet animals are often spoken to in the same
vein. It shows that the adult has stopped crediting the animal with
its animal nature. It has become a dumb child, in fur. Either way,
with child or animal, the result is that the adult is able to ooze his
surplus benignity over the creature, and dominate it, without
bothering about its real nature. Dickens' tone in the passage would
be as appropriate to any species of cuddly animal as it is to the young
Toodles. By chance we can compare his treatment with a realistic
account of almost the same scene. Emile Zola, in *Germinal*, tells the
story of a coal-mining community in mid-nineteenth-century
France. The miners and their families live on the threshold of
starvation, ignorant and oppressed. Maheu, father of the central
family, comes home one day to find that there is brawn for tea:

> He drank off a glass of water, and then fell to on the brawn. He cut off
> square chunks, spiked them on the end of his knife, and ate them on his
> bread, without a fork. Nobody talked while their father was eating . . .
> But the smell of the meat made Lenore and Henri look up from their game
> of guiding the spilt bath-water into little streams. They both came and
> took up their positions by their father, the little boy in front. They
> followed each piece with their eyes, full of hope as it left the plate, but of

consternation as it disappeared into his mouth. At length he noticed how
their faces grew pale and their lips moist with ravenous desire.

'Have the children had any?' he asked.

And as his wife hesitated, he went on:

'You know, I hate this unfairness. It takes my appetite away to see them
hanging round begging for scraps.'

At this the mother says that of course the children have had some
brawn, and gets one of the more obedient ones to back her up in the
lie. She turns on the others and tells them that all they do is cost
money, while their father works for it. Nevertheless Maheu takes the
two hungry children on his knee and shares out the brawn with them.

We are not allowed to survey Zola's scene from a serene distance.
There are no bantering Dickensian circumlocutions. Unlike
Dickens, Zola does not hide the children's greed under a mulch of
sentiment. Its symptoms are starkly recorded, though in fact Zola's
children are less greedy than Dickens' because they haven't had any
tea of their own. But though Zola's family is less prosperous, its
members are accorded the dignity of human beings. Though
destitute and ravenous, the children are less like animals than
Dickens' children, not more. Zola's style is simpler, yet it does more
justice to the complexity of the situation. To convey the involved
frictions within a family, as Zola does here, would have been beyond
Dickens' powers. His family frictions are straightforward panto-
mime affairs, featuring henpecked husbands or termagant wives.
Besides, he would not have considered that a family at this level of
society deserved such complicated treatment. Essentially Dickens'
passage is more carelessly written, for all its stylistic elaboration.
The antics of the Toodle children are not deliberately chosen – it
doesn't matter whether they dance or hop. Nor is the Toodle food of
particular significance – it just happens to be bread and butter
because that sounds likely at tea time. What a railway stoker coming
off duty would need and get to eat, is no concern of Dickens. But
Zola selects his children's game – guiding their father's spilt bath-
water into little streams – for a reason. He wants to draw attention
to the cramped housing conditions his miners have to endure. He
selects the brawn with distinct motive too. In fact brawn is better than
Maheu's usual fare: he realizes as soon as he tastes it that it isn't the
normal potted meat. The reader, unlike Maheu, has seen his wife
buying the brawn with five francs borrowed from the village shop-
keeper, who only made the loan because he has his eye on the

couple's young daughter. The miners' diet and their victimization by middle men are vital issues in Zola's book. Toodle and his children are fair representatives of Dickens because, despite the semblance of social protest in his novels, he designs to diffuse a genial and complacent air. The nice people, we can be sure, will always have enough money by the end. Zola, on the other hand, intends to be disagreeable.

The Toodle children are dwarfs, then, no less than Paul Dombey, though of a different kind. They represent the gay and he the solemn dwarf. Their purpose is to solace adults with a myth of gleeful childhood. Being the offspring of a railway stoker, they bring political comfort to the adult too. While the workers have such contented children, the middle classes may sleep safely in their beds.

Dickens produces dwarfs because he stops remembering what it was like to be a child. In his theories about education we can detect the same breakdown of memory. While reminiscing about his own childhood he never loses sight of the fact that children rightly consider education a boring irrelevance. He recalls how he was taken, as a birthday treat, to see a machine which demonstrated the motions of the heavenly bodies, and had been assembled in a local theatre. Olympia Squires, a small girl with whom he was in love at the time, was also of the party. They sat in the dark, and the planets and stars revolved with increasing tedium, while a gentleman with a wand explained them – tapping away at the heavenly bodies, Dickens remembers, 'like a wearisome woodpecker'. Both children fell asleep. Elsewhere Dickens relates that at school he consorted with the idlers and dunces, and refrained from asking the masters questions for fear of bringing down upon himself 'a cold shower-bath of explanations and experiments'. When in this mood Dickens stresses the absurdity of teaching children facts; all a child needs is to have its imagination stimulated by the *Arabian Nights* and, at a later age, by the novels of Fielding and Smollett – this being virtually the extent of his own education. Hence the schoolmasters M'Choakumchild in *Hard Times* and Bradley Headstone in *Our Mutual Friend* are denounced both for learning things themselves and for believing children should learn things.

But when Dickens visits schools for indigent children, these educational notions vanish in a flash. A child from the lower orders, it appears, should be gorged with facts, the aim of education being that it should raise its hand regularly during oral examination.

Dickens reports with pleasure that the pauper boys at the Boylston school in Boston 'answered correctly, without book, such questions as where was England; how far was it; what was its population; its capital city; its form of government; and so forth'. Why the population of England should be of the remotest significance to a pauper boy in Boston, Dickens does not reveal. To Dickens these indigent children are not children at all, but dwarfs – miniature adults, to be stuffed with the strange information which adults value. Similarly when visiting the schools of the Stepney Pauper Union at Limehouse Dickens enthuses over the rapidity with which the boys produce geographical facts when questioned, and the answers to problems in mental arithmetic. In the same tone he applauds their smartness at performing military evolutions – marching, counter-marching, forming in line and square – their brisk broadsword exercises and their naval drill. Meanwhile the girls are learning, as Dickens puts it, to 'clean up everything about them in an orderly and skilful way'. No question of stimulating the imagination here. The classrooms of the Stepney Pauper Union schools bristle with raised right arms at each new query. 'Ever faithful to fact,' cheers Dickens. How, we wonder, can this be the same Dickens who poked fun so divertingly at M'Choakumchild's school in *Hard Times* for being ever faithful to fact? The answer is that in a novel it is harmless, indeed delightful, to pretend that poorer children's imaginations should be nurtured gently, like flowers. Middle-class readers will be charmed by the fiction. But in the real world Dickens knows as well as they do that underprivileged children must be turned into well-drilled obedient menials as rapidly as possible, so that they can be exploited. The less imagination they have, the better. Dickens announces triumphantly that the products of the Stepney Pauper Union schools are in great demand among the better class of customer. A naval captain has written to say 'Your little fellows are all that I can desire.' The colonel of a regiment writes, 'We want six more boys; they are excellent lads.' Employers of all kinds, says Dickens, cry out 'Give us drilled boys, for they are prompt, obedient, and punctual.' And the girls, he adds, 'make excellent domestic servants'. What more could be asked of education?

Dickens realized at an early age that he was different from lower-class children. When he was 12 his parents accepted a position for him at Warren's blacking warehouse, his job being to label pots of blacking. His fellow workers were low boys such as Bob Fagin, an orphan, who lived with his brother-in-law, a waterman, and Paul Green, whose father was a fireman at Drury Lane theatre, and whose sister did imps in the pantomimes. 'No words can express the secret agony of my soul as I sunk into this companionship,' writes Dickens. 'I worked, from morning to night with common men and boys.' He did not not confide to his fellow workers, however, his opinion of their companionship. 'I never said, to man or boy, how it was that I came to be there, or gave the least indication of being sorry that I was there.' A relative of his mother's worked in the counting-house, and this enabled Little Dickens to feel superior – 'upon a different footing from the rest', as he puts it. Besides, he remained uncontaminated by the other boys. 'My conduct and manners were different enough from theirs to place a space between us. They, and the men, always spoke of me as "the young gentleman".'

The boy who particularly befriended him was Bob Fagin. When Paul Green rebelled against the 'young-gentleman' usage, Fagin, more devotedly servile, settled him rapidly. When the young gentleman had stomach-ache, Fagin filled empty blacking bottles with water, and applied them to his side to ease the pain. Being bigger and older he insisted on escorting him home afterwards. This was a terrible embarrassment to Dickens, since his father was at the time in the Marshalsea Prison.

I was too proud to let him know about the prison, and after making several efforts to get rid of him, to all of which Bob Fagin in his goodness was deaf, shook hands with him on the steps of a house near Southwark Bridge on the Surrey side, making believe that I lived there. As a finishing piece of reality in case of his looking back, I knocked at the door, I recollect, and asked, when the woman opened it, if that was Mr. Robert Fagin's house.

It may seem an odd reward for such fidelity that the young gentleman should have turned Fagin into the villain of his first novel – the leering Jew, who corrupts small boys and is eventually hanged. But the reward is really quite logical. Paul Green's enmity was a proper acknowledgement of social distinction. But by daring to offer his friendship, Fagin had threatened to drag the young gentleman down to his own level. Nothing could be so unforgivable as kindness in such circumstances. Bob Fagin's good nature justly earned him a place among the leading criminals of English fiction.

The weeks in the blacking warehouse permanently wounded

Dickens' mind, and helped to make him a great novelist. His whole nature was, as he puts it, penetrated 'with grief and humiliation'. I often forget in my dreams', he writes, 'that I have a dear wife and children; even that I am a man; and wander desolately back to that time of my life.' Dilapidated buildings, riverside waste land, and counting-houses haunt his fiction. They were the components of his childhood nightmare as described in his autobiography and repeated, almost verbatim, in the account of David Copperfield's experience at Murdstone and Grindby's. The blacking warehouse was a 'crazy, tumble-down old house', Dickens recalls, with 'a wharf of its own, abutting on the water when the tide was in, and on the mud when the tide was out'. It had panelled rooms, discoloured with dirt and smoke, decaying floors, a rotten staircase, and it was alive with vermin. 'The old grey rats swarming down in the cellars, and the sound of their squeaking and scuffling coming up the stairs at all times, and the dirt and decay of the place, rise up visually before me, as if I were there again. The counting-house was on the first floor, looking over the coal barges and the river.'

That Oliver Twist remains so virtuously uncontaminated, and so well spoken, during his sojourn with the thieves, has aroused the incredulity of some critics. We should realize, though, that Dickens is simply reasserting, in this part of the novel, the distinction between himself and the low boys in the blacking warehouse. It is a hymn to the purity of the middle-class soul. Fagin's den is quite recognizably the blacking warehouse: it has the rotten staircase, the vermin, and the panelled walls, black with neglect and dust. Monks' hide-out, where he interviews the Bumbles, is a dilapidated riverside house as well, and so is the thieves' lair on Jacob's Island where Bill Sikes is eventually run to earth. Monks' place had been 'formerly used as a manufactory of some kind', Dickens writes, and previous to that as a dwelling house. It has rats, rotten piles, and seems about to sink into the muddy water. Jacob's Island, we are told, was a thriving place once; now there are crumbling warehouses and deserted dwellings with crazy wooden rooms threatening to fall into the mud. The hint of former prosperity in the panelled rooms of Warren's warehouse is retained. To the blacking factory, in one guise or another, the evil spirits of the novel naturally flock.

Dickens goes on writing this fragment of his autobiography in novel after novel. The bright, pure child in the mouldering house is an image to which his imagination constantly returns. But after

Oliver Twist the child is always a girl. The change is natural enough. Dickens found it easier to associate purity with the female than the male. Besides, the contrast between himself, delicate, sensitive, and 'unusually small for his age', and his coarse workmates at Warren's, is suggestive of a girl among men. David Copperfield's nickname with his schoolfellows was, we recall, 'Daisy'.

At all events, the house to which Kate Nickleby has to move after her father's death is clearly Warren's though its address is no longer 30, Hungerford Stairs, the Strand. An 'old dingy house in Thames Street', 'gloomy, and black', with 'a wharf behind, opening on the Thames', it looks out on a riverside waste land containing 'fragments of iron hoops' and 'staves of old casks'. It has panelled rooms, and it has been a warehouse with 'rats and mice' and piles of dusty merchandise. Kate Nickleby, with her delicate ways, provides, Dickens points out, a beautiful contrast to the gloomy building. The pure, beautiful girl surrounded by lumber is the image from which *The Old Curiosity Shop* grows, too. The narrator declares at the start that he is haunted by the idea of Nell in her grandfather's shop:

All that night, waking or in my sleep, the same thoughts recurred and the same images retained possession of my brain. I had ever before me the old dark murky rooms . . . the faces all awry, grinning from wood and stone – and the dust and rust and worm that lives in wood – and alone in the midst of all this lumber and decay and ugly age, the beautiful child in her gentle slumber, smiling through her light and sunny dreams.

Master Humphrey's Clock, the serial out of which *The Old Curiosity Shop* developed, began with a similar contrast. Master Humphrey, the figure Dickens chooses to speak through, lives in a gloomy house which was, years ago, the resort of gay and brilliant society. Now it is decayed and worm-eaten. It has panelled walls and dark stairs and dust and dullness everywhere. But when he hears his footsteps echoing in it, Master Humphrey likes to imagine, he says, 'the rustling of silk brocade, and the light step of some lovely girl'. Master Humphrey, an old, almost friendless man, has been a cripple from birth, and as a result felt cut off from other children when he was small. The odd choice of this fictional surrogate for a young, healthy, popular author suggests perhaps, Dickens' sense of his own blighted childhood, with its unmentionable horror of descent into the working class.

The next pure child in a decaying house is Florence Dombey. 'Florence lived alone in the great dreary house,' Dickens begins

Chapter 23, 'No magic dwelling-place in magic story, shut up in the heart of a thick wood, was ever more solitary and deserted to the fancy, than was her father's mansion in its grim reality.' As the chapter proceeds it is something of a surprise to the reader to find Mr. Dombey's house crumbling into spectacular ruin. The patterns fade on the carpets. Floorboards creak and shake. Keys rust in locks. Damp starts out on the walls. Mildew and mould lurk in closets, and trees of fungus grow in the cellars. Rats squeak and scuffle at night through the dark galleries they have mined behind the panelling. We are back in Warren's warehouse. The monstrous improbability of Mr. Dombey's dwelling, with a full complement of servants in residence, getting into such a state, is not supposed to strike us. Dickens is intent on pursuing his dream. Realism is irrelevant. So Mr. Dombey's house, in what we were earlier told was 'a dreadfully genteel street between Portland Place and Bryanstone Square' becomes Warren's Blacking, Fagin's Den, The Curiosity Shop, The Threatening Place; and Florence remains pure in the middle of it. 'Florence lived', Dickens assures us, 'in her wilderness of a home, within the circle of her innocent pursuits and thoughts, and nothing harmed her.' As if harm usually came to wealthy children living between Portland Place and Bryanstone Square.

Little Dorrit is another heroine who retains her purity in threatening places. Her experience in the Marshalsea is based on Dickens' own, and Dickens' father, like hers, esteemed himself superior to the other prisoners. We are told that Clennam thinks of Little Dorrit as 'removed from . . . the common and coarse things surrounding her'. 'Her youthful and ethereal appearance, her timid manner, the charm of her sensitive voice and eyes' result, Clennam finds, in a 'strong difference between herself and those about her'. Curiously Little Dorrit continues to be the unsullied child surrounded by decay even when her family and she have got out of prison and started on their continental travels. Just as it is hard to imagine how Mr. Dombey's servants could have let his house become so ruinous, so it must puzzle the literal-minded reader to find that the Dorrits, though apparently heirs to almost unlimited wealth, should regularly select such dreary accommodation for themselves when they go abroad. We glimpse Little Dorrit waking up on her journey through Italy in what is described as 'a humbled state-chamber in a dilapidated palace', and breakfasting in 'another painted chamber, damp-stained and of desolate proportions'. The house the Dorrits take in

Venice also seems a dismal choice. It has, we learn, 'a mouldering reception room, where the faded hangings, of a sad sea-green, had worn and withered until they looked as if they might have claimed kindred with the waifs of seaweed drifting under the windows'. The breakfast room is little better – 'a faded hall which', Dickens says, 'had once been sumptuous, but was now the prey of watery vapours and a settled melancholy'. From this strange holiday home Little Dorrit visits another pure heroine in reduced circumstances, Pet Gowan. Pet's house, with barred windows that make it look like 'a jail for criminal rats', is on a little 'desert island' surrounded by 'ditches' – a Venetian version of Jacob's Island from *Oliver Twist* – smelling of bilge water, where even the scaffolding that holds up the buildings has fallen into decay. The ramshackle Italian villas intrigued Dickens. *Pictures from Italy* contains rapt accounts of their rottenness. Into these waterside ruins with their traces of vanished grandeur, he places small pure females to represent, in some sense, the small, pure child he saw himself as in the mouldering, panelled house by the Thames. Indeed, at the start of *No Thoroughfare*, the river near Hungerford Stairs, distinguished by its coal barges, slimy wharf, rotting piles and rusty mooring rings, is specifically likened to the Adriatic at Venice.

The Lazy Tour of Two Idle Apprentices, too, contains a spectacularly mouldering mansion, deserted save for a hapless maid – innocent to the point of imbecility – and her guardian, who later marries and murders her (rounding off his disagreeable career by braining her admirer with a bill-hook). The dark, panelled rooms and their crazed bride, 'trailing herself along the floor . . . a white wreck of hair, and dress, and wild eyes', raise thoughts of Miss Havisham. Estella presents another variation on the girl in the ruin. She disparages Pip among the rotting splendours of Satis House, and he watches her walk like a vision over the 'wilderness of empty casks' in the dilapidated brewery. Estella, as pure and unapproachable in her ramshackle palace as the star which her name invokes, makes Pip feel a common, labouring boy. She reopens the wound. Dickens expresses again through Pip the humiliation he felt in the blacking warehouse: 'I worked, from morning to night, with common men and boys.' Seven years later – and only three years before his death – Dickens wrote a story called *George Silverman's Explanation* – a sketch for a novel, which he left in its compact form – and here the girl and the ruin occur for the last time. George Silverman is a pauper child. When his parents die, he is sent to live on a farm. A beautiful girl of his own age lives there too, and though he loves her he is terrified he will contaminate her with the fever which killed his parents. Accordingly he hides himself away in a ruined mansion which adjoins the farm, pretends not to hear when he is called, and watches the beautiful girl from the windows. The mansion has the familiar marks of Warren's warehouse about it: rotten floors, ruined oak panels, rats at the bottom of the broken staircase, desolation and decay.

Kate Nickleby, Florence Dombey and Amy Dorrit celebrated the purity of the middle-class soul. But in these last two versions of the girl and the ruin, Dickens returns to the shame of the middle-class labourer. He becomes again the humiliated boy, inhabits the ruin and gazes at the bright, privileged life he seems destined not to share.

7

DICKENS AND SEX

Dickens and sex is an unpromising subject. It is generally agreed that the biggest gap in his achievement consists in his failure to portray even once, with any kind of fullness or understanding, a normal sexual relationship. There is no one, in the whole of Dickens' massive output, who, to quote Angus Wilson, 'gives woman the true dignity of a whole body and a whole mind'. Some critics, of religious bent, have even found the sexlessness a recommendation. Mr. A. E. Dyson remarks of *David Copperfield*:

One continuing strand in the book is the thought that love can be independent of sex and is greater than sex; this strikes me as true, a genuine insight acknowledged in most ages, and unaccountably mislaid by our own, to its very great loss.

But is the love of David for Steerforth, we may ask, really 'independent of sex', except for the most innocent of readers? Isn't it that sex in *David Copperfield*, as in other of Dickens' novels, is not banished but driven underground, to emerge in perverted and inhibited forms? More sophisticated readers than Mr. Dyson have found that even so apparently blameless a figure in *David Copperfield* as Mr. Peggotty is positively obsessed with unmentionable sexual urges. Mrs. Leavis, for example, entertains the severest doubts about Mr. Peggotty's affection for his niece, Little Em'ly. 'While Mr. Peggotty', says Mrs. Leavis,

seems at first sight to offer the pattern of disinterested devotion to the winning child he had fostered, what emerges is a horribly possessive love that is expressed characteristically in heat, violence and fantasies, impressing us as maniacal.

If this seems to be going a little far, Mrs. Leavis can produce as evidence the obsessive dreams which Peggotty says he has, in which his niece repeatedly falls down at his feet, and he raises her up whispering 'Em'ly, my dear, I am come fur to bring forgiveness' – forgiveness, Mrs. Leavis thinks, for loving Steerforth better than him, which is the one thing Peggotty can't get over, and which drives him on his strange hike through Europe on the offchance of hearing some news of his beloved.

We shall be returning to *David Copperfield* later. But perhaps we should first remind ourselves of Dickens' own encounters with the opposite sex in real life, since many critics have regarded these as determining the bias of his fiction. The first woman Dickens knew well was his mother, and his mother proved, at a crucial period of his life, something of a disappointment. When his father's financial irresponsibility brought the family to ruin, it was a relation of his mother's, James Lamert, who arranged for the 12-year-old Charles to go and work in Warren's blacking warehouse. It must have seemed a strange betrayal, for Lamert had been the boy's chief befriender in the amateur dramatics that so delighted him, and had also first taken him to a theatre. During little Dickens' ordeal, his mother was seen about the warehouse frequently, his father hardly at all. Eventually John Dickens grew ashamed that his son was being displayed in Warren's window as a little labouring hind, and remonstrated with Lamert, who flew into a rage and dismissed the boy. John Dickens was now determined that Charles should be sent to school, as he eventually was, but his mother was horrified at the thought of losing the 7 shillings a week which Charles had earned, and she called on Lamert to persuade him to take the boy back. 'She brought home a request', Dickens remembers, 'for me to return next morning.' We can all see, in retropsect, that Mrs. Dickens was wrong to be concerned about buying food for her family instead of providing posterity with a great novelist. Anyway, she was unsuccessful. John Dickens stood firm, and the boy went to school. But his mother's behaviour made a lasting impression on Charles. 'I do not write resentfully or angrily,' he declared, 'but I never afterwards forgot, I never shall forget, I never can forget, that my mother was warm for my being sent back.' If he ever had any warmth of affection for his mother, it doesn't seem to have survived this incident. Once he began to be successful, his parents were eager to prey on him, and he was furious to find they were asking for money from his publishers behind his back. He bundled them off to a cottage in Devonshire, much to their chagrin, and put a notice in the newspapers warning creditors that he wouldn't be responsible for debts contracted by people bearing the same surname as himself. Years later, when his mother was sunk in senile decay he seems to have found her a comic figure rather than anything else, commenting on her propensity to dress up in sables 'like a female Hamlet'. 'The instant she saw me', he writes, 'she plucked up a spirit, and asked me for "a pound".'

The second woman often blamed for blighting Dickens' view of the sex was Maria Beadnell, daughter of a successful banker, and a year older than Dickens, whom he fell passionately in love with when he was about 17. The penniless son of John Dickens, late of the Marshalsea, was hardly an eligible suitor, and the Beadnells hastily dispatched Maria to a finishing school in Paris. When she returned her feelings towards her admirer had apparently cooled. Besides, a mutual friend called Marianne Leigh had – in some way that isn't very clear – been upsetting the relationship by gossip. Deeply hurt, Dickens broke off the hopeless affair, and sent a bitter letter to Marianne. But the wound, if we are to believe Dickens himself, never really healed. It was the determination to win Maria that first heartened him to fight his way towards success. Writing to her years later, he says:

Whatever of fancy, romance, energy, passion, aspiration and determination belong to me, I have never separated and never shall separate from the hard-hearted little woman – you . . . My entire devotion to you, and the wasted tenderness of those hard years . . . made so deep an impression on me that I refer to it a habit of suppression which now belongs to me, which I know is not part of my original nature, but which makes me chary of showing my affections, even to my children, except when they are very young.

His love for Maria was transmuted into David Copperfield's for Dora. In 1855, when Dickens was an ageing, distinguished novelist and family man, unhappily married, he suddenly heard from Maria again, and arranged a meeting. She was now married also, to a merchant called Winter, and had two little girls, and she warned Dickens that she was 'toothless, fat, old and ugly'. He paid no attention to the warning, and hurried to meet her, his mind filled with images of the captivating teenager who had so tormented him as a boy. Confrontation with the grotesque reality was shattering. Maria's garrulity and her annoying giggle and her middle-aged girlishness are recorded in Flora Finching in *Little Dorrit*, who so embarrasses Arthur Clennam by her arch references to their previous attachment. Maria Beadnell had let Dickens down a second time.

The third woman to fall below his expectations was his wife, Catherine. Exactly when friction between husband and wife commenced is uncertain, but it seems to have been relatively early. In a letter of 1857 Dickens himself declares that he had foreseen the eventual breakup since the birth of his daughter Mary – only two years after the marriage took place. He can, indeed, be found lecturing her on her 'sullen and inflexible obstinacy' some time before the wedding. Catherine's physical clumsiness became an increasing source of exasperation to him. 'You recollect her propensity', Dickens writes to Forster six years after his marriage:

She falls into, or out of, every coach or boat we enter; scrapes the skin off her legs; brings great sores and swellings on her feet; chips large fragments out of her ankle bones; and makes herself blue with bruises.

In a statement by Dickens published in the New York *Tribune* at the time of his separation from Catherine he maintained, after asserting his own 'manly consideration' for his wife, that 'some peculiarity of her character' had meant that her children had never been devoted to her but had transferred their affections to their aunt Georgina, who lived with the Dickenses. He even hints that his wife is insane. She labours sometimes under a mental disorder which makes her unfit for 'the life she has to lead as my wife'.

The angelic counterpart to clumsy Catherine was her sister Mary Hogarth, worshipped by Dickens as an ideal of feminine purity, who died suddenly in his arms a year after the Dickens marriage, at the age of seventeen. 'I solemnly believe that so perfect a creature never breathed,' he affirmed. 'She had not a fault.' Her loss overwhelmed him with grief. For months afterwards Mary came back to him in visions every night – sometimes as a spirit, sometimes as a living creature. Interestingly these nightly visits stopped as soon as he told his wife about them. Mary appeared to him again once or twice in later years – for the last time in Genoa in 1844. 'I was not at all afraid,' Dickens recalls of this vision, 'but in a great delight, so that I wept very much, and stretching out my arms to it called it "Dear",' and awoke 'with the tears running down my face'. 'Recollection of her', he affirmed, 'is an essential part of my being, and is as inseparable from my existence as the beating of my heart is.' Occasions of spiritual uplift brought her image back to him with especial clarity. At Niagara, for instance, the large quantity of water inspired Dickens with elevated thoughts – 'It would be hard for a man to stand nearer God than he does there' – and he felt certain that Mary had been a regular visitor to the Falls in her celestial capacity: 'she has been here many times, I doubt not, since her sweet face faded from my earthly sight.' He desperately wanted to be buried in her grave, and was much put out when her grandmother, by dying first, displaced him. 'I cannot bear the thought of being excluded from her dust.' At first he contemplated having Mary dug up and stored in the catacombs before her deceased grandmother arrived. Finally, though, he satisfied himself by getting to the cemetery early and meditating in solitude on Mary's exposed coffin.

Little Nell and Ruth Pinch and Florence Dombey and David Copperfield's Agnes and the self-sacrificing Little Dorrit are all, it is generally agreed, partial reflections of Mary Hogarth's purity and blessedness. A live sister would have been a serious enough rival to poor Mrs. Dickens, especially as she could remain unsullied in Dickens' eyes by the connubial embraces which Catherine herself had to endure. But a dead one was utterly invincible. For ever young, and with her halo for ever untarnished, Mary nestled in Dickens' heart while his wife grew older and more clumsy. In the novels likewise an unbridgeable gulf divides the pure young maids from the nagging married women, stupid, sexless, aggravating, their dynasty extending from Mrs. Nickleby right through to Mrs. Wilfer. He brought himself to believe that his love for Mary was so pure that it was virtually paternal. 'In her', he affirms, 'I had the fondest father's pride.' The gruesome union of girl and aged man, which so appealed to Dickens, intimated in the closeness of Nell to her grandfather, and finally made official in the marriage of Dr. and Mrs. Strong in *David Copperfield*, plainly relates to this erotic paternalism. Such energies as Dr. Strong has seem to be consumed by lexicography, and we are left in some doubt about whether we should consider the marriage consummated. 'Oh my husband and father', cries Mrs. Strong confusingly. (Compare the chubby-fingered Mrs. Peerybingle in *The Cricket on the Hearth* – 'such a child', as she reminds her spouse, 'and you more like my guardian than my husband').

It's easy to see why the authoritative, paternal role in a love relationship should have attracted Dickens' forceful personality. He enjoyed flirting with young girls, and this was usually looked upon as amiable condescension or high spirits. The affair with Ellen

Ternan began when he hired her as an actress for a play he was stage-managing. Another curious episode in which Dickens asserted that his motives were superior and professional, concerned a Madame De la Rue, whom he met in Italy and whose nervous ailment he offered to cure with the mesmeric powers that he and others thought he possessed. When it turned out that the treatment included nocturnal visits to Madame De la Rue's bedroom, Catherine grew suspicious. Monsieur De la Rue would even come and fetch Dickens from bed in the early hours of the morning to attend to his wife's needs. Catherine's resentment grew so undisguised that Dickens had to pretend to the De la Rues that she was suffering from a nervous breakdown. Though she pleaded, with tears, that he should put an end to the intimacy, he rigidly and characteristically refused. Heated self-righteousness also marked his pronouncements about his relationship with Ellen at the time of his separation from Catherine. 'Upon my soul and honour', his letter in the New York *Tribune* read, 'there is not on this earth a more virtuous and spotless creature than this young lady. I know her to be as innocent and pure, and as good as my own dear daughters.' As with Mary Hogarth, Dickens needs to combine the roles of lover and father. The process keeps the girl unspotted and deprives her of her stature as a woman. Wives who regress so drastically as to resemble babies or toys are accounted particularly palatable. 'The little baby-like married woman', in tears over leaving her parents' home, is listed among delightful female types in Dickens' memorandum book. Mrs. Tott, aptly named, in *The Perils of Certain English Prisoners*, earns the hero's high praise: 'I never saw a woman so like a toy in my life.' Women adult enough to present a threat to man, have a certain horror for Dickens. Women in his world have no right to violent feelings, erotic or otherwise. Madame Defarge is a monster, fit only to be exterminated like a savage animal, for feeling vindictive towards the family which murdered her brother and sister. Carton, when he meets her, senses that it would be a good deed to lift her arm 'and strike under it sharp and deep'. Of course, Madame Defarge is French; hence her ungovernable temper. Dickens' only murderess, Hortense in *Bleak House*, suffers from the same handicap relative to her nationality.

Towards women who fail to be sexually attractive, which in Dickens' terms means women who are not girlish subordinates, the novels' routine attitude is loudly jocular. The frumps and widows

and spinster aunts, we're given to understand, are all out to inveigle
one of the master sex into marriage, whatever they may pretend.
They're hideously plain, and quite possibly bearded as well, like
Sally Brass in *The Old Curiosity Shop*. They belong to an utterly
different species from the tender, marriageable maidens. No con-
ceivable process by which the girl might grow into the middle-aged
woman ever seems to have presented itself to Dickens' imagination.
His heroines are, like Mary Hogarth, perennially young and pure. The
fear of ageing, an ever-present horror in a society that demanded
girlish women, never seems to trouble their heads at all. Furthermore, though spinsters are acknowledged to be laughing stocks, the
Dickensian heroine must display no eagerness to get hold of a
husband. Ideally she should be perfectly unaware of the facts of life,
and will imagine that the man who is forcing his attentions upon her
is really applying to become her brother or father. When Florence
Dombey welcomes Walter Gay home from his sea voyage, 'She had
no thought of him but as a brother,' Dickens assures us, though the
pair are to be married within half a dozen chapters. Florence's
embrace, he anxiously stipulates, is 'pure'. Walter, whose mind does
not happen to be running on brotherhood, is unable to meet her
'open glance of sisterly affection'. When Little Dorrit goes to the
Marshalsea to nurse Clennam, again within a few chapters of marrying him, we are hastily warned not to suspect that she has the feelings
of a normal, marriageable woman. 'She nursed him as lovingly, and
God knows as innocently, as she had nursed her father in that room
when she had been but a baby.' Many Victorian girls, as we know,
were so sheltered from the world that they had little conception of
what marriage entailed until their wedding night. They were often
revolted and terrified by the discovery. Florence and Little Dorrit
are true to this tradition. What is disconcerting is that Dickens
should plainly esteem it an ideal state of affairs. Moreover, by
describing as innocent and pure, heroines who are in reality dan-
gerously retarded, he leaves us to infer that even normal sexuality is
guilty or unclean. This seems to be what he believed, or wanted to
be thought to believe. *Sketches by Boz* contains a particularly sicken-
ing description of a little boy and girl at a wedding reception, whose
love for each other is offered to the reader as inherently preferable
to the love which comes after puberty:

They have dreamt of each other in their quiet dreams, these children, and
their little hearts have been nearly broken when the absent one has been

dispraised in jest. When will there come in after life a passion so earnest, generous, and true as theirs; what, even in its gentlest realities, can have the grace and charm that hover round such fairy lovers!

Believing this, the Victorian male would naturally want to marry a child, or a woman as like a child as possible. Little Dorrit is even child-size:

Arthur found that her diminutive figure, small features, and slight spare dress, gave her the appearance of being much younger than she was. A woman, probably of not less than two and twenty, she might have been passed in the street for little more than half that age.

Obviously a recommendation, for those in search of 11-year-old brides. The wife's childlike status was further emphasized in Victorian society by her entire dependence on the man who kept her. Keen to preserve this pattern in his novels, Dickens specializes in young women whose husbands are doing them a favour by marrying them. Rose Maylie in *Oliver Twist* describes herself as 'a friendless, portionless girl with a blight upon my name', and Harry Maylie shows himself a noble fellow by overlooking these shortcomings. Little Dorrit in the Marshalsea is also well suited to be a recipient of masculine condescension, and so is Lizzie Hexam, daughter of a Thameside scavenger, whom Eugene Wrayburn generously weds, though only when he thinks he hasn't long to live. The Dickensian bride should be as penniless, as well as pure, as a child. This will ensure her gratitude – a more becoming quality in a woman than sexuality.

Louisa Gradgrind in *Hard Times* is exceptional among Dickensian heroines because she has some inkling of the more passionate side of marriage and is even prepared to talk about it. That, anyway, seems to be what she is referring to in an interview with her father where they discuss her forthcoming marriage to Bounderby, though the phrasing is veiled enough for the modest reader to miss the point if he wishes. Louisa, having failed repeatedly to get her father to acknowledge the need for love in marriage, stares out of the window at the factory chimneys of Coketown so fixedly that he asks her why she's looking at them.

'There seems to be nothing there but languid and monotonous smoke. Yet when the night comes, Fire bursts out, father!' she answered, turning quickly.

'Of course I know that, Louisa. I do not see the application of the remark.' To do him justice he did not, at all.

This is a new kind of frankness, even if it escapes Mr. Gradgrind – and a new kind of woman. It's difficult to imagine much fire breaking out between Arthur Clennam and Little Dorrit at night. But Louisa is physically aware of Bounderby, and the awareness revolts her. When he kisses her cheek she feels so contaminated she tells her brother he can cut the piece out with his penknife.

Louisa is something of a breakthrough for Dickens, escaping the two categories of pure maid and frump. Generally his female figures fit comfortably into one or other of these two categories. The Victorian effort to restrict the role of women to such stereotypes, both in fiction and in real life, suggests a lurking awareness of woman's threat to male supremacy. The woman must be constrained to certain kinds of servitude – domestic pet, angel, mother, clown – to meet the male's need for entertainment or spiritual uplift. But behind the man-made categories women were waiting to get out – women with talents and intellects which the nineteenth century stifled. The phenomenon of woman expecting to be treated, in political or intellectual matters, as if she were a normal human being, provoked Dickens, in real life, to sportive derision: 'she has found out that she ought to go and vote at elections; ought to be competent to sit in Parliament; ought to be able to enter the learned professions – the army and navy, too, I believe.' For a woman to 'go out speechifying', besides being preposterous in itself, was to forfeit the 'hold' upon her husband which shrinking femininity could naturally reckon on. His own wife's bids to broaden her mind, he treated with little respect. 'Kate wants to know whether you have "any books to send her",' he wrote to Forster. 'If you have any literary rubbish on hand, please to shoot it here.'

Among those rightly upset by the portrayal of the public-spirited women in *Bleak House* was John Stuart Mill, who pronounced it 'vulgar impudence', and 'done too in the vulgarest way, just the style in which vulgar men used to ridicule "learned ladies" as neglecting their children and household'. Independent, professional women are represented in Dickens' fiction. But it's difficult to disguise from ourselves the fact that he normally regarded them patronizingly or with contempt. Miss La Creevey the miniaturist in *Nicholas Nickleby*, kind but untalented; Mrs. Gamp; Miss Mowcher, the sharp-tongued dwarf chiropodist in *David Copperfield*, who was going to turn out an evil character until Mrs. Seymour Hill, on whom Miss Mowcher was based, wrote in and complained; Miss Peecher,

the best qualified of the various schoolmistresses in the novels, who
is nevertheless sarcastically presented learning by rote the principal
rivers and mountains of the world in order to cool her passion for
Bradley Headstone. They hardly constitute an impressive argument
for female emancipation. The threat presented by women does not
get into the novels through these woebegotten strugglers-for-a-
living. It gets in through scenes where women with ordinary domestic instruments – scissors, needles – are suddenly thrown into
relief, malignant, uncomfortable. Madame Defarge and her knitting
needles immediately comes to mind – though Dickens, of course,
didn't have to invent her and her savage cronies around the guillotine. Miss Mowcher has clippings from a Russian prince's fingernails which she carries around as gifts to clients. She sneers at that
male fabrication 'the social system', insisting that it is nothing but 'a
system of Prince's nails'. Woman, as nurse and mother, closer than
man to the indecencies of birth and death, has haunted the masculine
imagination for centuries, as we may gather from the three women of
Greek mythology with their mundane instruments – the spindle, the
scissors – who spin and cut the thread of man's life. The Fates are
suggested unexpectedly by Miss Tox, the feeble spinster of *Dombey
and Son*, whom we find one morning at her housework, thinking of
her dead relations and the passage of time. She wears 'a pair of
ancient gloves, like dead leaves', and attends to her houseplants
'which', says Dickens, 'generally required to be snipped here and
there with a pair of scissors, for some botanical reason that was very
powerful with Miss Tox'. As she snips she wonders about Mr.
Dombey: 'Was he reconciled to the decrees of fate?' The arrival of
Mr. Dombey's sister to tell Miss Tox of his marriage doesn't put a
stop to the work of the scissors: 'arming herself once more with her
scissors,' Miss Tox 'began to snip and clip among the leaves with
microscopic industry'. The vindictiveness of the action – Miss Tox
has of course been hoping to marry Dombey herself – and the allusion
to fate's decrees, give the scene disturbing undercurrents. And there
is a strange circularity about the action, too: the gloves, like dead
leaves, cutting dead leaves out from among the living. Fear of the
scissored woman is felt earlier in *Dombey* when Good Mrs. Brown
has dragged the helpless Florence to her lair: 'Mrs. Brown whipped
out a large pair of scissors, and fell into an unaccountable state of
excitement.' After the scissors have hovered around the child's head
for some moments, Mrs. Brown relents, and Florence's golden locks

are spared. Mrs. Brown carries 'skins' over her arm, and her house is furnished only with a heap of rags, a heap of bones and a heap of ashes. Hardly a convenient scheme of interior decoration, if we consider Mrs. Brown as a real person. But with their suggestion of human remains the heaps take their place, like the scissors, as the attributes of woman as Death. Mrs. Sparsit in *Hard Times*, hopeful, like Miss Tox, of a profitable match, is likewise engaged with scissors when Bounderby comes to break the news that he is going, after all, to marry her rival Louisa Gradgrind:

> Mr. Bounderby sat looking at her, as, with the points of a stiff, sharp pair of scissors, she picked out holes for some inscrutable ornamental purpose, in a piece of cambric. An operation which, taken in connection with the bushy eyebrows and the Roman nose, suggested with some liveliness the idea of a hawk engaged upon the eyes of a tough little bird.

This ferocious concentration on a victim's eyes is repeated by Jenny Wren, the doll's dressmaker in *Our Mutual Friend*. Bradley Headstone comes upon her when, as usual, she's busy with needlework, and she expresses her hatred of him, Dickens writes, by 'making two little dabs at him in the air with her needle, as if she pricked him with it in his own eyes'. The needle stands repeatedly for womanly perceptiveness as well as womanly malice. Pip's spiteful sister emphasizes her words with it when delivering a reprimand: ' "That's the way with this boy!" exclaimed my sister, pointing me out with her needle and thread.' Mrs. Joe also has an unpleasant way of jamming the loaf firmly against her bib when preparing to cut a slice: 'where it sometimes got a pin into it, and sometimes a needle which we afterwards got into our mouths'. And Betsey Trotwood questions David Copperfield over her needlework, 'eyeing me as narrowly as she had eyed the needle in threading it'. The sinister opium woman in *Edwin Drood*, in those filthy den Jaspar lies drugged and helpless, uses a needle too: 'With the point of a needle she stirs the contents of the bowl.'

These women, with their insidious miniature weapons, adumbrate a threat to masculine superiority. Around them gathers a sense of the female power which will not finally be subjected to a man-made scheme. Lawrence felt the same about the scissored woman. Self-willed Mrs. Witt in *St. Mawr*, symbol of all Lawrence loathed in emancipated females, takes 'long scissors like one of the Fates' to deprive Lewis the groom of his masculine locks, 'holding those terrifying shears with their beak erect'.

Education increases a woman's menacing potential, and Dickens' only extended portrait of a cultured, intellectual woman – Rosa Dartle in *David Copperfield* – is significantly a diabolic amalgam of envy, hatred and malice, trademarked with a livid scar across her mouth, inflicted when Steerforth, in one of his wiser moments, threw a hammer at her. She terrifies David. When she sings an Irish song, accompanying herself on the harp, he goes into a trance at the strangeness of it. For a time, he relates, she stands beside the harp 'going through the motion of playing it with her right hand, but not sounding it'. Then she plays.

I don't know what it was, in her touch or voice, that made her song the most unearthly thing I have ever heard in my life, or can imagine. There was something fearful in the reality of it. It was as if it had never been written, or set to music, but sprung out of the passion within her; which found imperfect utterance in the low sounds of her voice, and crouched again when all was still. I was dumb when she leaned beside the harp again, playing it, but not sounding it, with her right hand.

The harp, familiarized by Romantic poets and novelists as the instrument of the ancient bards, the Celtic melody, David's trance, all conspire, a little obtrusively perhaps, to give this scene a mythic quality. It's less successful in this respect than Miss Tox among her houseplants, because more posed, more literary. We sense Dickens' resolve to exhibit the untameable, primeval passions of woman. The harp symbol had already let him down badly in his effort to depict the tempestuous Edith Dombey: 'dark pride and rage succeeded, sweeping over her form and features like an angry chord across the strings of a wild harp.' The arresting detail of Rosa Dartle's silent harping (compare the Dickensian silent laugh), before and after her song, presumably means that the song itself is only a brief audible fragment of the passionate turmoil which constantly consumes her inside. Rosa is one of Dickens' combustible characters, like Krook and Mrs. Clennam. 'Her thinness', David remarks, 'seemed to be the effect of some wasting fire within her, which found a vent in her gaunt eyes.' The thrilling snake woman of the romantics – Keats' Lamia or Coleridge's Geraldine – finds her Victorian counterpart in Miss Dartle. But she has no allure for Dickens. Her final venomous interview with Little Em'ly, who moans on the floor throughout, is evidently meant to brand Miss Dartle as a disgraceful outcast from that sweet sisterhood from which any prudent Victorian male would wish to choose his mate. The

passionate woman is a separate category for Dickens. She is easily
recognizable. Her bosom heaves; she tends to smite herself by way
of emphasis. What Dickens with his self-contained categories never
did and never could show was how in any individual woman the
passion of Rosa Dartle and the purity which he allocates to his
heroines and the humdrum household worries which occupy his
frumps intermingle, cohabit and work out through the complexities of
growth and experience a practical front to show to the world. Louisa
Gradgrind is a start in this direction, but he never got any further.

When it comes to describing sexual encounters – and it very
seldom does come to that – Dickens was handicapped by his
determination to cater for the Victorian family audience. Like Mr.
Podsnap he believed that art should avoid anything that would bring
a blush into the cheek of the young person. Besides, his own nature
and the habit of suppression which he blamed Maria Beadnell for,
seem to have made him chary of explicitness in this direction. He
was embarrassed by public displays of affection and had to conceal
this by grotesque hilarity. When the young wife of a dinner guest
called her husband 'darling' at Dickens' table, he was seized with
such a violent explosion of mirth that his chair fell over and he lay
helpless with laughter on the floor waving his legs in the air. He
became increasingly mealy-mouthed as Victorian propriety har-
dened. In successive editions of *Sketches by Boz* the language was
cleaned up, the 'legs' of the young lady in 'The Dancing Academy'
becoming 'ankles', and allusion to the aphrodisiac effect of oysters
being toned down. *Pickwick*, *The Old Curiosity Shop* and *Martin
Chuzzlewit* have love scenes. After that they almost disappear. The
scenes between Sam Weller and Barbara in *Pickwick* are narrated
with a lumbering roguishness which plainly derives from Sterne.

Whether it was that the pretty housemaid's face looked prettier still,
when it was raised towards Sam's, or whether it was the accidental consequence of their being so near to each other, is a matter of uncertainty to
this day, but Sam kissed her.

Still, Sam and Barbara's scuffles below stairs have at least some
tenderness and co-operation about them. When Kit Nubbles kisses
his Barbara and John Westlock makes advances towards Ruth
Pinch, Dickens' genial chuckles increase in volume, along with his
coy professions of ignorance about what's going on:

Oh! foolish, panting, frightened little heart, why did she run away!

Merrily the tiny fountain played, and merrily the dimples sparkled on its sunny surface . . . Oh, foolish, panting, timid little heart, why did she feign to be unconscious of his coming! Why wish herself so far away, yet be so flutteringly happy there?

Dickens positively hugs himself at the deliciousness of it all, and what he finds so delicious, we should note, is female alarm. Likewise with Kit Nubbles' Barbara: 'Why, she is trembling now! Foolish, fluttering Barbara!' The male appetite needs to be whetted by the fearfulness of its prey. When the Dickensian maiden does exhibit any consciousness of sex, it's obligatory that it should strike her all of a quiver. Marrying a child is pleasurable; but marrying a frightened child, more so.

After the early novels Dickens also becomes guarded about releasing details of his heroines' bodies. Dolly Varden, as Hugh sees her, and Little Nell, as Quilp sees her, are relatively succulent, even if they can produce nothing more than the standard components – ripe lips, cherry cheeks and so forth. 'What mortal eyes', asks Dickens excitely, as Dolly whimpers and trembles, 'could have avoided wandering to the delicate bodice, the streaming hair, the neglected dress, the perfect abandonment and unconsciousness of the blooming little beauty?' But with Esther Summerson or Amy Dorrit there is precious little for mortal eyes to wander over. Their bodies have no erotic charge. In *Dombey and Son*, when a wet nurse has to be found for Paul, Mr. Chick demonstrates his ignorance of maternal problems by suggesting 'Couldn't something temporary be done with a teapot?' But Dickens, by restricting the female breast to its role as receptacle for milk, and firmly ignoring its attractiveness to the male, is not very far from Mr. Chick's position. When David Copperfield meets Mrs. Micawber, she has a baby at her breast:

This baby was one of the twins; and I may remark here that I hardly ever, in all my experience of the family, saw both the twins detached from Mrs. Micawber at the same time. One of them was always taking refreshment.

For all the erotic response David registers, Mrs. Micawber might just as well be using a teapot. With hard, forbidding women, Dickens feels safe in drawing attention to their unerotic breasts as corroboratory evidence. Mrs. Merdle's, for example, come in for much jocular comment:

Mrs. Merdle's first husband had been a colonel, under whose auspices the bosom had entered into competition with the snows of North America, and had come off at little disadvantage in point of whiteness, and at none in point of coldness.

Positive, appealing counterparts to Mrs. Merdle's marble breasts are not to be found, however, on Dickens' women.

Of the later heroines Bella Wilfer is the one whose body is most sensuously evoked, though the method is suggestive rather than explicit. When Mr. and Mrs. Boffin call unexpectedly on Mrs. Wilfer, and ask to see Bella, Mrs. Wilfer haughtily replies:

'My daughter Bella is accessible and shall speak for herself.' Then opening the door a little way, simultaneously with a sound of scuttling outside it, the good lady made the proclamation, 'Send Miss Bella to me!' Which proclamation, though grandly formal, and one might say almost heraldic, to hear, was in fact enunciated with her maternal eyes reproachfully glaring on that young lady in the flesh – and in so much of it that she was retiring with difficulty into the small closet under the stairs, apprehensive of the emergence of Mr. and Mrs. Boffin.

The reader's – or at any rate the male reader's – imagination is craftily stimulated by this tempting morsel of information. 'In the flesh – and in so much of it'. Just what Bella's state of undress is as she struggles engagingly to squash herself into the little closet under her mother's angry glare, is a question on which the mind dwells with a certain fondness. Such prurient moments don't come often. Dickens can allow himself to convey the physicality of sex with a more brutal frankness when talking about textiles and furniture than when talking about bodies. In *Bleak House*, for instance, Inspector Bucket tramps up to search Lady Dedlock's bedroom after her flight. 'A spicy boudoir this', says Mr. Bucket. Opening and shutting drawers, rummaging in caskets he forces his rough presence into the intimacies of the place.

He has opened a dainty little chest in an inner drawer. His great hand, turning over some gloves which it can scarcely feel, they are so light and soft within it, comes upon a white handkerchief.

Inspector Bucket's masculine paw disembowelling the little female hide-out approaches nearer to sexual union than any of the loving couples in the book. So, too, Estella in *Great Expectations*, Dickens' most provocative girl, is skilfully fabricated out of a minimum of physical detail. To make her luminous and unattainable Dickens repeatedly hides her body and substitutes a star. On his first visit to Satis House, Miss Havisham commands Pip to shout for Estella. He finds himself standing 'in the dark in a mysterious passage of an unknown house, bawling Estella to a scornful young lady neither visible nor responsive'. The action, shouting her name in the dark, beautifully externalizes the need of Pip's soul. 'She answered at last,' he recalls, 'and her light came along the passage like a star.' Later, in the ruined brewery, he watches her 'go out by a gallery high overhead, as if she were going out into the sky'. A star again. On another visit she carries a lighted candle before him along a dark passage, and then stops suddenly, turning round 'her face quite close to mine'.

'Well?'
'Well, miss,' I answered, almost falling over her and checking myself. She stood looking at me, and of course I stood looking at her.
'Am I pretty?'
'Yes; I think you are very pretty.'
'Am I insulting?'
'Not so much so as you were last time,' said I.
'Not so much so?'
'No.'
She fired when she asked the last question, and she slapped my face with such force as she had, when I answered it.
'Now?' said she. 'You little coarse monster, what do you think of me now?'

A star which slaps its admirer's face is doubly provocative. We notice how tantalizingly a physical embrace is avoided by the blundering Pip – 'almost falling over her, and checking myself'. Tantalizingly for Estella, too, who evidently wants to arouse him, and is eventually reduced to telling him he can kiss her cheek. The girl's disdainful allure is irresistibly conveyed, yet not even Podsnap could object that Estella's body is ever immodestly shown. It is scarcely there at all.

We should not suppose that Dickens failed to notice the sexual inhibitions of himself and his audience. Two of his figures – David Copperfield and Esther Summerson – amount to extended studies of the deviations which Victorian attitudes to sex could promote. David is a confusing figure to analyse, because he's supposed to be the product of so many different parent–child relationships. Totting up his various parents, stepparents and surrogate parents, we find him first the doting son of a gentle widowed mother, then the persecuted son of a disciplinarian father, Mr. Murdstone, and his grim evangelical female counterpart who closely resembles Arthur Clennam's

mother in *Bleak House*; then the son of the feckless, amiable
Micawber, modelled on Dickens' own father; then the son of the
stiff, repressed Betsey Trotwood with her half-witted husband
substitute, Mr. Dick. The mind boggles at the prospect of calculat-
ing the effect of this variegated parenthood on a real child. Fortunately Dickens is not a clinical enough novelist to make the
exercise worthwhile. But equally clearly we're meant to relate
David's parenthood to his love-choices in certain definite respects.
He makes the mistake of marrying mindless, fluffy Dora because
she resembles his first love, his mindless, fluffy mother. The resemblance is firmly etched. Both are wilful, pettish, curly haired; Miss
Murdstone acts as wardress to both; both die young. When David
tries to educate Dora he realizes he is doing what Murdstone did to
his mother, and gives it up. 'I could not endure my own solitary
wisdom: I could not reconcile it with her former appeal to me as my
child-wife.' Dora is child, and domestic pet. Her pet dog is a representative attribute, and dies at precisely the same moment as his
mistress. Betsey Trotwood refuses to help educate Dora because,
she says, 'I want our pet to like me, and be as gay as a butterfly.' In
the disastrous housekeeping of the Dora marriage, Dickens faces
up to the impracticality of the child-wife idea. But it was at least an
idea which ensured play and gaiety and unreason, and he knew that
he and his contemporaries needed these attributes in a woman
before they could feel sexually attracted. Agnes, on the other hand,
has all the correct attributes for a wife, being responsible and staid,
but Dickens knows that most men feel sexually chilled by such
women, and this is how he shows David feeling. Agnes is no child:

Agnes, my sweet sister, as I call her in my thoughts, my counsellor and
friend, the better angel of the lives of all who come within her calm, good,
self-denying influence, is quite a woman.

Quite a woman, but predominantly a sister and an angel, and with
neither is sexual intercourse usually countenanced. David can love
Little Em'ly, because she's a pettish child like his mother and
Dora: 'I love little Em'ly and I don't love Agnes – no, not at all in
that way.' So little does he think of her 'in that way' that he can't
bring himself to so much as discuss with her his suspicions about
Mrs. Strong's affair with her cousin: 'It was not a subject I could
discuss with Agnes.' Agnes never has a chance. From the moment he
sets eyes on her, David decides she is to be a religious symbol for him:

I cannot call to mind where or when, in my childhood, I had seen a stained glass window in a church. Nor do I recollect its subject. But I know that when I saw her turn round, in the grave light of the old staircase, and wait for us, above, I thought of that window; and I associated something of its tranquil brightness with Agnes Wickfield ever afterwards.

To the end he insists on thinking she is made of stained glass. 'Ever pointing upward, Agnes; ever leading me to something better; ever directing me to higher things,' he remarks cheerfully, only two or three chapters from the end. 'She only shook her head; through her tears I saw the same sad quiet smile.' David's obtuseness is enough to make any girl weep. For Agnes has perfectly normal instincts, in fact, and is pointing not upwards but towards the bedroom. The inadequacy lies in David, not her. He is unable to associate maturity with sex. He can stomach it as a childish game, but not otherwise. Perhaps we're to blame Murdstone for this. Seeing his tender mother couple with a black-haired monster is enough to make adult sexuality repellent to any child. David's feeling that the road to maturity involves uncleanness (a feeling which we have seen Dickens endorsing) is conveyed when he says of himself as a little child at his mother's breast: 'I wish I had died then . . . I should have been more fit for Heaven than I ever have been since.' So loth is he to come to terms with what sex entails, that when he suspects Mrs. Strong is having an affair with someone her own age, his mind positively recoils in horror. His homosexual love for Steerforth – never progressing, needless to say, to the physical – can be easily related to this recoil, as it can to his desire for protection, the natural outcome of his stepfather's savagery. David is frank enough about his love for Steerforth. He even admits he never loved him more than when he ran off with Em'ly. And Steerforth's appetite for the female is stirred by David. At first meeting, he's disappointed to learn David has no sister: 'If you had had one, I should think she would have been a pretty, timid, little, bright-eyed sort of girl. I should have liked to know her.' He makes up for his disappointment by calling David 'Daisy'. To modern eyes Steerforth is the only really detestable Dickensian villain. Compounded of meanness and insolence, his treatment of Mr. Mell puts him beyond the pale early in the book. His appropriation of David's belongings when the latter arrives at Salem House is a good deal less excusable than the straightforward thefts of the outcasts on the Dover Road. With no more remarkable assets than a glib tongue and domineering manner,

Steerforth might at best have made a passable confidence trickster.
Yet the infatuated David believes to the end that, but for his lax
upbringing, he 'might have won the love and admiration of thou-
sands'. The only question is whether Dickens believed this too.
His denunciation of Littimer, Steerforth's servant, shows him
complacently adopting the middle-class theory that when a young
gentleman went wrong it was his servant's fault. On his second visit
to America he was waylaid on a railway train by an adoring little girl
who questioned him about the novels, and told him that her family
all cried so much over the death of Steerforth that their eyes were
too swollen to go to Sunday School. 'Yes, I cry when I read about
Steerforth,' replied Dickens. Perhaps, then, Steerforth really is
meant to be a portrait of squandered genius. At all events, his place
in David's sexual pilgrimage is plain enough. From him David
advances to Dora, a child, then to Agnes, a real woman. Readers
who come away thinking Agnes a sexless saint miss the point. David
sees her as that, but only because his own fear of a mature woman
forces him to turn her into something untouchable. Through David,
Dickens satirizes his own tendency to force women into watertight
categories – child-bride, frump, stained glass window. Agnes actually
combines purity and sexual desire and household efficiency. She
spans the Dickensian categories. Blind David just can't take it in
until she tells him – 'I have loved you all my life!'

Esther Summerson in *Bleak House* provides a counterpart to
David Copperfield. Her childhood guardians, like his, make adult
sexuality terrifying to her 'Your mother, Esther, is your disgrace,
and you were hers,' her godmother informs her. 'You are different
from other children, Esther, because you were not born, like them,
in common sinfulness and wrath. You are set apart.' To drive home
the lesson, her godmother has a stroke and dies just when Esther,
reading to her from the Bible, has reached the passage about the
woman take in adultery. Understandably impressed by this exhibi-
tion, little Esther goes out into the garden after her godmother's
funeral, digs a grave and buries her doll in it, thus renouncing
motherhood and its terrors. A homosexual phase follows, as with
David. The innocent kisses and embraces Esther shares with Ada
allow her to feel motherly without undergoing the contagion of the
male. Significantly she feels revulsion when she notices a 'hideous
boy' in Chancery Lane 'fondling and sucking the spikes' outside
one of the offices. Feminine men she can tolerate. Prince Turveydrop

appeals to her, she says, because of his 'innocent, feminine manner', which 'made this singular effect upon me: that I received the impression that he was like his mother'. Likewise paternal men present no threat; hence her acceptance of Jarndyce. Besides being like a father, Jarndyce is reassuringly dispassionate. He sleeps with his window open all the year round, so Esther tells us, 'his bedstead without any furniture standing in the middle of the floor for more air, and his cold bath gaping for him in a small room adjoining'. To be sure, one would not have suspected that Jarndyce needed to take such elaborate precautions against the sudden onset of passion, but his care on this score naturally makes him less alarming to Esther. He is able to give Esther children without any of the usual intimate preliminaries. 'If you please, miss, I'm a present to you, with Mr. Jarndyce's love,' says her little maid Charley on arrival. The features that make Esther unwholesome to the modern reader – her middle-aged postures, her self-disparagement, her eagerness for unsexing nicknames like 'Dame Durden' – are not mistakes in Dickens' portrayal of her, but shrewdly observed symptoms of a young girl's painful inhibitions about sex. Mr. Guppy's proposal naturally repels her. His smell puts her off, apart from anything else: 'he quite scented the room with his bear's-grease and other perfumery.' His crude bid to awake the sexuality she has carefully repressed at once reminds her of her ceremony of renunciation: 'I was in a flutter for a little while; and felt as if an old chord had been more coarsely touched than it had ever been since the days of the dear old doll, long buried in the garden.' The awakening of her love for Woodcourt is a much slower process. The little bunch of withered flowers she keeps as a memento of him mirrors her own sterility. She burns them when she accepts Jarndyce – her second gesture of renunciation – and but for Jarndyce's improbable nobility Woodcourt would never have had a chance to guide her into sexual maturity.

David and Esther, then, both combat tendencies in Dickens himself. The tendency to categorize women, which is David's failing. And the tendency to admire plucky, sexless heroines – Little Nell, Little Dorrit – with their unnatural attachment to older men. In Esther he shows us that the type is a perversion: the result of cruel pressures exerted in childhood.

The temptation is to make Dickens look more modern than he is. His affection for junk and dilapidation, for speech that refuses to communicate – soliloquy, somniloquy, bird talk – has a suggestive air for a generation conditioned by Beckett and Pinter. His imagination, haunting the frontier between the living and the inanimate, preying on effigies, corpses, artificial limbs, repelled by the female, inventing people who fall away into dead pieces, and buildings or furniture that seem to gather strength and become alive, prompts comparison with the unpredictable, alien worlds contacted in Kafka or Sartre – with, to take a specific example, the psychological predicament of Sartre's Antoine Roquentin, his sense of objects touching him 'as if they were living beasts', in *La Nausée*. When we recall Dickens likening dead children to 'pig's feet as they are usually displayed at a neat tripe shop', Roquentin seems a small step away:

I stopped in front of Julien's, the pork-butcher's shop. Through the glass I could see now and then a hand pointing to the truffled pigs' feet and the sausages. Then a fat blonde bent forward, showing her bosom, and picked up the piece of dead flesh between her fingers. In his room, five minutes' walk from there, Monsieur Fasquelle was dead.

From the start Dickens found it a problem to keep meat and people distinct, as the cannibalism in his novels suggests. Already in *Sketches by Boz* there occur ladies and gentlemen seated alternately 'like the layers of bread and meat in a plate of sandwiches', and 'one of those young women who almost invariably, though one hardly knows why, recall to one's mind the idea of a cold fillet of veal'. But if we pursue Sartre and Roquentin, their meat (and, we might add, Kafka's living meat in a piece like 'Ein altes Blatt') becomes, in the end, less Dickensian, more surely the content of a diseased mind:

The father of a family may go for a walk, and he will see a red rag coming towards him across the street, as if the wind were blowing it. And when the rag gets close to him, he will see that it is a quarter of rotten meat, covered with dust, crawling and hopping along, a piece of tortured flesh rolling in the gutters and spasmodically shooting out jets of blood.

What saves Dickens from this rather shrill surrealism is his humour – a humour so interfused with his creative processes that when it fails his imagination seldom survives it for more than a few sentences. His humour serves as weapon and refuge. It allows him both to cut through the fake of the 'real world', as we have seen, and to keep the terrors of his imagination at bay. Consequently there is a feeling of strain when one applies words like 'appalling' or 'horrifying' to his creations. The materials of horror may be there, but they are transmuted by humour into something more spirited and resilient. Laughter establishes Dickens' confidence, his superiority to menacing forces, and the confidence is deeply unmodern, connecting him not with Sartre or Kafka but with the eighteenth-century writers – Fielding, Swift – who influenced him as a boy. 'If I went to a new colony', he once asserted, 'I should force myself to the top of the social milk-pot, and live upon the cream.' This toughness helped to ensure his commercial success, but it can be traced, too, in the way he manipulates his imagination. Behind his defenceless children – David or Pip – there stands, smiling, the secure adult writer; it is the same figure who authoritatively converts his insidious scissored women into frumps and termagants. Dickens' imagination transforms the world; his laughter controls it.

ACKNOWLEDGEMENTS

Tolstoy's *War and Peace* is quoted on p. 41 from Rosemary Edmonds' translation; Sartre's *Words*, on p. 133, from Irene Clephane's translation; his *Nausea*, on pp. 175-6, from Robert Baldick's translation; and Zola's *Germinal*, on pp. 144-5, from L. W. Tancock's translation. All these are published by Penguin Books Ltd., Harmondsworth, Middlesex. On p. 154 the quotation from Mr. A. E. Dyson occurs in his *The Inimitable Dickens*, published by Macmillan; and that from Mrs. Leavis in *Dickens the Novelist*, by F. R. and Q. D. Leavis, published by Chatto and Windus.

INDEX